Springer Series in Design and Innovation

Volume 8

Springer Series in Design and Innovation (SSDI) publishes books on innovation and the latest developments in the fields of Product Design, Interior Design and Communication Design, with particular emphasis on technological and formal innovation, and on the application of digital technologies and new materials. The series explores all aspects of design, e.g. Human-Centered Design/User Experience, Service Design, and Design Thinking, which provide transversal and innovative approaches oriented on the involvement of people throughout the design development process. In addition, it covers emerging areas of research that may represent essential opportunities for economic and social development.

In fields ranging from the humanities to engineering and architecture, design is increasingly being recognized as a key means of bringing ideas to the market by transforming them into user-friendly and appealing products or services. Moreover, it provides a variety of methodologies, tools and techniques that can be used at different stages of the innovation process to enhance the value of new products and services.

The series' scope includes monographs, professional books, advanced textbooks, selected contributions from specialized conferences and workshops, and outstanding Ph.D. theses.

Keywords: Product and System Innovation; Product design; Interior design; Communication Design; Human-Centered Design/User Experience; Service Design; Design Thinking; Digital Innovation; Innovation of Materials.

How to submit proposals

Proposals must include: title, keywords, presentation (max 10,000 characters), table of contents, chapter abstracts, editors'/authors' CV.

In case of proceedings, chairmen/editors are requested to submit the link to conference website (incl. relevant information such as committee members, topics, key dates, keynote speakers, information about the reviewing process, etc.), and approx. number of papers.

Proposals must be sent to: series editor Prof. Francesca Tosi (francesca.tosi@unifi.it) and/or publishing editor Mr. Pierpaolo Riva (pierpaolo.riva@springer.com).

More information about this series at http://www.springer.com/series/16270

Nuno Martins · Daniel Brandão ·
Daniel Raposo
Editors

Perspectives on Design and Digital Communication

Research, Innovations and Best Practices

Springer

Editors
Nuno Martins
ID+ / School of Design
Polytechnic Institute of Cavado and Ave
Barcelos, Portugal

Daniel Brandão
CECS / Institute of Social Sciences
University of Minho
Braga, Portugal

Daniel Raposo
CIAUD / RETHINK / School of Applied Arts
Polytechnic Institute of Castelo Branco
Castelo Branco, Portugal

ISSN 2661-8184 ISSN 2661-8192 (electronic)
Springer Series in Design and Innovation
ISBN 978-3-030-49646-3 ISBN 978-3-030-49647-0 (eBook)
https://doi.org/10.1007/978-3-030-49647-0

This Springer imprint is published by the registered company Springer Nature Switzerland AG
The registered company address is: Gewerbestrasse 11, 6330 Cham, Switzerland

Preface

Digital technology has been assuming an increasingly relevant role in the transformation of communication paradigms in our current societies, more global and interconnected than ever. The challenges of Design are therefore equally greater. The field of action of Communication Design has expanded, where it is vital to recognize the importance of interdisciplinarity and the dilution of boundaries between different areas of knowledge.

Openness to plurality and the crossing of knowledge are essential requirements for designers to be better prepared to respond to the constant challenges of the current dynamics of the information society. It is based on this philosophy that the Digicom—International Conference on Digital Design and Communication was created, organized by the Design School of the Polytechnic Institute of Cavado and Ave and by ID+, Research Institute for Design Media and Culture.

This conference aims to be a space for reflection and analysis on the constant challenges of digital communication for society, institutions and brands. It brings together annually the work of researchers, academics and designers from around the world. Although Digicom is focused on the area of Communication Design, the objective is the promotion of an open, broad and plural discussion, aggregating different areas of knowledge, namely Arts, Technology, Communication Sciences and Education Sciences. The conference thus seeks to stimulate interdisciplinary relationships that contribute to a solid development of scientific activity.

The book presents preliminary and final results of research experiments and processes, which represent new contributions and an advance in scientific, academic and practical knowledge in the areas of digital design, communication design, web, multimedia and motion design, graphic design and branding, among other intersection areas.

The book can be viewed from a global perspective of design research as well as observed from specific components or from the specialty in design research.

Our aim is to open new perspectives and research paths, explaining the diverse processes and experiences carried out by different research groups, centres and institutions on an international scale.

The chapters are the result of an invitation, addressed by Digicom's Organizing Committee, to the authors of the best papers approved by blind peer review and presented in the 3rd edition of Digicom, in November 2019. This book gathers about 15 chapters written by researchers and professors of design and related areas.

The chapters cover the following topics:

- The communication technologies and the intersections between printed and digital media;
- The need to deepen the study of graphic interfaces specific components;
- Spatial and transmedia storytelling and the design of interactive narratives in virtual reality;
- The challenges of branding and new perspectives created by languages such as dynamic visual identities;
- The impact of digital design on people's daily lives;
- Digital Design commitment in socio-political agendas;
- The education and new learning process in and by Design.

Barcelos, Portugal — Nuno Martins
Braga, Portugal — Daniel Brandão
Castelo Branco, Portugal — Daniel Raposo

Contents

From Painting to Graphic Arts: The Unique Legacy of Armando Alves

Cláudia Lima, Heitor Alvelos, Susana Barreto, Eliana Penedos-Santiago, and Nuno Martins

Abstract This paper analyses the professional life and work of Armando Alves. Graduated in Painting from the School of Fine Arts of Porto, the artist distinguished himself in the field of graphic arts, not only for his academic contribution, but also for his intense activity in the field of design. Although he has a vast legacy of graphic works carried out in the last 60 years, this study is focused on his contribution to the establishment of the graphic arts subject in higher education, as well as in the analysis of a set of rare books, selected by Armando Alves as those that truly marked his career as a designer. More than graphic works, these books are design objects created to be stroked, experienced, sensed and visualised. It is argued from this evidence that the books in question prefigure a return to craftsmanship and limited editions, which can be found in contemporary design as an empirical and intuitive counterpoint to the prevalence of immaterial digital content and processes.

Keywords Armando Alves · Rare books · ESBAP generation · Graphic arts · Sensorial design

---

C. Lima (✉)
Faculdade de Belas Artes da Universidade do Porto / ID+ Research Institute for Design, Media and Culture; Universidade Lusófona do Porto, Porto, Portugal
e-mail: claudiaraquellima@gmail.com

H. Alvelos · S. Barreto · E. Penedos-Santiago
Faculdade de Belas Artes da Universidade do Porto / ID+ Research Institute for Design, Media and Culture, Porto, Portugal
e-mail: halvelos@gmail.com

S. Barreto
e-mail: susanaxbarreto@gmail.com

E. Penedos-Santiago
e-mail: elianapenedossantiago@gmail.com

N. Martins
Faculdade de Belas Artes da Universidade do Porto / ID+ Research Institute for Design, Media and Culture; Polytechnic Institute of Cávado and Ave, Porto, Portugal
e-mail: nunomartins.com@gmail.com

N. Martins et al. (eds.), *Perspectives on Design and Digital Communication*, Springer Series in Design and Innovation 8, https://doi.org/10.1007/978-3-030-49647-0_1

1 Introduction

From practice to academia, Armando Alves (Fig. 1) marked the first pedagogical essays of the School of Fine Arts of Porto (ESBAP) in the field of graphic arts, which would result, years later, in the creation of the first design course in higher education in northern Portugal. Graduating in Painting, in the beginning of the 1960s, Alves has always divided his time between painting and design. As most of Portuguese designers of this time, the learning of graphic arts was done through practice and experimentation, in an empirical way, with the first academic essays on this field at ESBAP driven by him.

It was in 1958 that Armando Alves began his graphic activity (Barroso 2014), to which he would dedicate himself particularly from 1973 onwards. His legacy of graphic works is vast, particularly in the field of poster design and editorial design, making him one of the most respected Portuguese designers of his generation (although existing bibliographical references do not do him justice).

Among his work are countless commemorative posters, such as the poster *Nicolau Nasoni Arquitecto do Porto*, for the commemorations on the 2nd Centennial of this architect, in 1973, and the posters for the International Women's Day and for the International Children's Day, both in 1975; exhibition catalogues for, e.g., the *Exhibition on the 30 years of Eugénio de Andrade*, in 1976, or the catalogue for the *Retrospective Exhibition of the First 50 Theatre Performances of Teatro Experimental do Porto*, in 1981; stamps design, including those for Centennial of Public Transport in the City

Fig. 1 Armando Alves. Portrait made during the interview held in his studio on December 5, 2018. Photography: @Cláudia Lima

of Porto, in 1973, stamps for the *Barcos da Costa Portuguesa* series, in 1977, or *Barcos dos Rios Portugueses* e *1st May* series, in 1981; and books such as the poetry collection *Indícios de Oiro*, in 1973, *Poemas do Último Século Antes do Homem*, in 1979, or the poetry collection *Obscuro Domínio* and *O Aprendiz de Feiticeiro*, in 1980. But when we ask him which works he considers the most remarkable of his career, the graphic artist does not hesitate to answer the special editions, rare books of great dimension thought of as design objects to be felt, handled, touched, experienced. Deliberately or intuitively, this production of special (and limited) editions reveals an unexpected attunement with the resurgence of manual production niches and renewed interest in the object in contemporary design. This resurgence, it is often argued, is so much more unexpected when the growing access to digital platforms for content creation and consumption seemed to prefigure a total surrender to this new paradigm, associated with the expected gradual abandonment of manuality by obsolescence.

This study is carried out within the framework of the *Wisdom Transfer project: towards the scientific inscription of individual legacies in contexts of retirement from art and design higher education and research* (POCI-01-0145-FEDER-029038), which stems from the evidence that there is insufficient inscription of individual knowledge and experience of retired professors and researchers in art and design. The testimony of Armando Alves and the analysis of his professional life and graphic work aim precisely at the inscription of the knowledge and individual experience of an artist whose path has greatly contributed to the introduction of design in higher education and to the history of graphic arts in Portugal.

2 Methodology

Although Armando Alves is a well-known designer, with around 60 years of activity, we found few bibliographical references regarding his legacy as a graphic artist. In this sense, and in the framework of the *Wisdom Transfer* project (https://endlessend.up.pt/wisdomtransfer/), the methods of direct observation and indirect observation were used (Quivy and Campenhoudt 2008). Two interviews were carried out with the designer, one in December 2018 and another in January 2019, in his studio, allowing the observation of his paintings and graphic works, namely a set of rare books (which are limited editions of difficult access) selected by him, as well as, the opportunity to witness first-hand, some of the practices that characterised his creative process.

Furthermore, interviews were conducted with some of his students (Appendix), allowing the reconstitution of a set of pedagogical practices adopted by Armando Alves in the field of graphic arts, a subject initially created by him in the context of the Painting course (Mendonça 2007; Lima and Barreto 2019). For the interviews, it was used a script with open-ended questions (Quivy and Campenhoudt 2008) focusing on the artist experiences as student and professor, the role of design in his professional life and methodologies adopted in his creative process. The designer was also asked to select a set of graphic works of his authorship which he considered more remarkable or representative of his graphic legacy.

The interviews were filmed aiming at creating memory support documents for the investigation process (Tinkler 2013). To this end, at the beginning of each interview, the participants were asked for permission to collect images and sound, through an informed consent signed by them, and explained the purpose of these materials (Banks and Zeitlyn 2015).

3 Armando Alves: The Rise of a Graphic Artist

Born in Alentejo (Estremoz, 1935), in the south of Portugal, Armando Alves revealed from an early age a deep interest in graphic arts, at a time when this field had not much presence in the country, with no higher education in Design. In Lisbon, he attended a Preparatory Course in Fine Arts, and later moved to Porto where he graduated in Painting at the School of Fine Arts of Porto (ESBAP) with full marks (Universidade Digital 2008).

It was during this period of training, between 1957 and 1962, that Armando Alves did his first graphic works. Back then, it was common for companies to recruit the best art students to collaborate with them. The first graphic work designed by Armando Alves was commissioned by the company Simão Guimarães e Filhos, for whom he developed graphics for the magazine *Lusíada*[1] (Mendonça 2007). After this work he was invited by Master Carlos Ramos, then director of ESBAP, to develop the catalogues and posters for the Magna Exhibitions and Extra Escolar Exhibitions. These events were held at the school: the Magna Exhibition, where artworks by students created in the school context and selected by the faculty were exhibited side by side with the artworks of the professors themselves; and the Extra Escolar Exhibition, a showcase of works by students carried out in the studios and, therefore, with a less rigorous character in relation to the parameters and guidelines of the course. These exhibitions were of great importance for the school and for the city of Porto itself, being, at the time, newspaper news and attracting a vast population interested in art. And these graphic experiences for the Magna Exhibitions and Extra Escolar Exhibitions were, as stated by Armando Alves, the ones that really aroused his interest in the field of design.

When he finished the course in 1962, he was appointed Assistant Professor at ESBAP where he taught until the early 1970s. Still in 1962, he took on a leading role in the introduction of graphic arts in the school by creating a subject in this field, in the Painting course, which would lead, more than a decade later, to the creation of Communication Design/Graphic Arts course. Armando Alves was then a professor of the discipline of Decorative Painting, a subject whose name dated back to the 19th century, and which proved to be of little interest to the professor in light of the artistic reality of the time. In this sense, and after a period of teaching it, he proposes

[1] Illustrated magazine of culture, art, literature, history and criticism.

to Master Carlos Ramos, as an alternative, a subject of initiation to Graphic Arts. This subject is thus introduced in the ESBAP Painting course. There was no written programme for the subject, nor academic background in Portuguese higher education that could be followed, but an idea of what it was intended to do based on Alves practical experience. The first year would be experimental and then, depending on the results obtained, the continuity of the subject would be evaluated. The approach to the graphic arts subject was then thought of and structured by the graphic artist, characterised by both craftsmanship and experimental work.

As there was no easy access to and exchange of information across borders at the time, his references were restricted to the national environment, the main one being Sebastião Rodrigues, including his graphic work for the publication *Almanaque*. Other existing reference materials were used, namely magazines such as *Marie Claire* or *Paris Match*, according to Armando Alves, publications "of great importance and great graphic quality"[2] (personal communication, December 5, 2018). These publications were analysed graphically in the classroom context and constituted working materials: their graphic contents were cut out and archived to be reused in new graphic compositions in a "cut and paste" process. With these materials, which included clippings of letters, titles, texts or photographs among others, several projects were designed as record covers, fictional book covers and posters.

At the end of the year, the results of this subject were exhibited at the Magna Exhibition and were highly appreciated by the academic community. The Graphic Arts subject, initiated on an experimental basis, was thus stabilised in the course of Painting at ESBAP, maintaining a similar approach over the following years: the analysis of existing graphic work and renowned publications—occasionally from abroad and oriented towards design, such as *Graphis*—and a practice characterised by experimentation and craftsmanship.

One of his students, Nuno Barreto, made an interesting and clarifying description of his classes:

> We made posters, covers, a Greetings card, we confronted ourselves with the dialogue of the illustration with blocks of text. Once again, what we did was on drawing paper, with gouache and papers cut out of magazines. There was no photography studio at the school, no serigraphy or lithography, that allowed us to simulate the final result of our work. As it turns out, we were still light-years away from the digital age, computers, PageMaker[3] and PhotoShop. It was little, just a start without follow up, an awareness raising for the students who, in their overwhelming majority, would, within a few years, be teaching Design, or Visual Education in High School. (Nuno Barreto, cited in Mendonça 2007, p. 62).

Occasionally, the works developed acquired a more experimental and artistic character, partly due to the nature of the course (of Painting) and to the School itself, which was very much oriented towards Plastic Arts and Architecture. This experimental approach paved the way for the development of more alternative projects, blurring the boundaries between art and design. For example Rodrigo Cabral, one of his students in the beginning of the 1970s, recalls a set of posters developed within

[2] All citations in this document are translated by the authors.

[3] Precursor software of Adobe InDesign.

this subject, composed of removable parts, which he called "sculptural objects" (personal communication, December 28, 2018). Nonetheless, it was also frequent for students to develop graphic works on real occasions or events, such as Extra Escolar Exhibitions, for which they designed posters and catalogues (Mendonça 2007).

4 A Painter Dedicated to Graphic Arts

Alongside his academic activity at ESBAP and his activity as a painter, Armando Alves has dedicated himself to a vast production of graphic works covering areas such as poster design, stamp design and catalogue design for several exhibitions, but above all, editorial design. In this field, he produced an extensive work for publishing houses such as Editorial Inova, since its foundation in 1968, Editorial Limiar, founded in 1975 and of which he became graphic director that same year, and Editorial Ouro do Dia, Inova's successor publishing house, of which he took over the graphic direction in 1980, editorial graphic work that Francisco Providência (2016) characterised as "a rare creative example that, despite different visual languages, accentuates common features, where the laconic elegance of silence and rigour prevails, which lent identity to the cultural elite, marked by a new graphic attitude" (p. 12).

In 1973, Armando Alves left ESBAP and dedicated himself exclusively to graphic arts and painting, since he realised it was not possible to successfully conciliate academy and graphic arts outside the school, because "both required great dedication". In fact, since 1968 he was art director of Editorial Inova (Barroso 2014), for which he developed hundreds of books, along with other projects such as commemorative and advertising posters or exhibition catalogues. According to him, back then "there was a great appetence" for graphic works "with a certain quality", and Inova was publishing around 30–40 books per month whose design was of his own authorship (personal communication, December 5, 2018).

From this period, several prestigious works with artistic direction by Armando Alves are worth mentioning, many of them produced with the Portuguese Poet Eugénio de Andrade. Among these works are the 1968 book *Daqui houve nome Portugal: antologia de verso e prosa sobre o Porto*, a commemorative publication of the 1100 years of the city of Porto, organised by Eugénio de Andrade which includes texts by authors such as António Nobre, Aquilino Ribeiro or Miguel Torga; *Memórias de alegria: antologia de verso e prosa sobre Coimbra no centenário da Geração de 70* also organised and prefaced by Eugénio de Andrade, in 1969, with artistic selection and direction by Armando Alves (Barroso 2014); or *Ostinato Rigore*, from 1971, a work highlighted by the graphic artist himself for his graphic and material quality. This book of small dimensions includes a drawing of his authorship and poems by Eugénio de Andrade. With a graphic language ruled by simplicity, the book is presented inside a black cardboard package with a photograph of a puppet he made printed. The design and textured material in which the packaging is produced and

Fig. 2 *Ostinato Rigore*, 1971. Photography: @Cláudia Lima

the book itself inside appeal to greater handling, valuing the experimentation of the work and the sense of touch (Fig. 2).

In the decades that followed Armando Alves had an intense activity, both in the field of graphic arts and painting. Although these areas have crossed, and even contaminated, in the work he produced, the graphic artist has always recognised the specificity of the visual and communicational language of each one of them, considering that over the years he has been able to conciliate these areas "doing different things" (personal communication, December 5, 2018).

Nevertheless, the presence of a more artistic side is recurrent in his graphic works, either by his own intervention when to the graphic layouts he combines his own drawings, or by the collaboration of other artists such as the sculptor José Rodrigues, the painter Almada Negreiros or the poet Eugénio de Andrade.

His graphic work is usually characterised by simplicity, often minimalism, being frequent the use of sans serif typefaces, such as *Avant Garde*, *Helvetica* or *Frutiger*, as he stated, marking a style that Providência defines as being "more modernist than the postmodern aspiration" of Dario Alves or João Machado, designers who stood out in the city of Porto also at this time. The preference for sans serif typefaces is visible in several graphic works he has developed, such as the cover of the aforementioned book *Ostinato Rigore*; the cover of the book *O texto de João Zorro*, from 1974; or the book *Poemas a Guevara*, published in 1975 by Editorial Limiar, where *Futura* is used in a light version and combined with another sans serif typeface.

In fact, the option for minimalism and use of sans serif typefaces tends to be predominant in his most recent graphic works. *Armando Alves: 60 anos de pintura*,

Fig. 3 *Poemas de Veneno e Asas Frias* by Puri Fontes, 2012. Photography: @Cláudia Lima

published in 2017, is an example of a catalog by himself with a hardcover where his name is printed with a light sans serif typeface on a black fine paper. From the same year, *Armando Alves: uma antológica breve*, a catalogue for the anthological exhibition of the artist held in Paris at the Fauve gallery, is another example of this approach. Both these catalogs have a cover and back cover printed separately on fine paper glued to cardboard. The inside pages are sewn and the booklets glued to a fabric that unifies both cover and back cover. These sophisticated finishings are a frequent feature in Armando Alves' graphic work, giving it greater elegance and appealing to a more sensorial experimentation of the work.

Although the preference for sans serif typefaces is visible in his graphic work, there are also notable examples where the author uses serif typefaces without losing his graphic identity. Among them, the book produced in 2012 for the painter Puri Fontes, *Poemas de Veneno e Asas Frias* with a cover where the title is presented in uppercase serif typeface followed by an illustration of the painter thoroughly drawn in graphite (Fig. 3).

This work, of an admirable refinement, opens with a green page with a die-cutting in square format, as if it was a window, on which the first illustration of the painter appears (printed on the next page). On the remaining pages, Puri Fontes' illustrations interpose Laura Costa's texts in a composition guided by minimalism and a monochromatic palette with a wide range of grey tones that convey more realism to the gradients of the drawings given by the graphite.

As a designer, Armando Alves has seen a whole evolution in the graphic arts field fostered by the development of techniques and technologies, both in graphic design and printing production. The introduction of digital systems, in particular, seems to the author a natural way of evolution of things. Thus, he understands the potential of the computer as an execution tool and uses it in the development of his works, though he does not master this technology. To this end, he relies on a collaborator to whom he gives indications on what he intends to do.

Currently 84 years old and retired, Armando Alves keeps his activity as a graphic artist and painter, working daily in his studio, located in Matosinhos (northern

Portugal). The pace and requests for graphic works slowed down, eventually leaving room for the author to devote himself to one of the design aspects that he most appreciates and that most marked his career as a graphic artist: the design of special editions/catalogues, rare books thought of as design objects to be handled and sensorially experienced.

5 From Graphic Design to the Object Design

Although Armando Alves' legacy in the field of graphic arts is very extensive (according to him, by way of example, he developed "thousands of books" for Editorial Inova), it was the special editions, the rare books he developed as true pieces of art, that gave him the most pleasure and that he considers the most remarkable of his career. In these graphic works it is possible to perceive a concern that goes far beyond the organisation of elements and contents on the work surface, being evident a concern with the selection of materials and papers used in the production, the printing technics, as well as the finishings thought out in detail and often handmade. According to Armando Alves, "books are objects and, as objects they are, they also have tact", therefore, their materiality, the way they can be touched and felt, is a determining aspect of the special editions he develops (personal communication, January 15, 2019).

As he told us, when he is asked to develop a graphic work, namely these special editions, he reflects on the whole process: "There is a time to think [about the work] and there is a time to do it". In this sense, he previously seeks and experiments with different materials and the way they combine so that the final result becomes an interesting and original object of design.

One of the special editions highlighted by Armando Alves was *Variações sobre um Corpo*, published in 1972. This is a rare book he developed together with Eugénio de Andrade and José Rodrigues, that he considers as an object of design, paying special attention to the way it can be handled and touched. Indeed, this is a principle underlying his graphic works—the way the public experiences the handling of the book—and therefore he values the sensory side of the work appealing not only to the visual sense, but also to the sense of touch. Inside, poems of well known Portuguese writers are worked with the *Avant Garde*, a typeface that marked the 1960s and that Armando Alves has always considered very elegant, having used it in his graphic works very often until nowadays (Fig. 4).

For *Variações sobre um Corpo* 20 copies were produced, numbered from I to XX plus 6 copies (not for selling) numbered from A to F, printed in *Damier* paper with 200 g. This special edition has reproductions of 26 drawings and an original drawing by José Rodrigues, as well as a handwritten poem by one of the authors included in the publication. The small number of copies produced and the originals included made this work very expensive and rare. As reported by Armando Alves, at the time,

Fig. 4 *Variações sobre um Corpo*, special edition organised by Eugénio de Andrade with drawings by José Rodrigues, graphic work by Armando Alves, 1972. Photography: @Cláudia Lima

the selling price was PTE 7000[4], a cost that was justified not only by the value of the production itself, but also by the value of the original drawing and the handwritten poem.

In this context of rare works developed by the author, *Maternidade*, published in 1982 for Imprensa Nacional, also stands out. This rare book has a hardcover binding covered with leather with a foil stamped in gold. Inside, the pages of the book are presented separately, without binding, with reproductions of 26 drawings by Almada Negreiros, all made in March 1948, 1 painting by this same author as well as texts by Ernesto de Sousa about the Motherhood. Although Almada Negreiros' drawings are reproductions, the book includes an original by this author. About this work, Armando Alves highlights the quality of the reproduction of the drawings (an image whose quality is very close to the originals, as we could verify), printed in the old Inova Printing House, in Porto. In the interview, he appreciated and praised the printing, done in offset lithography, stating that, even looking closely "it really looks like the original" (personal communication, January 15, 2019), since the printing dot is not perceptible to the naked eye, but only using the printing loupe (it is a very fine dot). Thus, when we look at the reproductions of José Rodrigues, we have the sensation of observing the originals, the detail of the pencil, the texture of the charcoal (Fig. 5).

Another special edition highlighted by Armando Alves was *Dunas*, a catalogue by João Avelino with texts by Eugénio de Andrade, published in 1989, whose production required intense craftsmanship. In this work, the photographs were printed on photographic paper and glued manually (one by one) on heavy paper lightly textured.

[4]PTE (Portuguese Escudo) was the Portuguese currency used in the 20th century (before the entry of the euro). The existence of a minimum wage in Portugal dates back to 1974 (Decree-Law No. 217/74 of 27 May 1974), when the value of PTE 3300 was established, a value that "represented a scandalous increase for many people", as Avelino Pacheco Gonçalves, then Minister of Labor, reported in an interview to Faria (2014).

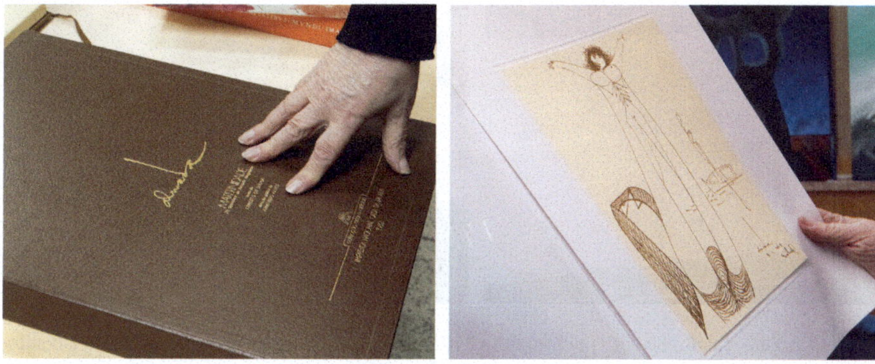

Fig. 5 *Maternidade*, special edition with text by Ernesto de Sousa, drawings and painting by Almada Negreiros, graphic work by Armando Alves, 1982. Photography: @Cláudia Lima

The pages are packed in a transparent acrylic box whose hinge is sewn by hand with brown thread, giving it an elegant handmade look (Fig. 6).

In this work the author uses a sans serif typeface in upper case, in a graphic approach ruled by simplicity and minimalism, a frequent characteristic of his graphic works.

In the context of rare books, *Príncipio* also stands out, a catalogue from 1990 with photographs by João Avelino Marques and texts by Mário Cláudio, for which only 20 copies were produced, of which 15 were numbered from 1 to 15 and 5, that were not for sell, numbered from I to V. All copies have the signature of the authors and the photographs are originals printed in Fujichrome paper. Packed in a transparent acrylic box, as *Dunas*, this work is printed in large format on *Moulin du Gue* paper of 270 g, a textured heavy paper. The texts are worked with a serif typeface whose drawing refers us to the typography of the typewriter, giving the catalogue a greater refinement while conveying a more artisanal character (Fig. 7).

Fig. 6 *Dunas*, catalogue with photography by João Avelino Marques and text by Eugénio de Andrade, graphic work by Armando Alves, 1989. Photography: @Cláudia Lima

Fig. 7 *Princípio*, catalogue with photography by João Avelino Marques and text by Mário Cláudio, graphic work by Armando Alves, 1990. Photography: @Cláudia Lima

For these works, Armando Alves insisted on following the whole production process at the printing company: "I spent many nights there in lithography" (personal communication, January 15, 2019). As in all works, there were deadlines. Part of the production process was manual and time consuming. Sometimes it was necessary to make corrections, often on the printing machine itself, directly on the plate.

Special editions like these presented here are the graphic works that he considers the most outstanding of his career and true challenges where he feels the creative act. When asked about possible links between his paintings and his graphic work, the author argues that these two areas tend to have a different approach and language. He observes that many of his paintings are characterised by the work of colour, namely by vivid colours, contrary to his graphic work which is more focused on depuration and minimalism. Nevertheless, we verified in his studio the existence of a set of works of art where the approach is also characterised by minimalism, works that he considers "very graphic" designating them as *painting-objects* (personal communication, January 15, 2019). In these *painting-objects* that he showed to us, we can sense a symbiosis between his paintings on canvas, often with vivid colours, and the clean approach that characterise his graphic works.

Works such as *Maternidade*, *Variações sobre um Corpo*, *Dunas* or *Princípio* are special editions whose quantity produced is generally between 10 and 20 copies. These are expensive graphic works targeted mainly to bibliophiles[5]. Given the nature and specificity of these editions, the author observes that, in these cases, no financial constraints are imposed, since the publishers already have a predetermined idea of what they want and a notion of the associated costs. These are rare works, printed in a very small number and, inevitably, they become expensive. Nevertheless, by limiting the number of copies, their production becomes viable. They are considered to be rare bibliographic collections, being much more than books or catalogues: they are design objects.

[5]In fact, for all these editions there were versions of small format, without the originals of the artists, with a less expensive binding and, therefore, at a more affordable price.

6 Conclusions

Graduated in painting, and with an extensive work in this field, Armando Alves has always lived between art and design, exercising an intense activity that allowed him a national recognition and abroad, as a painter and as a designer.

In higher education, although empirically, Alves introduces the subject of graphic arts, establishing the first practices in this field much based on experimentation and craftsmanship. We can argue that his practical approach has greatly contributed to the understanding of design in ESBAP, subsequently having repercussions in the formatting of the Graphic Arts subject and the Design (Graphic Arts) course itself.

Although there are no evident similarities in the works he carried out in the domains of art and design, it is clear that the artist's sensitivity and approach is transversal, especially when we observe the rare books and catalogues, highlighted by him as the most outstanding graphic works he has made. In fact, his artistic roots can be seen in the numerous graphic works that resulted from collaborations with other Portuguese artists such as José Rodrigues or Almada Negreiros, as well as in those where he illustrates the graphic work with his own drawings.

In the special editions, his approach goes beyond the domain of graphic design, prevailing the idea of object design. Hence, he explores the sensorial side of the work and the way in which the public experiences it, not only through the visual sense, but also through the sense of tact. Thus, when we observe these works, when we handle and experience them, we realise that his approach transcends the strict context of graphic design: what we observe are objects of design and true pieces of art. Furthermore, we verified that there is a whole conceptual thought around the design object that makes each one of these special editions unique, though we can find certain graphic patterns that characterise the graphic style of the artist.

From a contemporary perspective, it is argued that this aspect of Armando Alves's work reveals great harmony and relevance with design niches that today operate an unexpected return to manual processes and a re-inscription of the material object, as a multiple form of complement to the prevailing immaterial digital culture.

Acknowledgements The authors wish to thank the Foundation for Science and Technology for the financial support of the Wisdom Transfer project (POCI-01-0145-FEDER-029038).

Appendix

List of interviewees participants of the *Wisdom Transfer* project between December 2018 and November 2019

Name	Course	Start	End	Date of the interview
Ana Campos	Communication Design/Graphic Arts	1976	1981	27th June 2019
Antero Pinto	Communication Design	1979	1987	10th January 2019
António Mendanha	Painting	1979	1986	10th January 2019
António Quadros Ferreira	Painting	1966	1971	12th April 2019
Armando Alves	Painting	1957	1962	5th December 2018 15th January 2019
Carlos Barreira	Sculpture	1968	1973	8th January 2019
Carlos Carreiro	Painting	1967	1972	16th January 2019
Carlos Marques	Sculpture	1967	1975	11th December 2018
Elvira Leite	Painting	1957	1962	15th January 2019
Graça Morais	Painting	1966	1971	31st January 2019
Haydée De = Francesco	Sculpture	1956	1961	21st January 2019
Helena Abreu e Lima	Painting	1963	1968	23rd January 2019
Helena Almeida Santos	Painting	1961	1966	7th January 2019
Isabel Cabral	Painting	1967	1973	28th December 2018
João Machado	Sculpture	1963	1968	1st March 2019
João Nunes	Communication Design/Graphic Arts	1976	1981	26th February 2019
Jorge Pinheiro	Painting	1955	1963	16th April 2019
José Paiva	Painting	1968	1986	19th December 2018
Leonilde Santos	Painting	1981	1986	14th December 2018
Lima de Carvalho	Painting	1967	1972	31st January 2019
Lúcia Matos	–	–	–	24th January 2019
Manuela Bronze	Painting	1975	1981	4th January 2019
Maria José Aguiar	Painting	1967	1972	14th January 2019
Maria José Valente	Painting	1968	1977	22nd January 2019
Mário Américo	Painting	1962	1972	25th January 2019
Mário Moura	Architecture	1961	1967	5th November 2019
Paula Soares	Painting	1973	1978	8th April 2019
Pedro Rocha	Painting	1967	1972	30th January 2019
Purificação Fontes	Sculpture	1964	1972	22th January 2019
Rodrigo Cabral	Painting	1968	1973	28th December 2018
Sobral Centeno	Painting	1969	1978	20th December 2018
Zulmiro de Carvalho	Sculpture	1963	1968	7th January 2019

References

Banks M, Zeitlyn D (2015) Visual methods in social research. SAGE Publications

Barroso EP (2014) Escutar uma Pintura. Modo de Ler, Porto

Faria N (2014, April 13). A criação do salário mínimo em 1974 foi um impulso para a economia. Público. Retrieved from https://www.publico.pt/2014/04/13/sociedade/noticia/a-criacao-do-salario-minimo-em-1974-foi-um-impulso-para-a-economia-1631964

Lima C, Barreto S (2019) Caminhos cruzados de Armando Alves. Revista Gama, Estudos Artísticos. Retrieved from http://gama.fba.ul.pt/G_v7_iss13.pdf

Mendonça R (2007) O Cartaz e a Escola_Um Estudo Centrado nos Autores e no Curso de Design das Belas Artes do Porto (Dissertação de Doutoramento). Faculdade de Pelas Artes da Universidade do Porto

Providência F (2016) João Machado: comunicar com o mundo. In: Providência F, Bártolo J, Silva HS (eds) João Machado. Cardume Editores, Matosinhos, pp 8–29

Quivy, R., & Campenhoudt, L. V. (2008). *Manual de Investigação em Ciências Sociais*. Lisboa: Gradiva

Tinkler P (2013) Using photographs in social and historical research. Sage Publications

Universidade Digital (2008). University of Porto Famous Alumni: Armando Alves. Retrieved from https://sigarra.up.pt/up/en/WEB_BASE.GERA_PAGINA?P_pagina=1001299

Designing for Cinema Trindade: Graphic Communication in Contemporary Portuguese Cinemas

Igor Ramos and Helena Barbosa

Abstract After eighty-three years of existence, Cinema Trindade didn't resist the economic monopoly that big multiplex cinemas had over the national market of film exhibition and closed its doors in 2000. In 2017 it reopened to the public, with a renewed project that has benefited from a favourable situation and enthusiastic reception by the city habitants ('portuenses') and the Portuguese film industry. This article speaks about the role of design in the development of graphic objects, printed and digital, destined to communicate and promote the weekly programme and the events organised by Cinema Trindade, explaining how the curatorship of films, the cinema's audience and other variables have influenced the creation of such objects. Without wanting to reclaim a "case-of-study" status, Trindade does constitute a unique reality since it is, currently, the only neighbourhood cinema open everyday in Porto, and represents an indelible mark in the memory of several generations of Portuenses and the city's history. The partnership with Cinema Trindade has been proving the advantages of having an in-house designer giving response, on a daily basis, to the challenges of visual communication.

Keywords Neighborhood cinema · Graphic design · Cinemas of Porto · Cinema Trindade · Film exhibition

1 Introduction

As part of a broader investigation currently being developed at the Doctoral Programme in Design of the University of Aveiro, focused on the history of the Portuguese film poster seen through the lens of design, the opportunity arose to collaborate with Cinema Trindade in the graphic idealization and design of its communication supports, which serve as a vehicle to promote the weekly programme and

I. Ramos (✉) · H. Barbosa
University of Aveiro / ID+ Research Institute for Design, Media and Culture, Aveiro, Portugal
e-mail: igor.ramos@ua.pt

H. Barbosa
e-mail: helenab@ua.pt

N. Martins et al. (eds.), *Perspectives on Design and Digital Communication*,
Springer Series in Design and Innovation 8, https://doi.org/10.1007/978-3-030-49647-0_2

other special events. Since the reopening of this historical neighbourhood cinema, located in downtown Porto, in February 2017, the project has represented a window for theoretical and practical learning about the national circuit of film distribution and exhibition from a designer's point of view.

The present chapter accounts for this three-year journey, explaining how design has been, right from the beginning, considered to be of the upmost importance to the communication with audience and visitors. In order to do so, it's initially presented a brief incursion into the historical background of Cinema Trindade and the circumstances that led to its closure, in the year 2000, and further reopening in 2017. Then the current status of film exhibition in Portugal is briefly presented, in terms of market dynamics and design approach, before introducing, in more detail, the strategy idealized for Cinema Trindade and exploring how graphic design has been a tool to build and promote the identity of this particular cinema. After presenting examples of several materials designed, the eyes are set on the future to present some clues towards new challenges for Cinema Trindade—and independent cinemas at large—and also further studies regarding this subject matter.

2 The Past and the Present

2.1 A Brief History of Cinema Trindade

Cinema Trindade was inaugurated on the 14th of June, 1913, as 'Salão Jardim da Trindade', meaning Hall Garden of Trindade, 'Trindade' being one of the main areas in the city centre.[1] It was a venue destined to welcome a wide variety of cultural events and spectacles such as theatre, musical and dance plays as well as film screenings. With a great hall of around 1200 seats, cabins, restaurants and an outside garden (with terrace, bandstand and shooting school) in its precinct, it was described by the press at the time as "the most luxurious and comfortable venue" in the city of Porto (Gonçalves 2018, p. 70). It closed its doors for the first time between October, 1st and November, 10th 1930, at the end of the outdoors summertime cinema sessions, to proceed with the installation of technological apparatus that would allow the screening of sound films (2018, p. 88).

Following the inauguration of new venues in the city of Porto with a more modernist architecture, such as the Coliseu (in 1941) and Cinema Batalha (in 1947), a work permit application was made in 1946 to modernize the installations of Cinema Trindade, developed by modernist architects Viana de Lima (1913–1991) and Agostinho Ricca Gonçalves (1915–2010). Although it was approved by the City Council, it never came to fruition. Only in 1956, after twenty-five years since the

[1] Historically because of the Trindade Church, located right behind the Aliados square and the City Council Building, and nowadays due to the Trindade subway station, epicentre of the Porto subway line system and surrounded by a large concentration of services, hotels, office buildings and commerce.

last modernization works were carried out in the premises, did António Ferreira Neves, head of 'Empresa do Cinema Trindade' (the company that owned Cinema Trindade) submit a remodeling project for the building, very similar to one from 1946. Agostinho Ricca became the lead architect and was later joined by Architect Benjamim do Carmo (2018, pp. 107–109).

With the dawn of television,[2] VHS tapes and the arrival of large-scale cinemas integrated into shopping malls, neighborhood cinemas such as Trindade struggled in terms of audience turnout and financial viability, particularly in the last quarter of the 20th century. In order to prevent closure, extensive works were carried out between 1989 and 1990: the great hall, which had a very high ceiling, was converted into three floors, giving place to two smaller screening rooms (on the ground floor) where the cinema kept working, and a larger room (first and second floors) home to a Bingo parlor. Cinema Trindade resisted until de year 2000, when it was forced to close, eighty seven years after its inauguration, with an average number of just 7.3 people per session (Marques 2016).

The Bingo helped in some capacity to preserve the building, its structure and the two cinema rooms, allowing them to be used sporadically: in 2008, to host and week-long extension of the Indielisboa film festival, and in 2014 and 2015, during three days, to welcome the Desobedoc film cycle. In September 2016, plans were announced in the press to reopen Cinema Trindade, explored by film distributor Nitrato Filmes that was going to be leasing the cinema from Empresa Neves & Pascaud, owner of the property. The main goal was to restore daily cinema sessions in downtown Porto, which up until that point only took place sporadically at cinema-bar Passos Manuel and Rivoli Theatre. The installation of a digital projection system that would allow films to be reproduced from a DCP—*Digital Cinema Package*[3] represented the main financial investment to reopening the cinema, upon which there were also requalification works so that the venue, closed for sixteen years, would comply with the legislation, safety and hygiene standards inherent in the operation of cinemas in Portugal. Only after that the two rooms, one with 169 seats and the other with 183, were ready to welcome back the people from Porto into the cinema.

2.2 *Cinemas and Film Exhibition in Portugal*

Film distribution in Portugal is made essentially through major and minor distributors that own or lease the cinemas where the films are to be exhibited and/or establish agreements with other cinemas to exhibit the films they're distributing, who then collect a percentage of the ticket sales money. Production, distribution and exhibition can be intertwined within the same structure as different companies: as an

[2]The first Portuguese TV channel, state-owned RTP1, began its regular transmission in 1957, and a second channel, RTP2, in 1968. In the 1990 s, they were joined by private TV channels SIC (1992) and TVI (1993).

[3]Package of files necessary to the projection of the film, which are encapsulated into a hard drive.

example, producer Paulo Branco operates on all three sectors with Leopardo Filmes (production and distribution) and Cinemas Medeia (distribution and exhibition) and is the leading entity in terms of *auteur* cinema exhibition in Portugal.

Cinemas NOS, UCI Cinemas, Cineplace and Cinema City dominate large-scale film exhibition since they're present in major shopping malls in cities across Portugal. According to official data from 2019 by ICA (National Institute of Cinema and Audiovisual), together they amassed 89.3% of the total number of admissions in Portuguese cinemas, and 91% of the GBO (Gross Box Office), the money generated in ticket sales. The majority of these cinemas are multiplexes—big venues with eight or more screening rooms: in 2019 there were in Portugal a total of nineteen multiplex cinemas, representing 65.5% of all cinema screens and 48.8% of the total number of admissions (ICA 2020).

This, of course, reveals a great asymmetry that leaves small cinemas with narrow margins within the film exhibition market.

Big exhibitors offer audiences a wide range of films, from the biggest Hollywood blockbusters to the occasional, lesser-known titles coming from independent studios and world cinema. The large-scale nature of their business allows financial investment by distributors in major publicity campaigns, promoting films that are beforehand expected to generate big box-office returns. At the same time, smaller films usually go more unnoticed in this reality and instead find a niche audience in smaller cinemas, which can prove more profitable in the long run, because they cater to a different kind of public, more interested in the alternative film circuit.

Since the majority of small film distributors don't own cinemas, their films can be exhibited in multiplexes (where every week they face tough competition from big blockbusters for session times and rooms), or smaller venues such as neighbourhood cinemas and small cinema rooms, cine-theatres and cultural/educational associations that exist outside shopping malls and retail stores. In Lisbon, distributor Midas Filmes explores Cinema Ideal, a neighbourhood cinema that reopened in 2014 and mirrors the situation of Cinema Trindade, in Porto, which is explored by Nitrato Filmes since 2017. Medeia Filmes explores cinemas in Lisbon (Espaço Nimas, Fernando Lopes room in Lusófona University), Porto (Rivoli/Campo Alegre), Setúbal (Cinema Charlot), Figueira da Foz (CAE), Braga (Theatro Circo) and Coimbra (TAGV), among others. In other cities, film sessions can be held daily, once or several times a week, and are organized by cine-clubs and the cities' municipalities (cultural cabinets). It's common for some films to spend some weeks screening in major cities and simultaneously or afterwards begin a tour through smaller cities, concentrating audiences in just one day/screening session.

The downturn of the very well structured and optimized communication strategies from big cinemas is the homogenization of supports and languages to a wider audience, while small cinemas in some capacity tailor the films and contents to their costumers. This is possible by maintaining a more intimate approach to the cinematic experience, printing physical objects, fostering a relationship with the visitors, highlighting some films based on their stories and organizing special sessions with directors, actors, film critics, journalists or other personalities. The struggle for self-sufficiency and profit forces them to be more creative with fewer resources and to think about their programme and distinctive offers on a weekly basis.

It was clear from the start that this was the segment where Cinema Trindade would be operating.

2.3 Reopening and Strategic Approach

After two collaborations[4] with independent film distributor Nitrato Filmes in the last trimester of 2016, there was an invitation to outline a communication strategy to promote the weekly programme of Cinema Trindade. The inauguration took place on February 5th, 2017 and regular daily sessions began on the 16th, running uninterrupted until the present day.

The sustainability and considerable success[5] in the reopening of Cinema Trindade can be attributed to five key-factors. First, the tourism boom in the city of Porto: it was both cause and effect for the revival of the city's downtown and its infrastructures, and is responsible for a considerable number of tourists visiting the cinema and watching films there. Likewise, the deterioration of the political climate in Brazil since the election of President Jair Bolsonaro in 2018 has led to a new wave of Brazilian emigration in Portugal: whether looking for a short or long-time residency, studying or working, the number of Brazilian visitors to Cinema Trindade has risen considerably during the last year.

A second important key-factor was the support given by the City Council of Porto to cultural promotion and particularly to cinema through initiatives such as the monthly publication (online and printed) of 'Agenda do Cinema Independente,[6] (Independent Cinema Schedule) and creating the Tripass card, which would allow discounts in Downtown ('Baixa') cinemas—Rivoli Theatre, Passos Manuel and Trindade—thus fostering dynamics and audience loyalty to this circuit.

The absence of a cinema venue with regular, daily sessions in the center of Porto and the subsequent need for people to go to shopping malls in order to watch films on the big screen also represented a window of opportunity to give back to 'Baixa' this cultural offer. The location is also relevant: located at number 412 of Rua do Almada, Trindade benefits from the proximity to public transports (subway and buses) and a concentration of services, commerce, bars, cafes, restaurants and other spots that are important do the day life and night life of Porto. Going to Cinema Trindade can

[4]Design of the graphic materials for distribution of the Portuguese film *The Ornithologist* directed by João Pedro Rodrigues, and development of the identity for the 20th edition of the Luso-Brazilian Film Festival in the town of Santa Maria da Feira.

[5]In the first year open, the cinema as received around 50 000 visitors. "Reopening a neighbourhood cinema felt like and adventure, an idea far too romantic, but it has been a surprise. The people from Porto have embraced it. It opened at the right moment, a time of great cultural and touristic movement" declared Américo Santos to Lusa—Portuguese news agency (Porto City Council, 2018).

[6]Compiles all cinema sessions happening throughout the city of Porto, outside the big exhibitors.

be a relaxed way to end a long day or the starting point to a night out in the city, since it's at a walking distance to all major points of interest in the city center. Rua do Almada, a parallel to Avenida dos Aliados, is an emblematic street and an easy point of reference to visitors and residents alike.

The selection of films is another significant factor, perhaps the most important one. The curatorship developed by Américo Santos has privileged, since day one, *auteur* cinema[7]: films from all around the world, from directors recognized and celebrated for having a distinctive point of view on cinema at the art of filmmaking, usually with a remarkable path through the national and international film festival circuits. Even though Cinema Trindade's weekly programme sometimes includes films also screened in big cinemas, it mostly aims to represent an alternative to them, organizing often special screenings with directors, actors or other special guests in attendance, followed by Q&A's between them and the audience. Programming or hosting small-scale film festivals/cycles or special events in collaboration with entities from Porto is another common practice at Cinema Trindade: by doing so not only it welcomes new visitors but also promotes cultural dynamics within the city.

Finally, a latent feeling of 'nostalgia' cannot be overlooked when considering the public engagement with this project. The success of Cinema Trindade also results from a desire to return to a purest way of enjoying the cinematic experience, without all the 'noise' that surrounds large shopping-mall cinemas: trailers, advertising spots, intermissions, popcorns... and the consumerism and confusion that are inherent. At Trindade all films start on time, no food is available and there are also some DVDs, books and film soundtracks for sale.

At the same time, an investment was made in terms of communication, both printed and digital, through which the weekly programme is disseminated to the Porto city audience. It is in this context that design became essential.

3 The Role of Design

3.1 Weekly Programme

The weekly programme of Cinema Trindade usually consists of a selection of five to eight films, but in more atypical weeks that number has oscillated between three and twelve films. Like in every national cinema, the weekly programme changes every

[7]*Auteur* theory is theory of filmmaking in which the director is viewed as the major creative force in a motion picture (...) The auteur theory, which was derived largely from Astruc's elucidation of the concept of *caméra-stylo* ("camera-pen"), holds that the director, who oversees all audio and visual elements of the motion picture, is more to be considered the "author" of the movie than is the writer of the screenplay. In other words, such fundamental visual elements as camera placement, blocking, lighting, and scene length, rather than plot line, convey the message of the film. Supporters of the auteur theory further contend that the most cinematically successful films will bear the unmistakable personal stamp of the director (Encyclopædia Britannica 2020).

Fig. 1 Façade of Cinema Trindade (view from Rua do Almada) showcasing the weekly poster

Thursday, with new films premiering, others leaving or continuing in different timetables, with more or less sessions, considering how their commercial performance has been during the week before.

Although special sessions or reruns of classic films are sporadically programmed, the line-up consists mostly of new, contemporary films, following the national calendar of film premieres. It is announced and promoted to the public by recurring to print (poster and flyer) and digital mediums (website, newsletter, Facebook and Instagram accounts).

Three copies of the 70 × 100 cm poster with the programme are printed and displayed inside the cinema, on the façade facing Rua do Almada (Figs. 1 and 2) and on the glass window on the other entrance to the cinema, through the Bingo staircase access (Rua Dr. Ricardo Jorge). The print run of the flyer (Fig. 3) consists of around 500 copies, in A5 format and 180 g. weight.[8] The majority of copies stay in the cinema, where everyday dozens of people usually walk into grab their flyer, but a small number is also distributed in cafes and social spaces around Cinema Trindade. The newsletter is sent every Wednesday to the approximately 7000 subscribers. The contents are the same in poster, flyer and newsletter: title of the film and corresponding image, the director's name, technical specifications (country of origin, year, run time,

[8]During the first year, the flyer format was smaller (10 cm × 21 cm) with a lighter paper weight, essentially for greater savings in printing costs.

Fig. 2 Façade of Cinema Trindade (view from Rua do Almada) showcasing the weekly poster

Fig. 3 Front side of several flyers showcasing the grid adaptation to a variable number of films (April and May 2019)

age rating), small synopsis, indication of awards/selections to festivals and screening times. The image and block containing the written information are adjacent and complementary to each other through a chromatic coordination.

Given the very short window of time for its graphic execution,[9] the poster, flyer and newsletter keep cohesion among them by recurring to a grid template that allows a quick adaptation accordingly to the number of films that need to be included every week. The font Universe is used across the different graphic supports, where different weights and sizes allow good legibility and understanding of the information conveyed. It was considered important to display a clear hierarchy of information and a sober graphic approach, not too conservative but not too bold either, considering the diversity of visitors that attend Trindade in terms of age and social-cultural background.

Besides the special care in selecting the images representing each film, the highlights given to directors' names and awards/selections in film festivals were planned taking into account and expressing the criteria valued by the curatorial approach. In addition to the indication of the dates that mark the weekly programme (beginning and end), there are 'stickers' signaling when the film is a premiere, special session or event, contacts of the cinema and institutional logos of the Porto City Council, ICA and the Europa Cinemas network.

The contents are also subsequently transferred to the website and throughout the week are published various posts in the Facebook (+15,000 followers) and Instagram (+5000 followers) accounts of Cinema Trindade promoting the films in exhibition. Facebook has been, since the beginning, the privileged channel for digital communication with the audience, because of how omnipresent and transversal it is across different target audiences, for allowing to quickly and intuitively share contents, interact and respond to followers, and allowing to create events to which they can subscribe and get notifications. The cover image on the Facebook page works as a header where the weekly programme is always visible, and is updated on Wednesday nights or Thursday mornings, announcing the new programme[10] (Fig. 4).

The current logo of Cinema Trindade (Fig. 5), designed by Márcia Novais and Tiago Carneiro,[11] was idealized before the inauguration: a collaboration that didn't continue with the cinema's management. It's evokes the movement of frames, and uses the font Prophet Medium. Despite being present in all the communication materials, it was never further explored in terms of graphic or typographic deconstruction or applications, mainly because these hypothesis and explorations resided with the two designer's vision, and since they were no longer involved with the project it didn't feel appropriate to continue it.

[9]Usually the programme is closed during Tuesday evening/night and the materials are printed on Wednesday morning/afternoon, so that they're available in the cinema's facilities on Wednesday night or Thursday morning.

[10]Featuring the list of films and their screening times throughout the week.

[11]**Márcia Novais** (www.marcia-novais.com) and **Tiago Carneiro** (www.tiagocarneiro.com).

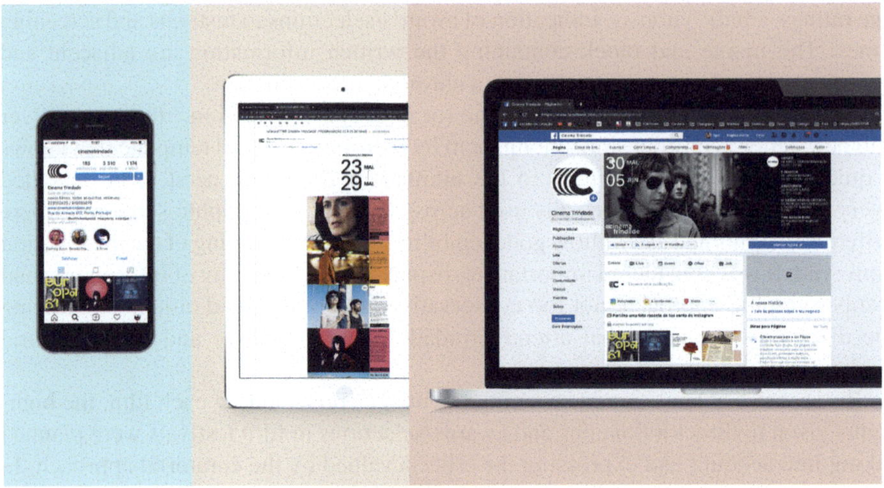

Fig. 4 Instagram account, weekly *newsletter* and Facebook page of Cinema Trindade (May 2019)

Fig. 5 Current logo of Cinema Trindade

3.2 *Special Events*

In parallel with the weekly programme, Cinema Trindade keeps presenting other challenges from a design point of view, regarding more occasional events that require their own communication while still having to be in some way coherent and connected with the weekly program graphic language. The most significant of these events

Fig. 6 Posters for the birthday weeks of Cinema Trindade (February 2018, 2019 and 2020)

is the birthday week, which takes place every year, between the 5th and 16th of February, and consists of a parallel programme that includes nearly three dozens of films distributed across four axis: Premieres, Director in Focus, Portugal Cinema (2018, 2019 and 2020) and Country in Focus (2018, 2019)/Docs Cinema (2020). The design of a commemorative poster (Fig. 6) serves as a starting point to develop a graphic identity which in then applied to a flyer, informative MUPI's for each axis, timetable, promotional card, digital contents and other materials. The posters for birthday weeks have been exploring and representing the same idea of cinema as a potential path/portal to access other stories and other worlds, thus evoking an imagery that combines inspirations related with astronomy and the magic and surrealism found on the cinema screen.

Other highlights from the last three years were the film cycles *Especial João Nicolau* and *Especial Gabriel Mascaro* in November 2019 (Fig. 7),[12] *Universo Bressane* in September 2018 (Fig. 8),[13] *Cinema Francês em Estreia* during May and June 2018 (Fig. 9),[14] and the premiere of the film *Don't Worry, He Won't Get Far on Foot*,[15] which was accompanied by an illustration showcase featuring artworks by

---

[12]Each week was dedicated to one director: first was Brazilian director Gabriel Mascaro (b.1983), with the premiere of his new film *Divine Love* (2019) and reposition of two previous films *Neon Bull* (2015) and *August Winds* (2014). Followed by Portuguese director João Nicolau (b.1975), who attended the premiere of his new film *Technoboss* (2019), and also *John From* (2015) and *The Sword and the Rose* (2010).

[13]'Bressane Universe': three films directed by Brazilian director Júlio Bressane (b.1943).

[14]'French Cinema on Premiere': Premiere of six French films, two of which starred French actress Isabelle Huppert (n.1953), who was featured in the communication materials designed for this film cycle.

[15]Biopic directed by Gus Van Sant (b.1952), about the life of American cartoonist John Callahan (1951–2010).

Fig. 7 Flyers for the film cycles *Especial João Nicolau* and *Especial Gabriel Mascaro* (November 2019)

Pudim Studio[16] (Fig. 10), in July 2018, that required planning out the exhibition design within the cinema's wall.

The large white wall in the cinema is a place to showcase graphic objects regarding the films and events whenever necessary, and also has a "Coming Soon" section where are continuously being revealed the premiere dates for upcoming films, keeping the visitors' curiosity alive. There's also a small show window, in the lobby leading up to the two screening rooms, where are exhibited some objects related with the world of cinema and filmmaking, which also displays a selection of photos from the first three years of memories at the cinema.

3.3 *Looking at the Future*

Following the celebration of the third birthday, the main communication vehicles of Cinema Trindade and its identity are well defined and established. The goal continues to be the expansion of this audience, while keeping in mind the clear contrasts

[16]Collective of three illustrators living and working in Porto: Carmena, Raquel Sem Interesse and Vicente Nirō.

Fig. 8 Bifold brochure for the film cycle *Universo Bressane* (September 2018)

between a neighborhood cinema and multiplexes, which despite operating on the same market have distinct resources available, strategic visions and communication vehicles.

The slogan of Cinema Trindade—"cinema, right next door"—finds its expression in the graphic materials designed; in its personalization and adequacy to the cinema's own identity which is simultaneously defined by them in some capacity. Small rituals like stopping in front of the cinema to see the poster with the weekly programme, or stepping inside to get one of the flyers and see the posters of the films in exhibition are part of the routine of the visitors. Since the reopening of Trindade that the work developed by the designer has complemented the day-to-day efforts of those who are truly responsible to keep the cinema running: the programmer, the manager, the people working at the front desk/ticket office and the projection technics (Fig. 11).

In strategic terms, there's an intention to keep creating more contents oriented towards Instagram, a social network increasingly more relevant amongst teenagers and young adults, a segment of audience that still prefers to watch films on shopping malls, streaming platforms or through illegal downloads. The website is another aspect that in the upcoming months will be restructured and redesigned to offer a better interface and allow booking tickets online through an appropriate platform, since currently this is only possible by calling or sending an e-mail to the cinema, which is not always practical for visitors, particularly in special sessions with high-demand of tickets, that sell out quickly.

Fig. 9 Bifold brochure for the film cycle *Cinema Francês em Estreia* (May 2018)

On the long term there's also an intention to design a new logo based on a concept and graphic argument that would allow it to be used in a more integrated and articuled way through all the communication supports.

Even thought it's not intrinsically related with Cinema Trindade, it would be useful to pick up on the idea of the Porto City Council of a Schedule of Independent Cinema and expand it to all the country or its regions. Because small, independent cinemas such as Trindade (in Porto), Ideal (in Lisbon) and all the others in different Portuguese cities and villages exist as 'small islands' in the film exhibition market, it could be interesting and helpful to create an official network and online platform that was able to congregate data and information on all the sessions taking place throughout the country, just like the big exhibitors do. Combining and communicating the activities of all small venues in one place and optimizing the digital user experience might instigate more people to see the films outside the big cinemas even it means waiting a little bit more.

Fig. 10 Exhibition design for the illustration showcase *Don't Worry, He Won't Get Far on Foot*, with the team from Pudim Studio (July 2018)

4 Conclusion

This article has outlined a global vision about the history and design strategy of Cinema Trindade, the only neighborhood cinema in downtown Porto with daily film sessions. Inaugurated in 2017, after an interregnum of sixteen years, it has resorted to design in order to create several communication supports that matched the film curatorship and also its target audiences in order to create routines and loyalty habits amongst them.

By combining printed and digital mediums, Cinema Trindade has built a community of thousands of followers, subscribers and visitors who are indispensable for the success of this comeback. By not trying to compete directly against the shopping mall multiplexes, and providing a different kind of cinematic experience, Trindade has made a sustainable and sustained path in which design finds expression and is valued.

Neighborhood cinemas struggle for survival is fought everyday and every week: the main challenge for Cinema Trindade—and design at its service—will be trying to expand its audience by developing new communication strategies and initiatives that promote the cinema and inspire the community, with design continuing to play and inseparable role.

Fig. 11 The team behind Cinema Trindade (February 2019)

Note All figures featured in this article were created and belong to the authors.

Acknowledgements This work is funded by national funds through the FCT—Foundation for Science and Technology I.P., within the scope of project <UID/DES/04057/2019> with the PhD scholarship grant number <PD/BD/135279/2017> .

References

Encyclopædia Britannica (2020) Definition of 'auteur theory' [In line]. EUA, Chicago. [Consult. 28 Febryary 2020]. Availabe at WWW: https://www.britannica.com/art/auteur-theory

Gonçalves A (2018) Salão Jardim da Trindade: Um cinema palimpsesto (1912–2017). Orient. Hugo Daniel Silva Barreira. Faculdade de Letras da Universidade do Porto, Porto, 2018. 75 f. Dissertação de Mestrado em História da Arte, Património e Cultura Visual

ICA (2020) Cinema Audiovisual de/from Portugal 2020: Dados Estatísticos/facts and figures. Instituto do Cinema e Audiovisual, Lisbon. ISBN 978-989-33-0330-6

Marques M (2016) Porto volta a ter cinema no centro da cidade [In line]. Jornal de Notícias, Porto (28/09/2016). [Consult. 30 May 2019]. Availabe at WWW: https://www.jn.pt/local/noticias/porto/porto/interior/trindade-volta-a-dar-cinema-ao-centro-da-cidade-5413198.html

Porto City Council (2018) A "ideia romântica" de reabrir o Cinema Trindade valeu a pena: num ano chamou 50 mil pessoas [in line]. Porto. o portal de notícias do Porto, Porto (04/02/2018). [Consult. 30 Maio 2019]. Availabe at WWW: http://www.porto.pt/noticias/a-ideia-romantica-de-reabrir-o-cinema-trindade-valeu-a-pena-num-ano-chamou-50-mil-pessoas

When Knowledge Meets Digital: A Systematic Literature Review About Digital Platforms and Knowledge Flow

Liliana Gonçalves and Lídia Oliveira

Abstract The evolution of the new information and communication technologies brings new dynamics to the knowledge flow. The use of digital platforms in our society to access information and share knowledge is much more democratic and gathers a lot of advantages. But it also brings some challenges regard infocommunicational practices, attitudes and interaction between digital users, or the relevance of virtual communities in social media. In this chapter, we present a systematic literature review, based on 18 academic publications published in the last 5 years, about "digital platforms" and "knowledge" issues. This analysis will identify the key factors to share knowledge, the different stakeholders engaged in the knowledge flow process and the main challenges regarding knowledge flow in the cyberspace. The main goal of the chapter is to systematize and understand the digital platform role in the knowledge flow.

Keywords Knowledge sharing · Digital platforms · Science communication

1 Introduction

It is undeniable the growing presence of new technologies in our daily's life. Thus, it is inevitable using digital platforms as tools to access and share knowledge. The constant evolution of new technologies has resulted in new formats to share information, new approaches to produce and consume contents and a range of available digital platforms. Therefore, it is crucial to develop an epistemological systematization of scientific knowledge in order to understand the digital platforms role in the knowledge flow.

L. Gonçalves (✉) · L. Oliveira
Digimedia-Digital Media and Interaction Research Centre, University of Aveiro, Aveiro, Portugal
e-mail: lilianabgoncalves@ua.pt

L. Oliveira
e-mail: lidia@ua.pt

N. Martins et al. (eds.), *Perspectives on Design and Digital Communication*, Springer Series in Design and Innovation 8, https://doi.org/10.1007/978-3-030-49647-0_3

Based on a systematic literature review, this chapter proposes an analysis to systematize the digital infocommunicational practices about users' access, attitudes and interaction to understand the importance of online communities and the relevance of social media and other digital platforms in the knowledge flow. The main goal is to contribute to a global understanding about digital impacts on knowledge flow. Finally, this analysis will also identify the main challenges, to the different stakeholders, regarding knowledge flow in the cyberspace.

2 Methodology

This chapter presents a systematic literature review with the goal of mapping the impact of new technologies in the knowledge flow. In order to achieve it, we collected academic literature, published in the last five years (2014–2019), available in the multidisciplinary databases Scopus and b-on. The terms explored were "digital platforms", "knowledge", "science", "digital", "knowledge sharing" and "science communication", with a combined search of the terms/expressions in the title, keywords and abstract (see Fig. 1). The research was limited to Social Sciences;

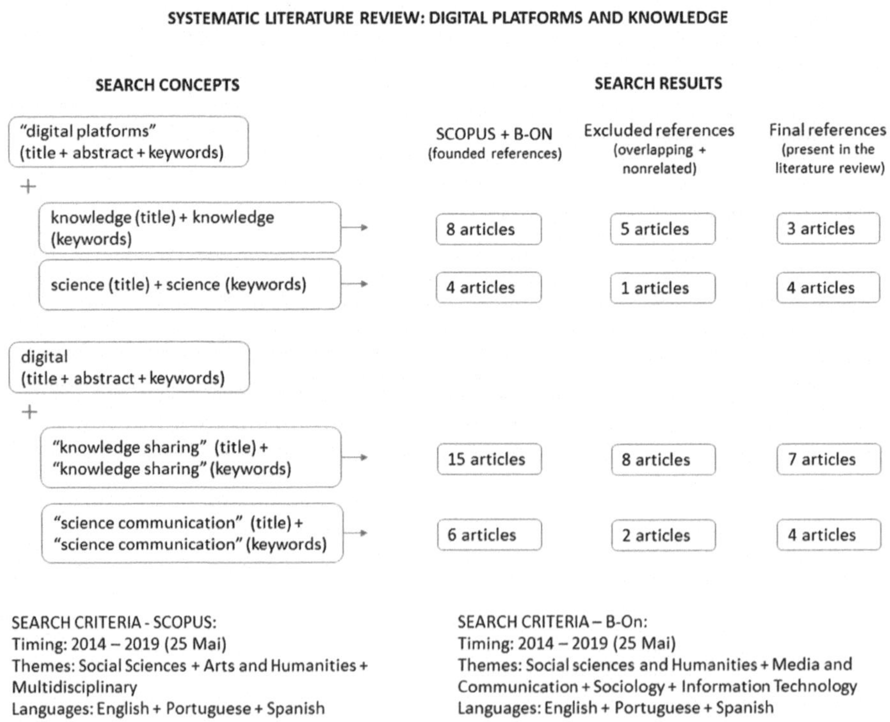

Fig. 1 Systematic literature review plan

Arts and Humanities and Multidisciplinary areas in Scopus; and Social Sciences and Humanities; Communication and Mass Media; Sociology and Information Technology areas in b-on. We considered this fields of study most appropriate to integrate the study of knowledge flow and we considered articles in English, Portuguese and Spanish.

30 references were found, 27 of them were validated after excluding duplicate references in both databases. A previous selection was made, based on reading all the abstracts, excluding 9 references and resulting in a total of 18 articles validated and analyzed. References whose central themes were not in the field of Digital Platforms were excluded, as well those that, even addressing this theme, presented research focused on the educational, business/industrial, digital libraries or data security scopes. This analysis considered all kinds of publications: editorials, articles, book reviews, book chapters, conference proceedings, etc.

The analysis identified 10 case studies, 1 comment, 1 critical book review and 5 articles dedicated to discussing/reflecting on the theme. In terms of methodologies, 6 use literature reviews, 4 are based on the analysis of quantitative data, through surveys, 1 uses qualitative data analysis, through interviews and 6 use mixed techniques such as direct observation, content analysis, data analysis and metrics from digital platforms or visual analysis. Regarding the themes, there was a wide variety of subjects addressed in the references, for example: virtual communities (3), social media (3), knowledge sharing in specific contexts (4), technology-based learning spaces (4) or access and use of information (2).

3 Are Digital Platforms the New Arena to Share Knowledge?

Knowledge sharing process takes place between people, communities, organizations or groups and shapes as exchange of experiences, skills or knowledge (Mahmood et al. 2016, p. 1). The definition founded in the literature seems simple at the first sight, however, there is a wide range of disciplines, themes and stakeholders involved, along with different theories, techniques and methodologies about it, which make knowledge sharing a very complex process (van Biljon et al. 2017, p. 464). This complexity becomes even more evident when the number of stakeholders involved is high, which may include government institutions, companies, non-profit organizations, educational institutions, research organizations, professionals, citizens, among many others (Leeuwis et al. 2018, p. 149).

In addition to this social complexity inherent in the knowledge sharing, there is also a technical complexity that knowledge management requires, which, sometimes, reveals information gaps, insufficient data, inconsistent metrics and models, lack of monitoring systems or uncoordinated actions in data collection (Leeuwis et al. 2018,

p. 149). This is particularly relevant in the current context, where big data present cultural, social and technological challenges and require new technical skills and new epistemological and methodological approaches to deal with a massive volume of information, especially in scientific knowledge (Pitrelli 2017, p. 4). On the other hand, ethical issues are also highlighted, seen here as a way of protecting social groups (Nazemi and Secko 2018, p. 74). Mostly, these issues arise in knowledge sharing about controversial scientific themes, since the information shared on digital platforms has no longer the mediation that journalism or documentaries used to do in non-virtual contexts (Urens and Dadzie 2015, p. 3), and that raises issues about responsibility for contents shared in emerging digital spaces (Nazemi and Secko 2018, p. 74).

4 Knowledge Flow in Digital Environments

In the context of knowledge sharing and learning, literature suggests different approaches to emphasize these processes. Socialization emerges as a strategy to support sharing knowledge, value co-creation and innovation (Bjursell 2015, p. 286). In her study about intergenerational learning, the author focuses on working environments with several generations of employees, where knowledge flow is usually seen as a knowledge transfer in a vertical process: from the oldest to youngest or vice versa. However, this kind of knowledge sharing can create friction based on stereotypes, especially with young, used to digital environments and with other experiences and interests. In this context, accordingly to the study, it is necessary to integrate multigenerational social dynamics, with a long-term vision, based on reciprocal and horizontal processes of co-creation to blur the differences between employees and thus avoid the generational gap. The experience reported in Bjursell's work (2015) included entrepreneurs with extensive experience in business and young people with advanced technological skills, concluding that knowledge sharing based on a horizontal perspective, where everyone can contribute with different types of knowledge, encourages sharing and learning between different participants—especially among young people, who feel valued—and benefits the work environment (Bjursell 2015). Still in the work field, literature also suggests informality in knowledge sharing. Here the emphasis is on informal activities among members, external to the work environment itself, since the work contexts already integrate formal processes to exchange information (Jarrahi 2018). The study suggests that sharing knowledge through informal activities outside the work environment allows employees to cross organizational boundaries and integrate different skills and perspectives (Jarrahi 2018, p. 38).

Participation is another approach pointed out in the literature for knowledge sharing. There are several examples, like workshops, to ease the access to knowledge and to knowledge-building techniques. This kind of practical environments can create bridges between different stakeholders and allow mutual understanding and participation (Gransard-Desmond 2015). In this way, apomediated spaces (virtual or real) are an alternative to guarantee the access to knowledge and knowledge flow, particularly in developing countries. Here, users with different backgrounds and expertise use these kinds of spaces to enable access to resources, information and knowledge, encourage relationships between group members, create bridges between communities and foster knowledge visibility in order to transform these apomediated spaces into trust areas to communities, who can see themselves empowered and motivated to learn and engage (Kwanya et al. 2015, p. 10).

Thus, literature points to an individual and collective benefit in knowledge sharing, promoting collaboration among participants (Mahmood et al. 2016, p. 4), increasing knowledge and, consequently, skills and expertise in different themes, enhancing to get in touch with different perspectives (Jarrahi 2018, p. 38) or even stimulating user engagement in communities (Faraj et al. 2016, pp. 6–7). Regarding the use of digital platforms for knowledge sharing, the advantages are speed of information spreading and a bigger impact of knowledge in users' culture and behavior (Bernardi et al. 2019).

In this context, the challenges of this knowledge sharing multi-complexity include different approaches and formats to share knowledge and to engage several actors. For example, crowdsourcing. This approach was implemented in a toponymy and disaster management project in Indonesia. It encouraged participation of several stakeholders—citizens, government institutions and non-profit organizations—in a project to map towns, villages and small locations of the country. The project distributed tasks among several participants groups and they were encouraged to share their knowledge about names and stories of the places they know through digital platforms—OMS, Facebook Place Editor, Swarm Foursquare, Google Local Guide, mobile apps, etc. The geographical information produced individually in this project was made available to everyone and used in emergency situations (Perdana and Ostermann 2018, p. 7). Literature also sees citizen science as an approach to share knowledge. For example, the BeeWatch program, implemented in United Kingdom. The program has its own digital platform to users' access and share information about edible plants pollinators and cultivation practices. The information shared on the BeeWatch digital platform allows the creation of an open database about different local ecosystems, biodiversity and ecology. This created sharing practices and dynamics among participants, who otherwise would not have contact with each other or access to different places ecological activity (Sharma et al. 2019).

In both cases, crowdsourcing and citizen science are approaches to ease the resolution of information gaps in knowledge production. By collecting data in a decentralized way (through different participants), crowdsourcing and citizen science benefit learning adapted to contexts, particularly in complex issues (Leeuwis et al. 2018). These types of knowledge sharing approaches achieved a special boost with the democratization of digital platforms.

5 Why Do We Share Knowledge?

To create new knowledge through sharing and interaction is a creative process (Faraj et al. 2016, p. 6) influenced by several factors (see Fig. 2). Literature points out the social capital as the main knowledge flow mechanism. Here, there are several factors such as shared goals, trust, as knowledge sharing facilitator, or network ties, which includes relationships, time and frequency of communication between community members (Bernardi et al. 2019, p. 3). These network ties are also strengthened with emotional intensity and reciprocity (Jarrahi 2018, p. 39).

In their research about different approaches to knowledge sharing concept, Mahmood et al. (2016) find a range of motivations that lead to knowledge sharing: cultural organization, trust, social norms, expectations, risks, ethics, leadership, motivation and organizational support. But the study refers mainly to social capital as an influencing factor in knowledge sharing, integrating dimensions such as context, motivations, participation and social relationships. Here, the greater the perceived social capital, the better social relationships, trust and established network ties, the higher will be the possibilities to share individual knowledge (Mahmood et al. 2016, p. 6).

Thus, the central premise behind the concept of social capital is based on the value of knowledge sharing to the members of the network, in terms of offered resources, social practices or the contribution to knowledge sharing (Jarrahi 2018, p. 39). In other words, the social capital of knowledge sharing networks implies, for example, that members find useful knowledge, find alternative sources of knowledge or realize the importance of their contribution through the sharing of their own knowledge (Jarrahi 2018, p. 39). Applied to a business/work context, for example, the social capital of knowledge sharing can be perceived by members as a way to solve problems, to increase expertise and even to contribute to the company success (Mahmood et al. 2016, p. 1). In organizational contexts, the concept of social capital is interconnected with network ties, since the strength of network ties determines the effectiveness of knowledge sharing (Jarrahi 2018, p. 39). The author defines that network ties include time spent, emotional intensity and reciprocity as characteristics to determine strong or weak network ties. Usually, strong network ties reflect personal relationships with family and close friends, which increases knowledge sharing (Jarrahi 2018, p. 40).

The case about intergenerational learning, mentioned above, is an example of social capital as a key to knowledge sharing. Here, the socialization among participants—young people with technological skills and adults with business experience—was the trigger to sharing knowledge and the reciprocity was decisive to break intergenerational barriers and stereotypes of passing knowledge from seniors to young, placing participants in equal circumstances in knowledge sharing, highlighting the skills held by each group (Bjursell 2015).

Other factors mentioned in the literature that enhance knowledge flow are risk perception, expectations, ethics, motivation, organizational culture or social norms. One example is the case presented by Ou et al. (2014) about the "guanxi" influence in knowledge sharing in online environments in a Chinese workers community.

"Guanxi" refers to a set of rules in social and work relationships mandatory by Chinese society. Something intrinsic that includes trust, presence and mandatory reciprocity in interpersonal relationships. According to the study, "guanxi" is the main element to identify sharing knowledge behaviors in online environments in that community. Here, motivation is seen as a result of Chinese social norms and should be seen by the organizations/companies as a positive process in high levels of performance and efficiency of online networks (Ou et al. 2014).

Perception of information resources and expectations are also decisive when it comes to sharing knowledge in online environments (Liu et al. 2014, p. 684). In this study, the authors focus on CreativeCommons mechanisms and find trust as the main factor to use CreativeCommons. Personal and community expectations are also important characteristics and they are related to the context of knowledge sharing through CreativeCommons. Here, CreativeCommons users'—in this case, the study was applied to students—value mutual trust between community members. Peer support is also valued and increases relationship processes among members with same goals. Realizing the importance of sharing resources among the community, CreativeCommons users understand this mechanism as a way of personal and community fulfillment (Liu et al. 2014, p. 692). In this context, CreativeCommons mechanisms allow to create new formats of knowledge sharing, particularly through the sharing of contents developed not only for knowledge, but also for reuse and modification by community users (Liu et al. 2014, pp. 681–682). Thus, social cohesion of a community increases the feeling of belonging and self-fulfillment and, consequently, increases knowledge sharing (Bernardi et al. 2019, p. 3) (Fig. 2).

Thus, digital platforms, particularly social media where participatory processes take place, contribute to the creation of social capital (Jarrahi 2018, p. 42). Therefore, it is a process based on strong and/or weak relationships amplified with the use of these digital platforms, where emerge informal networks to connect different users, communities and/or organizations and allow members to access knowledge through social interaction, enhancing knowledge sharing (Jarrahi 2018, p. 42). The author also mentions that social media benefits social capital, especially in the context of weak ties. Particularly at the organizational level, the knowledge sharing network is articulated between a reduced set of strong and close relationships and a broad set of weak and peripheral relationships (Jarrahi 2018, p. 40). Usually, these weak ties connect users with different backgrounds and expertise, allowing them access to a wide range of sources of information (Jarrahi 2018, p. 41). So, more than strong connections, weak network ties allow members to find specialists and access to specialized knowledge through informal social contacts, using social media—such as Twitter, LinkedIn or other social digital platforms for business like Yammer—turning these into spaces for discussion and knowledge sharing (Jarrahi 2018, p. 41).

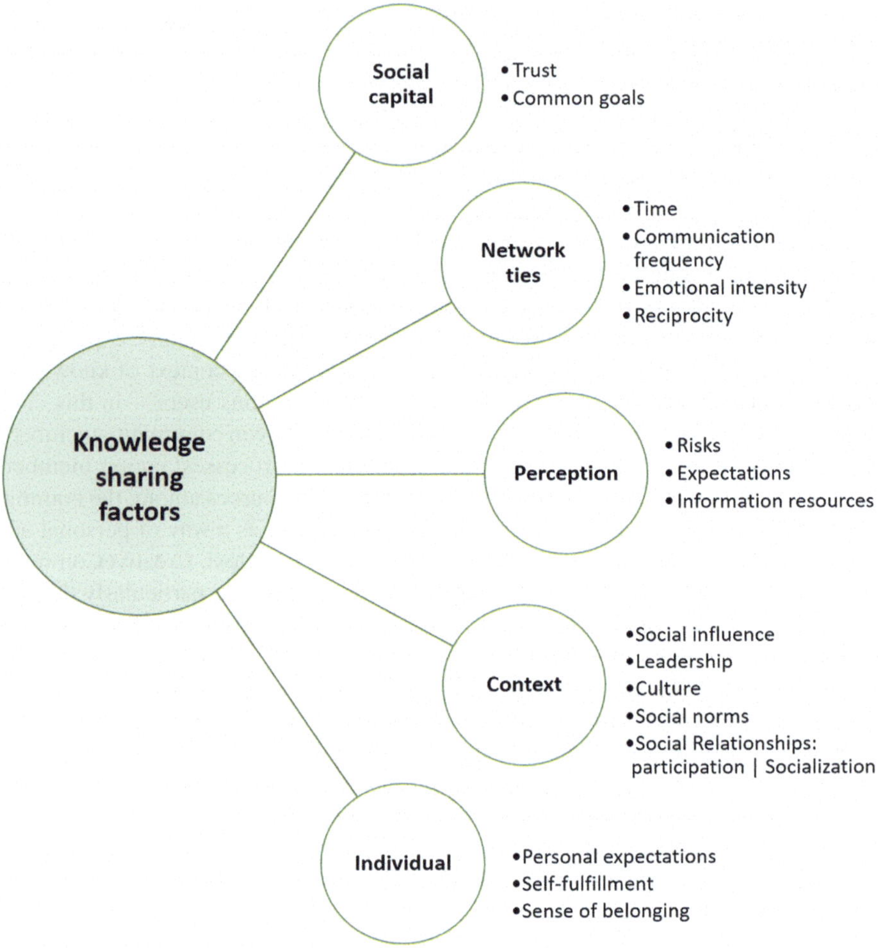

Fig. 2 Knowledge sharing factors plan

6 Digital Environments Facilitating Knowledge Sharing

In the process of knowledge sharing in digital environments, it is necessary to pay attention to issues such as user experience, platforms usability, digital literacy and technical skills needed to interact through different types of platforms (van Biljon et al. 2017, p. 481). However, frequently, stakeholders do not realize they are engaged in a collective process in which knowledge sharing to create something common depends directly on the contribution of all individually. That is why it is necessary to raise awareness of mutual interdependence and collective nature of knowledge sharing (Leeuwis et al. 2018, p. 155). In this context, it is essential to consider a wide range of stakeholders with different information needs and different ways of understanding and processing knowledge. Here, knowledge presentation and accessibility, digital platforms usability and accessibility and even security, privacy, and copyright issues differ according to each stakeholder individually (van Biljon et al. 2017, p. 480).

Several types of stakeholders were found in the literature. In this review they are grouped into three major categories: knowledge promoters/producers; knowledge mediators and public (individual users and communities).

Knowledge Promoters/Producers: This category includes stakeholders that produce knowledge and promote knowledge sharing. The range of knowledge promoters is vast and can range from governments or local/national authorities, to scientists or technical specialists, etc. Scientific organizations recognize the web 2.0 as a public relations space with an organizational impact, allowing access to scientific knowledge, to discuss scientific issues in digital environments. Scientists are increasingly aware of the importance of public engagement through digital platforms and, therefore, scientific communities have been adopting social media as spaces for informal communication with different stakeholders (Urens and Dadzie 2015, p. 2). In the case presented by the authors Perdana and Ostermann (2018) regarding the toponymy project mentioned above, knowledge promoters were national authorities, who triggered the project. As a collaborative-based project, several stakeholders such as scientists, toponymists and technical specialists had participated. This collaborative approach required national authorities to adjust work dynamics to collaboration with other stakeholders, considering social, political and territorial issues. It demanded that experts bring specific knowledge about places, ensuring accuracy of shared knowledge, but also considered guidelines for stakeholder participation in the context of digital platforms and information management (Perdana and Ostermann 2018, p. 15).

Knowledge Mediators: This stakeholder has been gaining importance, particularly in cyberspace. Considering the characteristics of knowledge sharing in digital environments, especially geographical dispersion, the figure of the "boundary spanners" emerges. They are individuals "who facilitate knowledge sharing by establishing connections between two or more different groups" (Jarrahi 2018, p. 42). These stakeholders' role is to identify specialists, to find knowledge, and to disseminate it to communities, helping other stakeholders to expand weak network ties and ensuring that the flow of knowledge goes beyond barriers (Jarrahi 2018, p. 42). As an example, the case presented by the author Gransard-Desmond (2015), regarding archeology workshops in digital environments to bring together scientists and society, the figure of the scientific educator is crucial. He conceptually creates the workshops, he bridges scientific communities and users, he ensures that communication is adapted to both communities, and he establishes dynamics of reciprocity and evaluation, contributing to create scientific knowledge (Gransard-Desmond 2015, pp. 314–315). This category also includes journalists, whose mediation role has been gradually changing with the massification of digital media (Nazemi and Secko 2018). Journalists—and in the case of scientific knowledge also documentary filmmakers—used to be the information gatekeepers but have been losing space in the mediation process between sources and public, however, there has been a progressive adaptation of traditional media to the new online environments (Urens and Dadzie 2015, p. 2).

Public: This is the most comprehensive category. The public can be seen as members of a society (Gransard-Desmond 2015), local inhabitants (Perdana and Ostermann 2018), workers or even business organizations (Jarrahi 2018). In the process of knowledge flow, they are active participants whether in citizen science projects, in collaborative processes or in digital communities. In this category, it is important to remember the changing nature of social interaction processes mediated by technology, demanding public to adapt to the new socio-technological dynamics to knowledge sharing (Jarrahi 2018, p. 44).

Behavioral factors, such as trust, social norms or expectations, create knowledge sharing (Mahmood et al. 2016), but the reverse also happens, with knowledge sharing having effects on behaviors, particularly in online environments (Bernardi et al. 2019). There are some studies on consumer behavior in the literature, such as the study presented by Bernardi et al. (2019) about alternative food networks. The authors conclude knowledge sharing in digital environments has direct effects in changing consumption and purchasing behaviors—by comparison, knowledge sharing in physical environments only have an impact on purchasing behavior as an immediate act—because information shared digitally tends to spread more quickly, affecting the culture of consumers (Bernardi et al. 2019). Regarding knowledge sharing and user engagement in online environments, there are some key factors to trigger products and services learning: personal experience, strong network ties (family and friends) (Jarrahi 2018), perceived social benefits, empowerment and self-improvement (Yuan et al. 2016). The case presented by Yuan et al. (2016) about sharing knowledge in travel contexts, divides users between active "posters" and passive "lurkers". External factors, such as reciprocity, play an important role in lurkers' motivations to share knowledge. On the other hand, posters have internal factors that triggered knowledge sharing, such as: satisfaction, self-assessment, self-perception of a high knowledge about consumer practices, subjective knowledge that gives them more confidence to share useful knowledge to the communities. Posters are innovative users, they are available to try new experiences, they adopt new technologies easily, they are active sharers of knowledge about travel products and services. That is why they became opinion leaders and market experts. Also, another key factor to share knowledge in travel context is the nature of the experience: when users have extremely good or extremely ruined experiences, they show greater availability for knowledge sharing in online environments (Yuan et al. 2016, p. 72).

In digital environments, when it comes to knowledge co-creation processes, they demand more engagement then knowledge sharing processes. Here, the interest in the theme and curiosity are the main factors to motivate users to co-create knowledge (Urens and Dadzie 2015). Literature reveals gamification as a strategy to use by knowledge promoters to increase co-creation, since funny experiences seem to keep motivation and users' engagement standards at different levels of co-creation process (Perdana and Ostermann 2018).

7 Online Communities and Digital Platforms: Knowledge Flow Spaces

Composed by a large number of participants geographically disperse who share activities, interests or a common identity, online communities are based on digital technologies and take shape of global collective spaces to knowledge flow (Faraj et al. 2016, pp. 1–2). Ruled by principles such as cooperation, communication and information reliability (Leeuwis et al. 2018, p. 147), online communities are also seen as new organizational forms and innovative sources of value to products, services and innovation processes (Faraj et al. 2016, p. 2). Here, value creation includes also perceived value, which feeds user engagement and interaction with communities and, consequently, knowledge flow (Faraj et al. 2016, p. 2). As an example, a study about online travel communities argues that these brought high benefits both to consumers and companies: consumers can see many issues resolved just by consulting online forums and feel their experiences are valued when sharing useful knowledge; companies benefit from the users' knowledge sharing by reducing costs in customer support services, by interacting with consumers to collect information on shared opinions to develop new consumption strategies (Yuan et al. 2016, p. 68).

Literature points out some challenges, especially to online communities' management, which may face problems such as: interdependence and/or overlap with other online communities, social contexts that shape them, collaboration from different stakeholders and definition of own communities' goals (Leeuwis et al. 2018, p. 155). Nevertheless, online communities' benefits from vast opportunities for learning, sharing opinions and causes, creating value in knowledge flow, without physical barriers from non-virtual contexts (Faraj et al. 2016, pp. 12–13).

Digital platforms enable connection and interaction between users and ease knowledge sharing and co-creation. Yet, they are not self-sufficient, i.e. they depend on communities' activity and participants' actions to create economic and social value (Faraj et al. 2016, p. 4). In this context, social media have been a real game-changers in knowledge flow, by enabling new connection formats between users and by arising new communities (Faraj et al. 2016, p. 4; Jarrahi 2018, p. 39). Here, social media includes public sharing platforms, such as blogs or wikis, social networking platforms, such as Facebook, Twitter or LinkedIn, and even corporate networking platforms used by organizations, such as Jive, Yammer, SocialCast or SocialText (Jarrahi 2018, p. 37). They play a crucial role in network ties allowing users to access a wide range of information sources, even if these ties are weak. With social media it is easier to find specialists since these digital platforms allow their self-promotion, for example in Twitter or LinkedIn (Jarrahi 2018, pp. 40–41). Thus, the way people interact and communicate shapes their own social networks, fostering a digital transformation that should be considered by organizations, since social media are technological tools for effective communication, even in working environments (Jarrahi 2018, p. 44). Science organizations have already identified value by using digital platforms to share information and scientific knowledge. Many of them use digital platforms, particularly social media, as an institutional communication vehicle, to build informal communication networks (Urens and Dadzie 2015, p. 3) or even in citizen science programs, like BeeWatch, to collect data, to share knowledge about species and to user interaction (Sharma et al. 2019).

Thus, interactive digital tools invite users to use and share knowledge and experiences (Sharma et al. 2019, p. 18). Social media are a communication channel, but mainly they are a social space (Pitrelli 2017, p. 2) that benefits from a range of formats to share knowledge (Nazemi and Secko 2018, p. 74). Image has proved to be crucial for science communication (Hwong et al. 2017, p. 481). This study focused on aspects that influence audience engagement in posts about space (astronomy) on Facebook and Twitter and it has identified several aspects crucial to communication success: image (videos and photos), visual description, anger, authenticity of the messages, URL, hashtags and number of followers (Hwong et al. 2017, p. 491). Literature also shows new metrics for data analysis such as visual analysis (Urens and Dadzie 2015), psychometric analysis (Hwong et al. 2017), data mining, social network analysis, computational models, augmented reality or geospatial analysis (Pitrelli 2017, p. 2). These new metrics result from technological development and are valuable to assess the use and interaction in digital platforms.

8 Conclusion

The systematic literature review presented in this chapter highlight knowledge sharing as multicomplex process. It is necessary to pay attention to social and technological complexities, especially when it comes to use formats like crowdsourcing or citizen science to promote interaction and knowledge sharing in digital contexts. Throughout the review it was possible to list different users and stakeholders that take an active part in knowledge sharing process, along with the factors that influence their behavior in knowledge sharing in digital environments. Literature also notices the growing importance of online communities, digital platforms, and particularly social media, for the knowledge flow, but it was also emphasized that value creation depends on online communities' interaction. The relevance of digital platforms and social networks, especially in business and scientific contexts, is enhanced by new tools and formats available to foster interaction between users. Finally, it was pointed out different possibilities presented by the new technologies regarding new data analysis methodologies, which allow measuring knowledge flow on digital platforms with greater precision.

In this context, it was possible to identify challenges when it comes to sharing knowledge in online environments. First, different types of digital platforms require different technological skills and digital literacy from users; second, several stakeholders engaged in knowledge sharing processes in digital environments presents social issues to deal with; third, new inclusive formats to share knowledge are arising—like crowdsourcing and citizen science—and knowledge promoters and mediators should be aware of their functionalities; fourth, it seems to be advantages in mediation and apomediation, the challenge here is to understand what kind of approach fits better when it comes to create online communities; fifth, online communities can arise only by user action, but these "free" scenarios have to deal with online communities overlapping, undefined identity or goals and social context from participants. All these challenges made knowledge sharing and knowledge flow very complex processes. In order to create value, particularly knowledge promoters and mediators should be aware of it.

Acknowledgments This research was supported by the Portuguese Foundation for Science and Technology (FCT) through the FCT fellowship [SFRH/BD/140247/2018].

References

De Bernardi P, Bertello A, Venuti F (2019) Online and on-site interactions within alternative food networks: sustainability impact of knowledge-sharing practices. Sustainability 11:1–14. https://doi.org/10.3390/su11051457

Bjursell C (2015) Organizing for intergenerational learning and knowledge sharing. J Intergener Relat 13(4):285–301. https://doi.org/10.1080/15350770.2015.1108952

Faraj S, von Krogh G, Monteiro E, Lakhani KR (2016) Online community as space for knowledge flows. Inf Syst Res, Articles in Advance 27(4):1–17. https://doi.org/10.1287/isre.2016.0682

Gransard-Desmond JO (2015) Science educators: bridging the gap between the scientific community and society. World Archaeol 47(2):299–316. https://doi.org/10.1080/00438243.2015.1020964

Hwong YL, Oliver C, Van Kranendonk M, Sammut C, Seroussi Y (2017) What makes you tick? The psychology of social media engagement in space science communication. Comput Hum Behav 68:480–492. https://doi.org/10.1016/j.chb.2016.11.068

Jarrahi MH (2018) Social media, social capital, and knowledge sharing in enterprise. IT Prof, 37–45. https://doi.org/10.1109/MITP.2017.265105759

Kwanya T, Stilwell C, Underwood P (2015) Apomediated marketplace: effective ba for knowledge sharing and learning among local civil society organizations in developing countries. Inf Dev 31(5):1–12. https://doi.org/10.1177/0266666914521827

Leeuwis C, Cieslik KJ, Aarts MNC, Dewulf ARPJ, Ludwig F, Werners SE, Struik PC (2018) Reflections on the potential of virtual citizen science platforms to address collective action challenges: lessons and implications for future research. NJAS—Wageningen J Life Sci 86–87:146–157. https://doi.org/10.1016/j.njas.2018.07.008

Liu CC, Lin CC, Deng KY, Wu YT, Tsai CC (2014) Online knowledge sharing experience with Creative Commons. Online Inf Rev 38(5):680–696. https://doi.org/10.1108/OIR-12-2013-0280

Mahmood J, Dahlan HM, Hussin ARC, Ahmad MA (2016) Review on knowledge sharing behavior studies: theories and research approaches. Indian J Sci Technol 9(34):1–8. https://doi.org/10.17485/ijst/2016/v9i34/100834

Nazemi P, Secko D (2018) Recent books in science communication: practice, ethics, and a perspective on new spaces in digital videos. J Commun 68:73–75

Ou CXJ, Davison RM, Wong LHM (2014) Contextual preferences and network-based knowledge sharing in China. In: 20th Americas conference on information systems, AMCIS 2014 (2013), pp 1–12. Retrieved from https://www.scopus.com/inward/record.uri?eid=2-s2.0–84905996666&partnerID=40&md5=b2acdbbf29c99b87663a0ce2959f5324

Perdana A, Ostermann F (2018) A citizen science approach for collecting toponyms. ISPRS Int J Geo-Inf 7:2–18. https://doi.org/10.3390/ijgi7060222

Pitrelli N (2017) Big data and digital methods in science communication research: opportunities, challenges and limits. J Sci Commun 16(2):1–4

Sharma N, Greaves S, Siddharthan A, Anderson HB, Robinson A, Colucci-Gray L, Wibowo AT, Bostock H, Salisbury A, Roberts S, Slawson D, van der Wal R (2019) From citizen science to citizen action: analysing the potential for a digital platform to cultivate attachments to nature. J Sci Commun 18(1):1−35. https://doi.org/10.22323/2.18010207

Urens V, Dadzie A-S (2015) Public scientific communication on Twitter : a visual analytic approach. Aslib J Inf Manag 67(3):1−34. http://dx.doi.org/10.1108/AJIM-10-2014-0137

van Biljon J, Marais M, Platz M (2017) Digital platforms for research collaboration: using design science in developing a South African open knowledge repository. Inf Technol Dev 23(3):463–485. https://doi.org/10.1080/02681102.2017.1328654

Yuan D, Lin Z, Zhuo R (2016) What drives consumer knowledge sharing in online travel communities? Personal attributes or e-service factors?. Comput Hum Behav 63:68–74. https://doi.org/10.1016/j.chb.2016.05.019

The Graphic Interface Design of the ALU13 Online Store

Nuno Martins, Francisco Pires, and Daniel Brandão

Abstract This research project consists in the development of the graphic interface of the online store ALU13. This brand is dedicated to the manufacture and trade of aluminum products for the exterior of the housing. It was intended to create an online store, in order to cut intermediaries in the commercialization of products, enhancing the contact between the brand and the consumer. In this sense, it was necessary to carry out the planning of the interface and the necessary approach. For the development of the graphical interface of the ALU13 online store, the state of e-commerce in Portugal was studied, the habits of use and purchase of the Portuguese consumer and it was necessary to understand the factors that can influence the user's trust with the online store. The online selection, purchase and sale processes and digital product exposure guidelines for homes were deepened. We explored the design and fundamentals of linking e-commerce aspects with the design of the online store. We investigated the interaction design, which has as fundamental concepts the design of experience (UX Design) and the design of interfaces (UI Design). In the end, we carry out usability tests to see the user's reaction with the prototype.

Keywords E-commerce · Experience · Interface · Interaction · Usability

N. Martins (✉)
Polytechnic Institute of Cávado and Ave / ID+, Barcelos, Portugal
e-mail: nunomartins.com@gmail.com

F. Pires
Polytechnic Institute of Cávado and Ave, Barcelos, Portugal
e-mail: franciscojapires@hotmail.com

D. Brandão
University of Minho / CECS, Braga, Portugal
e-mail: daniel.c.brandao@gmail.com

N. Martins et al. (eds.), *Perspectives on Design and Digital Communication*, Springer Series in Design and Innovation 8, https://doi.org/10.1007/978-3-030-49647-0_4

1 Introduction

ALU13 is a brand, founded in 2016, dedicated to the manufacture and sale of aluminum products for the exterior of homes. The company produces articles such as exterior doors with thermal insulation, double-leaf gates, sliding gates, garage gates, and railings.

Currently, the commercial activity of this company depends on several intermediaries. Taking this into account, the brand defined as its main strategic objective, the direct marketing of its products to the consumer, to reduce the dependence on intermediaries. In this way, electronic commerce appears as a means to achieve this goal.

According to Her Majesty's Stationery Office (1995), in electronic commerce "good design can significantly value products, lead to sales growth and enable the exploration of new markets and the consolidation of existing ones" (Stamm 2003).

It is in this context that this article emerges, with its main objectives: to acquire knowledge about electronic commerce in Portugal, specifically in products for housing; understand the online shopping habits of the Portuguese consumer; obtain guidelines on interface design that can be applied in the design of the ALU13 online store, in order to create valid solutions for the fulfilment of its objectives of strengthening its relationship with its customer, as well as a purchase support tool, capable of to enhance their effectiveness of the contact between the brand and the consumer (Nielsen 2018; Wills 2018).

1.1 E-Commerce

Electronic commerce, also known as e-commerce, consists of buying and selling products or services over the internet. E-commerce allows consumers to access a variety of products, which is not always possible through traditional purchases.

The acquisition of products in Portugal has been increasing in recent years, having exceeded 70 billion euros in 2017, which represents about 38.1% of the country's Gross Domestic Product (GDP) (ACEPI 2018). The construction sector in Portugal has also seen a recovery, since 2016, which can be seen through the observation of some indicators, namely investment and increased credit for the acquisition and remodeling of houses (IMPIC 2018). Growth and greater investment in this sector have thus contributed to a greater demand for products characterized by technological innovation, quality, and durability (ACEPI 2018).

According to data from the National Statistics Institute (INE), the percentage of Portuguese consumers who make purchases online, with a value greater than 1000 Euros (€) per transaction, is only 15%. This data allows us to conceive, as an explanatory hypothesis of this phenomenon, the reduced confidence of consumers to carry out online transactions with values considered high. In this sense, the need to invest in creating a relationship of trust, which appears as an essential condition for the success of the interaction between the user and the brand, appears to be evident (IMPIC 2018).

In the context of electronic commerce B2C (Business-To-Consumer) and B2B (Business-To-Business), the visual presentation, the navigation structure and the form of information presentation are fundamental for the user's satisfaction.

2 Sale of Housing Products in Portugal

2.1 E-Commerce

The growth of E-commerce in Portugal is entirely linked to the use of the Internet. According to the Digital Economy Association (ACEPI), in 2017, more than 7.5 million Portuguese people used the internet for different activities, with around 50% of these users making purchases of products or services online (ACEPI 2018).

In 2017, the Portuguese used the internet mainly to search for information about goods or services. As a result, that same year, 34% of people between 16 and 74 years old residing in Portugal, made purchases online (INE 2018). Although there are still no statistics for the years 2018 and 2019, estimates point to a continued increase in these numbers.

We also found that the use of electronic commerce in Portugal is below the European average. These values can be influenced by the fact that we are a country with a wide range of shopping centers. The Portuguese consumer prefers to make their purchases traditionally. This can be explained by the fact that digital literacy in Portugal is lower compared to other European countries. The type of product may also be an explanatory element of the differences mentioned, as it may be more practical for the consumer to purchase the product at the physical store (CTT 2017).

Although the number of users using mobile devices for online shopping is growing significantly, the desktop remains the preferred device for this type of action (Carter 2019). One of the factors that can explain this phenomenon is the fact that many users come into contact with the product for the first time through the mobile device, but prefer to make the purchase later, through the desktop (ACEPI 2018).

Regarding the household items sector—in which ALU13 is inserted—this represents 28% of the Portuguese online purchases, although they are mostly products of lower value, compared to ALU13.

Online shopping is more frequent in the areas of Lisbon and Porto and to the age groups up to 34 years old, falling gradually as age advances. The preferred means of payment for the Portuguese continue to be bank transfer, ATM and credit card. However, it should be noted that the use of means such as PayPal and MBway, has been growing. (ACEPI 2018).

2.2 Portuguese Online Buying Habits

After an analysis of electronic commerce in Portugal, the most searched online stores by the Portuguese were identified: OLX, La Redoute, eBay, Amazon, Worten, Fnac, Booking, and Prozis (Peixoto 2018). One of the factors that continue to inhibit the Portuguese from resorting to e-commerce is the lack of confidence and the fact that they privilege personal contact with traders. (CONFAGRI 2018).

Through this analysis, it was also found that in the furniture housing sector, in Portugal, the biggest online stores are the interior decoration stores, such as IKEA, AKI, Leroy Merlin, Moviflor and El Corte Inglês (Alexa 2019; Kadazza 2019).

2.3 Online Selection, Purchase and Sale Processes

Analyzing the shopping experience, Nuno Reis Martins argues that it "must interact with the customer to satisfy and create value" (Reis Martins 2017, p. 15). The customer, in turn, "interacts with the organization, products and possibly other customers" (Reis Martins 2017, p. 15). The author also admits that, from the consumer's perspective, the shopping experience can be conditioned by factors such as the layout of the website and the presentation of the product. But all of this is susceptible to being monitored and changed by the company, so that, in this way, it can meet the customer's needs and thus retain customer loyalty.

Although we know that the layout of the website can affect the consumer's experience, it is important to note that an online store, to achieve its goal, will have to focus primarily on selling. The design of an online store cannot devalue the sales process to enhance design and experience. Thus, it is understood that the graphic elements and the various interactions outlined should not be any interference in the purchase process, even if the user experience does not dissociate them (Kujala et al. 2017).

In order to define the elements and content that potentially persuade the user to purchase the product, Sales Funnel Stages can be used (Fig. 1). It is a system that identifies the user at the different stages of the product acquisition process. Thus, it is possible to idealize the information that the consumer needs to make the purchase (Yalanska 2017).

2.4 Digital Display of a Home Product

Over the years, advertising images have been used to convey information about products and brands, as well as to provoke emotional responses in consumers. Thus, the images of the product, assume a relevant role in its digital display, being considered a decisive element for the purchase decision, by the user. It is essential to develop

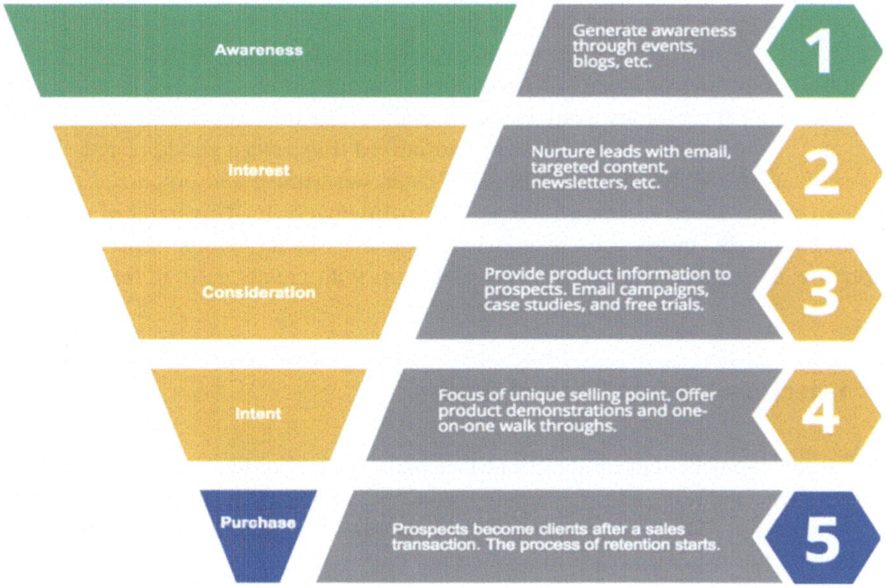

Fig. 1 Sales funnel stages process (Cacoo 2019)

them correctly, as they directly influence the appearance of the online store and consequently affect conversion rates and sales, in addition to influencing the amount of organic traffic arriving at the online store (Thomas 2019).

According to Cyr (2014), when idealizing the design of images for websites, the elements of balance, aesthetics, homogeneity of graphic appearance and an appealing intention of an emotional nature should be valued. For this, it is possible to resort to the use of photographs, the manipulation of colors, shapes and the type of font, and thus create a design that corresponds to the objectives defined for the digital store (Garrett 2003).

To create concept images, to promote emotional response, various techniques can be used, such as human interaction with the product; introduction in a concept environment (depending on the product); use of phrases that capture attention on a banner; consistency in all images and interaction with navigation.

Cultural elements are also relevant to the exhibition of the product. The definition of the target audience and country of sale and promotion can influence the creation of concept images, due to architectural, climatic, or social issues. Taking this into account, it is admitted that the names of the products can also be influenced by the culture of the country where it will be sold.

Smart Insights (December 23, 2016) addresses a study on images generated by users and reveals that 77% of them, at the time of purchase decision, demonstrate preferring to contact with photographs taken by other customers, rather than professional photos. This will be associated with the fact that this type of amateur photographs, appear to look more realistic, which possibly increases the level of user confidence in the online store. In this way, the use of this type of photographs is assumed as a strategy of exposure and valorization of the product.

In the perspective of Harley (2018), users of online stores should be able to easily understand all the options available so that they can make decisions in the least time and effort possible. All of this is materialized if there is a good presentation of the products available. That is, it must be clear, descriptive and organized through categorization, which facilitates the usability of the website. This trend of category and listing pages, inspired by responsive designs, gives a practical sense to online shopping, as users can make informed selections with greater ease, in fewer clicks.

3 Interface Design Methodologies

For the development of the graphic interface of the ALU13 online store, it is necessary to investigate and reflect on fundamental concepts of linking aspects of e-commerce with the design of the online store. The interaction and usability are directly interconnected, but it is necessary to understand their concepts, to know how to apply them.

3.1 UX and UI Design

The fundamental concepts of interaction design are experience design (UX Design) and interface design (UI Design). Thus, to complete the process of developing an online store, it is essential to focus on the study and seek to understand these basic concepts (Jansen et al. 2019).

Kolko (2011) states that "Interaction Design is the creation of dialogue between a person and a product, system, or service. This dialogue is both physical and emotional and is manifested in the interplay between form, function, and technology as experienced over time".

The harmony of user interaction with the online store is only achieved with the connection between the user interface design and your browsing experience. According to UX Planet (February 24, 2019), these are different concepts, but dependent on each other, since they guarantee simultaneous success.

The wireframes and flowcharts (Fig. 2) of the online store were then defined, focusing on the user experience and working on the project flow, that is, the definition of the tasks that the user is expected to accomplish.

The interface design (UI Design) refers to the thought and definition of visual elements, taking into account the visual brand identity, which then will help set the color schemes, layout, graphics, drawing and reaction buttons, use typography, white space, interactions and all other aspects necessary for the interface design (Martins et al. 2020).

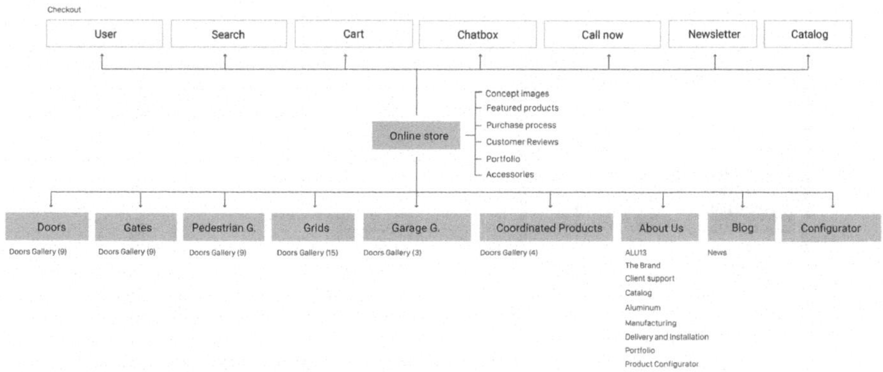

Fig. 2 Flowchart of contents and features, necessary for the ALU13 homepage

Therefore, we proceed to the development of the layout, visual elements and the respective color palette of the application, through the Figma software.

As we can see in Fig. 3, in addition to structuring the content, it was decided that the use of concept images and product details are the necessary bet to captivate the user to interact with the online store.

Thus it was established a standard in the application of colors, buttons, typography and icons throughout project design in order to create consistency, rather than user confusion. This allows them to complete tasks more effectively, resulting in an engaging experience.

In the development of the visual compositions of the application, we used two different chromatic palettes (Figs. 4 and 5):

Palette 01 corresponds to the colors used to design all the pages of the project, gray with different variations is the accent color present in almost all graphic elements. In turn, the use of green tone, in a moderate way, served to complement and highlight the main actions, this is because its vibrant color captures the user's attention.

Palette 02 was chosen in order to assign a color to each product category. The blue color (# 4ec4f4) corresponds to the doors; the salmon color (# ff7060) corresponds to the gates; yellow (# fedb5b) refers to pedestrian gates; brown (# cdaa82) to the bars; and, finally, orange (# f69352) was assigned to garage gates. This solution was thought and elaborated in order to help the segmentation and differentiation of product categories. It also facilitates user memorization, which helps to create empathy with the online store.

Considering now the creation of the typographic scale for the project, two typographic families were used, first the Regulator Nova (font applied to the visual identity) available in Adobe Fonts (Fig. 6). This was used for almost all written content, from titles, subtitles, highlights, buttons and quotes. This ensured the complementarity of identity, ease of use and overall graphic balance. In turn, the second font chosen was Open Sans, made available by Google Fonts. This was only used on the typographic scale for large amounts of text and information, in order to increase legibility and be visible on reduced screens. It should be noted that the space between

Fig. 3 ALU13 interface screens

Fig. 4 Color palette 1

Fig. 5 Color palette 2

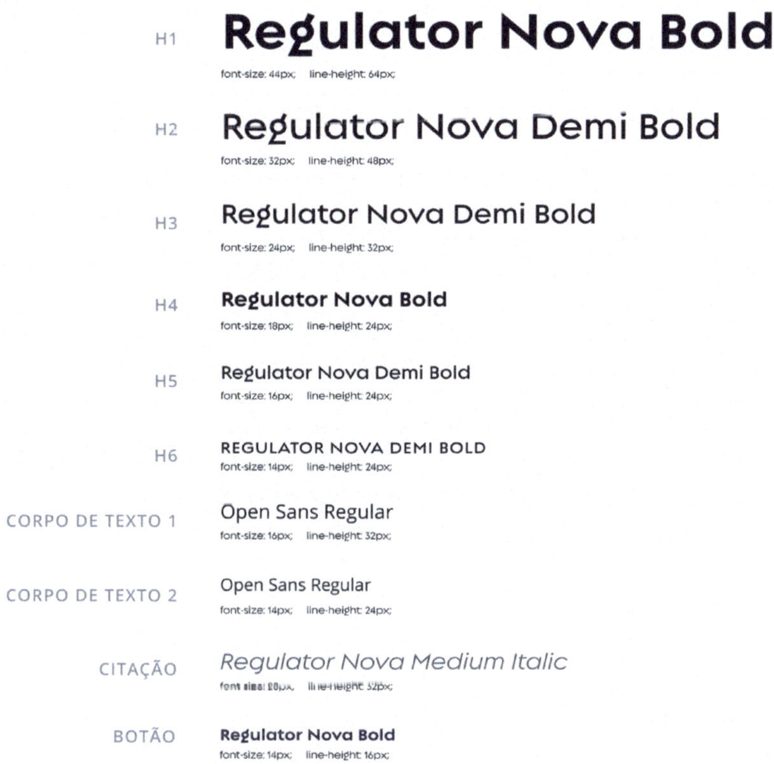

Fig. 6 Typographic scale for the interface design

the lines was taken into account, since it also becomes fundamental for legibility. So it was important to test and find the best solution together with the typography.

In the design of the project interface, the definition of the buttons is essential as they play a fundamental role in the interaction between the user and the system. When

Fig. 7 Proposed buttons and their states for the interface design

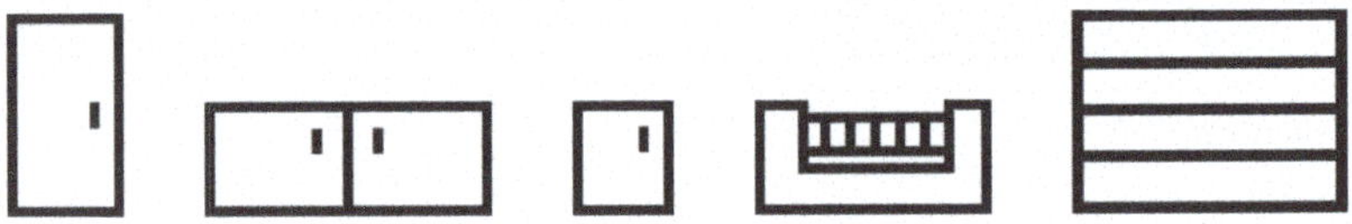

Fig. 8 Proposed graphic icons for each type of brand products

users click or interact with the button, they expect the project interface to respond with appropriate feedback.

Therefore, 5 types of buttons were then designed (Fig. 7), differentiated by the relevance of the action they perform, since, in an online store, the button that brings the user closer to finalizing the purchase should be the most prominent. In this way, the green background color and the uppercase text were used to make it stand out before the user.

In Fig. 7, the buttons pressed (botões pressionados) are the respective reactions of the buttons to the interaction. The status of these serves to exemplify when a button is not active.

It is also important to note that graphic icons (Fig. 8) were developed to identify and represent the types of products. This aspect helps to identify the solutions that ALU13 offers in terms of products and facilitates segmentation, which can be fundamental to reduce the time to search, select and purchase products.

3.2 *Prototyping*

To implement the prototype, the Invision digital platform was used. This is a free platform for developing prototypes of digital products. It should be noted that it supports the advantage of downloading and updating the wireframes developed in Figma automatically. It also allows the development of interactive and animated prototypes, using tools such as the assignment of action to buttons (Fig. 9) and the sharing of the prototype.

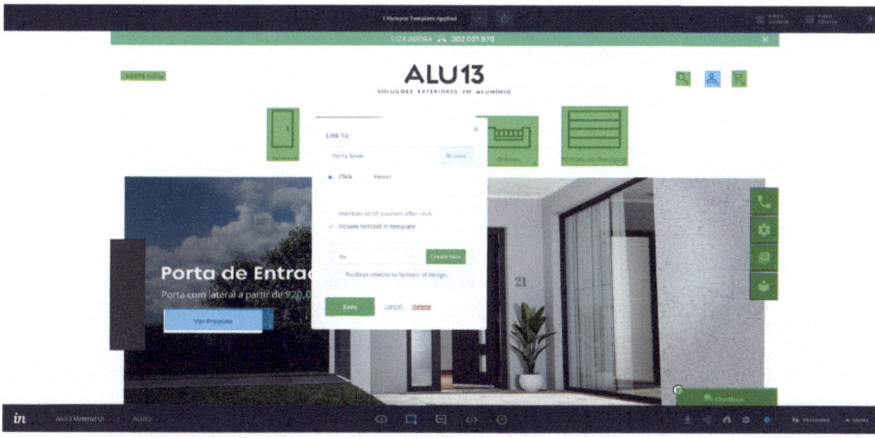

Fig. 9 Invision Platform—assigning actions and creating buttons

3.3 *Usability Tests*

> Usability is about making the product effective, efficient, and easy to use; by doing this, we provide satisfaction to the user when he interacts with our product. (Calonico et al. 2017)

It is known that, given the market overload, users are looking for a product that is effective and efficient. The offer is wide and therefore the possibility of empathizing with a brand is broadened. Thus, it is the company's responsibility to provide a service that meets the user's expectations (Calonico et al. 2017).

Bearing this in mind, it is admitted that testing usability makes it possible to check whether the service provided by the online store is easy for consumers to use.

Therefore, the first phase of this process, in this project, was to decide what should be tested. In this way, three main metrics were met: efficiency, effectiveness and satisfaction (ISO/IEC 9126–6).

To assess the degree of satisfaction of the participants, the interpretation and user satisfaction with the prototype of the online store, a questionnaire (QUIS) was developed. In this questionnaire, users were asked about issues such as the ease of interaction with the application, the quality of the data generated and presented, the utility of the application in diagnosis, the level of digital literacy and the overall appreciation of the application.

The questionnaire was divided into five assessment parts. The first part: ease of use (related to user interaction); the second part: thermology and information from the online store (related to the interface and data interpretation); the third part: utility (related to the purpose of the application); the fourth: digital literacy (related to the level of knowledge); and finally the fifth part: global assessment of the online store (the degree of satisfaction with the application) (attachment 1).

In the second phase, a list of tasks was elaborated that the user intended to perform, to observe how he behaves when executing them and, at the same time, to collect the necessary data, which will be analyzed and converted into opportunities to improve the project. The task list was as follows:

1. Buy Porta Ágata and choose the delivery day;
2. Register at the online store and consult the user area;
3. Report a claim;
4. Consult the information about the company;
5. Read an article on the ALU13 Blog;
6. Make a contact request.

The tests were carried out with five users, with approximate profiles of the personas model, and common users, in order to validate the potential of the online store. The tests lasted an average of 10 min and were performed in person, on a portable computer (Nielsen, 1994, 2012).

The analysis of the usability tests resulted in a set of points of interest, which includes aspects of the design that caused problems and difficulties in carrying out the tasks, as well as navigation aspects that should be improved (Norman and Nielsen, 2016).

All of this facilitated decision-making in relation to the design of the interfaces and the validation of the options taken, based on facts (Staats, 2019).

Observing the results obtained in the questionnaire (Table 1), we verified that in general, the answers were positive. In more detail, analyzing the answers to the questions regarding "Ease of Use" (question 1.1 to 1.5), it was found that 80% of users consider the online store to be clear and understandable; 100% of users consider that it does not require a high mental effort, being intuitive and easy to use; 60% of them are aware that they can freely browse and use the online store; finally, 100% say that the visual aspect is very pleasant.

Regarding the questions related to the "Terminology and information of the online store" (question 2.1 to 2.3), It was observed that 100% of the users consider the information in the online store perceptible and clear; 40% say they understand and easily interpret the terms applied; and that 80% agree that the online store reports on its progress and usage status.

In questions regarding the purpose of the application, "Utility" (question 3.1 to 3.5), 60% of respondents believe that the online store can replace the physical purchase of a product for the outside of the home, such as those provided by ALU13. It was also found that the responses were unanimous with regard to the appreciation of concept images, the possibility of getting in touch quickly to clarify doubts, increasing confidence with the available manufacturing information and increasing knowledge about a product that has little notoriety in Portugal.

As for "Digital Literacy" (question 4.1 to 4.5), 100% of users have already made purchases online; 40% of them say they have made purchases for their homes online; and only 20% of users made purchases over 1000 euros.

Finally, regarding the "Global Appreciation", all users found the online store very appealing, showing the potential to assert themselves in the Portuguese online market.

Table 1 Results of the online store evaluation questionnaire

1. **Ease of use**	I agree	Indecision	I disagree	Satisfaction (%)
1.1 My interaction with the online store is clear and understandable	4	1		80
1.2 The interaction with the online store does not require a high mental effort	5			100
1.3 The online store is intuitive, easy to use	5			100
1.4 I can do what I want in this online store	3	2		60
1.5 The visual aspect of the online store is very pleasant	5			100
2. **Data quality**	I agree	Indecision	I disagree	Satisfaction (%)
2.1 The quality of the data generated is very good	5			80
2.2 I easily understand and interpret the data generated	2	3		40
2.3 I have no problem with the data quality	4		1	80
3. **Utilidade**	I agree	Indecision	I disagree	Satisfaction (%)
3.1 The online store can replace the physical purchase of a product for the exterior of the dwellings	3		2	60
3.2 The concept images of the product help to visualize the same applied in my room	5			100
3.3 The possibility of getting in touch with the commercial quickly, helps to clarify doubts	5			100
3.4 The information available on manufacturing increases credibility and confidence in the online store	5			100
3.5 The online store increases my knowledge of aluminum products for homes	5			100
4. **Digital literacy**	I agree	Indecision	I disagree	Satisfaction (%)
4.1 I have already made online purchases	5			100
4.2 I have already purchased products for my home online	2		3	40
4.3 I have already purchased a product over 1000 € online	1		4	80
5. **Global appreciation of the online store**	I agree	Indecision	I disagree	Satisfaction (%)
5.1 The online store is very appealing	5			100
5.2 The online store is appealing				
5.3 The online store is not very appealing				
5.4 The online store is not appealing				

The face-to-face evaluation helped to understand some difficulties of use and receive positive feedback to continue to improve several aspects in the scope of user experience.

In short, the visual compositions, the structuring of the contents, the levels of organization in order of relevance, as well as the chromatic properties, were praised and a high degree of satisfaction was obtained in terms of the functioning of the online store.

4 Conclusion

In short, the framework and theoretical approach carried out within the scope of the research project on the interface development of the ALU13 online store was demonstrated.

In this sense, the contextualization of electronic commerce in Portugal, the understanding of the Portuguese online shopping habits, the perception of what are the best practices for selling home products, the study of methodologies and interface design guidelines, facilitated the design of it, validating the options taken to benefit the user and the business of ALU13.

The high-fidelity prototype can be found at the link: https://invis.io/XBTEIS36GK2.

The website is currently being implemented and is expected to be fully available to the public by the end of 2020.

References

A SMART INSIGHTS (2016) How Instagram can Elevate your E-commerce Store in 7 Steps, 23 Dec 2016. Accessed 7 May 2019, in https://www.smartinsights.com/social-media-marketing/instagram-marketing/instagram-can-elevate-ecommerce-store-7-steps/

ACEPI—Associação da Economia Digital em Portugal (2018) Economia Digital em Portugal. Accessed 7 May 2019, in http://www.aip.pt/uploads/Bibliotecas_de_Areas/Internacionalizacao/aico/apresentacoes/02102018_IDC_Estudo_ACEPI_Conclusoes.pdf

Alexa (2019) Top sites in Portugal. Accessed 7 May 2019, in https://www.alexa.com/topsites/countries/PT

CACOO (2019) Sales funnel software. Accessed 19 May 2019, in https://cacoo.com/examples/sales-funnel-software

Calonico S et al (2017) rdrobust: software for regression-discontinuity designs. Stata J 17(2):372–404

Carter J (2019) More people browse on mobile but buy via desktop. Accessed 28 April 2019 in https://www.smartinsights.com/ecommerce/more-people-browse-on-mobile-but-buy-via-desktop/

CONFAGRI—Confederação Nacional das Cooperativas Agrícolas e do Crédito Agrícola de Portugal (2018) Nem ecommerce nem centros comerciais: "millennials" portugueses preferem o comércio local. Accessed 28 April 2019, in https://www.confagri.pt/ecommerce-centros-comerciais-millennials-portugueses-preferem-comercio-local/

CTT (2017) e-Commerce report. Accessed 7 May 2019, in https://www.ctt.pt/contentAsset/raw-data/fcc210c5-f740-4f86-942a-99fc7888f02a/ficheiro/eCommerce_Report%20CTT%202017.pdf?byInode=true

CYR (2014) The encyclopedia of human-computer interaction, 2nd edn. Accessed 7 May 2019, in https://www.interaction-design.org/literature/book/the-encyclopedia-of-human-computer-interaction-2nd-ed/emotion-and-website-design

Garrett JJ (2003) The elements of user experience: user-centered design for the web. Thousand Oaks, USA, New Riders. Accessed 7 May 2019, in https://www.researchgate.net/publication/255710637_Exploring_Human_Images_in_Website_Design_A_Multi-Method_Approach

Harley A (2018) UX guidelines for ecommerce homepages, category pages, and product listing pages. Accessed 7 May 2019, in https://www.nngroup.com/articles/ecommerce-homepages-listing-pages/

Her Majesty's Stationery Office (1995) White paper on Competitiveness, citado por Bettina Stamm, (2003). Obtido de Managing Innovation, Design and Creativity. Accessed 7 May 2019, in https://books.google.pt/books?id=IlC7bN94zWgC&printsec

IMPIC—Instituto dos Mercados Públicos, do Imobiliário e da Construção, I.P (2018) Relatório Semestral do Sector da Construção em Portugall 1º Sem. 2018. Accessed 7 May 2019, in http://www.impic.pt/impic/assets/misc/relatorios_dados_estatisticos/RelConst_2018_S1.pdf

INE—Instituto Nacional de Estatística, Statistics Portugal. (2018). Destaque – informação à comunicação social – Sociedade da informação e do conhecimento – Inquérito à utilização de tecnologias da informação e da comunicação nas empresas 2018. Accessed 15 May 2019, in https://www.ine.pt/ngt_server/attachfileu.jsp?look_parentBoui=233842264&att_display=n&att_download=y

Jansen CP, Donker SF, Brumby DP, Kunc AL (2019) History and future of human-automation interaction. Int J Hum Comput Stud 131:99–107. https://doi.org/10.1016/j.ijhcs.2019.05.006

Kadazza (2019) Casa & Jardim. Accessed 7 May 2019, in https://www.kadaza.pt/casa-jardim%23

Kolko J (2011) Thoughts on interaction design. Accessed 7 May 2019, in https://medium.com/designstrat/thoughts-on-interaction-design-2011-5b38ddb107c1

Kujala S, Mugge R, Miron-Shatz T (2017) The role of expectations in service evaluation: a longitudinal study of a proximity mobile payment service. Int J Hum Comput Stud 98:51–61. https://doi.org/10.1016/j.ijhcs.2016.09.011

Martins N, Campos J, Simoes R (2020) Activerest: design of a graphical interface for the remote use of continuous and holistic care providers. Adv Sci Technol Eng Syst J 5(2):635–645. http://dx.doi.org/10.25046/aj050279

Nielsen J (1994) 10 Usability heuristics for user interface design. Accessed 7 May 2019, in https://www.nngroup.com/articles/ten-usability-heuristics/

Nielsen J (2012) Usability 101: introduction to usability. Accessed 7 May 2019, in https://www.nngroup.com/articles/usability-101-introduction-to-usability/

Nielsen (2018) Mais tempo e menos esforço: é isto que pede o consumidor. Accessed 7 June 2019, in https://www.nielsen.com/pt/pt/insights/article/2018/more-time-and-less-effort-what-consumer-asks-for/

Norman D, Nielsen J (2016) The definition of user experience (UX). Accessed 7 May 2019, in https://www.nngroup.com/articles/definition-user-experience/

Peixoto N (2018) Lojas online portuguesas para fazer as compras de Natal, Black Friday e Cyber Monday. Accessed 7 June 2019, in https://tsecommerce.com/blog/lista-lojas-online-portuguesas/

Reis Martins N (2017) E-Shopping experience em Marcas de Luxo. Accessed 7 May 2019, in https://recipp.ipp.pt/bitstream/10400.22/11786/1/nuno_martins_MMD_2018.pdf

Staats R (2019) 10 usability heuristics that all UI designers should know. Accessed 7 May 2019, in https://www.secretstache.com/blog/usability-heuristics/

Stamm B (2003) Managing innovation, design and creativity. John Wiley & Sons, London

Thomas (2019) Ecommerce product images: best practices that help you sell more. Accessed 7 May 2019, in https://acquireconvert.com/ecommerce-products-images-best-practices/

UX Planet (2019) What is UI design? What is UX design? UI vs. UX: what's the difference, 24 Feb 2019. Accessed 7 May 2019, in https://uxplanet.org/what-is-ui-vs-ux-design-and-the-difference-d9113f6612de

Wills B (2018) 18 Major benefits of e-Commerce business for retailers & customers 2018. Accessed 7 May 2019, in https://medium.com/@briannawillsss/18-major-benefits-of-e-commerce-business-for-retailers-customers-in-2015-63c5fc87f679

Yalanska (2017) UX design for E-commerce: principles and strategies. Accessed 7 May 2019, in https://tubikstudio.com/ux-design-for-e-commerce-principles-and-strategies/

Sensor Variable Font: A Model to Improve the Process of Signification of Graphic Interfaces Through Variable Fonts and Data Collected by Sensors

Iván Huelves and Lourdes Marco

Abstract Cities are rapidly developing into so-called *Smart Cities,* where the Internet of Things (IoT) and the hyperconnectivity of citizens are shaping new paradigms of coexistence, so further research is needed on how to improve the user experience through design. One of the revolutions in recent years in the typographic framework are variable fonts, which have the potential of turning typography into something *alive* that reacts to the environment. In response to this context, we present a model that lays the foundations for improving the process of signification of graphic interfaces through variable fonts, establishing a relationship between typography and the data collected by different sensors, resulting in more satisfactory user experiences. The research is contextualised by a literature review focused on semiotics, graphic design systems, interaction design, graphic and natural interfaces and variable fonts. Then, it describes the elements and the architecture flow of the model and advanced model cases. Finally, the model is evaluated by developing some prototypes. As an outcome of the early approaches to model evaluation, we can confirm that the proposed model has enough level of abstraction and flexibility to be successfully applied to multiple interactive projects in fields such as IoT, games, data visualization, branding or motion graphics.

Keywords Typography · Variable fonts · Interaction design · Graphic interface · Semiotics · Sensors

> Today's city—the city of end twentieth century—is the postmodern city: untamed, shrew, capricious, ever-changing; actually it is not a city but a text; a text written by millions of unknown writers, unaware that they are writers, read by millions of readers, each reading his or her own personal and subjective story in this ever-changing chaotic text, thus changing and recreating and further complicating it.
>
> Portugali (2000)

I. Huelves (✉) · L. Marco
Escuela Superior de Diseño de Madrid, Madrid, Spain
e-mail: ihuelves@esdmadrid.es

L. Marco
e-mail: lmarco@esdmadrid.es

N. Martins et al. (eds.), *Perspectives on Design and Digital Communication*, Springer Series in Design and Innovation 8, https://doi.org/10.1007/978-3-030-49647-0_5

1 Introduction

According to the World Urbanization Prospects report (United Nations 2018), by 2030 the planet is expected to have 43 mega-cities with more than 10 million inhabitants each. Moreover, nowadays 55% of the world's population lives in cities and it is expected to reach 68% by 2050, which means 2.5 billion more people. Portugali (2000) highlights that the city has become a text to be read, in which not only institutions write, but citizens are increasingly the main characters of the city's story. Cities have transformed from being a planned object to becoming a self-organised system. Today, we find ourselves immersed in an increasingly interrelated world, shaped by complex systems that our senses are unable to perceive in their entirety. The information explosion has given rise to new sciences such as Big Data, which analyzes and visualizes large amounts of economic, social, environmental and cultural data. Due to living in the information age, cities are rapidly moving towards the so-called *Smart Cities*, where the Internet of Things (IoT) and the hyperconnectivity of citizens at the micro and macro levels are creating new paradigms of coexistence and interaction. According to Cisco (2016) by 2030, 500 billion devices with sensors are expected to collect data, interact with the environment and communicate through the Internet. In this context of hyperconnection and continuous interaction with the environment, disciplines such as interaction design and data visualization are key.

One of the revolutions that we have been experiencing in recent years in the typographic framework are variable fonts, which can enhance the user experience in the context defined above, improving the process of signification, since their potential lies in turning typography into something *alive* that reacts and adapts to the environment. According to Vincens and Hornus (2017):

> Typography is the primary interface between this information and the city residents who benefit from access to it. The building blocks of that interface are fonts, typefaces of a certain style and size that render a text or icon recognizable to us. They bring our printed matter, screens and signage to life. In short, fonts are our most basic tool of communication. In an increasingly digital world, our communications are occurring at the intersection of typography and technology. One enables the other, and vice versa. Typography is ubiquitous. It is essential to communicate and gives information its shape.

From the literature review, we can affirm that typography is a central element of graphic interfaces and is one of the main means to access and interact with information on digital screens (Kahn and Lenk 1998; Yee 2006; Jeong et al. 2017 and Lee et al. 2019). Authors such as Salminen (2016) predict that the future of typography applied to graphic interfaces lies in their ability to adapt to the physical, textual and user context. In the same vein, Vincens and Hornus (2017) state that fonts can help to tune into our senses, sounds, feelings and smells, and translate abstract concepts into typography.

Several authors claim that typography has enormous potential for improving the process of signification (Childers and Jass 2002; Doyle and Bottomley 2009; Nørgaard 2009; Rath 2015). According to Rocha (1993), typography can "lend meaning or serve as signifiers or creators of identity". In the same text the author collects Barthe's and Massin's opinion that letterforms are more than a signifier for the character's signifies, but also carry ideas, thoughts and emotions. The process of meaning-making is achieved through the different styles and variations of typefaces. According to Doyle and Bottomley (2004) the congruency between a product and the selection of the typeface used, influence people's choice behavior. In short, "the ease of access to a variety of fonts no longer required written text to serve as an invisible means of communication, but as a visible means for communication" (Serafini and Clausen 2012).

From the context defined above, this chapter presents a model that lays the foundations for improving the process of signification of graphic interfaces through variable fonts, establishing a relationship between typography and the data collected by different sensors. Firstly, the research is contextualised by theoretical framework and a literature review focused on the definition of the fields involved: semiotics, graphic systems, interaction design, graphic and natural interfaces and variable fonts. Secondly, it describes the elements and the architecture flow of the model, and lays out a basic example and advanced model cases. Then, the model is evaluated by developing some prototypes. Finally, conclusions and limitations are drawn and future research is proposed.

2 Theoretical Framework and Literature Review

In this section a theoretical framework has been defined, which allows us to establish a solid ground for this research work from the perspectives of semiotics and graphic design systems. In addition, we have completed the study with a review of the current literature regarding the key aspects of this work, so that the concepts of interaction design, graphic and natural interfaces, and variable fonts are defined.

2.1 Signification from a Semiotic Perspective

According to Peirce (Peirce et al. 1998) semiotics is the study of signs and signification. A sign is anything that stands for something else to someone's understanding. The author developed a triadic model consisting in what Chandler (2007) would later reconfirm: "what is represented (the *object*), how it is represented (the *representamen*) and how it is interpreted (the *interpretant*)". Note that the interpretant must not to be understood as the person who interprets, but the sign that is generated in the mind of the interpreter. The study of signification is always conditional, since the meaning of a sign can change depending on the context. It is what Peirce calls the *ground* of the representamen. Therefore, the Peirce's third-order relationship is that in a particular ground context, a representamen stands for its object to an interpretant.

Once defined what semiotics and its main components are, we proceed to give a more precise definition of what the process of signification is. Signification can adopt different interpretations as: what is signified, the relationship between the object and the interpretant, a representation and the process of signification (semiosis). We will focus on the last one, semiosis, which refers to: "the process of meaning-making—specifically to the interaction between the representamen, the object and the interpretant" (Chandler 2007). Note that, nowadays the word meaning is usually avoided by semioticians due to the confusion it can cause, preferring to use the term signification (Skaggs 2017). We should keep in mind that the signification practices, are not only carried out by visual designers, but also by readers (Grayson 1998). Moreover, the signification is always incomplete, otherwise the representamen will be the object. In short, in words of A. J. Greimas (cited in Chandler 2007), "signification is… nothing but… transposition from one level of language to another, from one language to a different language, and meaning is nothing but the possibility of such transcoding".

In order to define what the process of signification is, Skaggs (2017) creates the following metaphor: "If we think of the triadic relation of sign,[1] referent,[2] and interpretant as a flexible leaf of paper, a sign's work can be thought of as an attempt to bend the interpretant toward the referent. One hopes that the understanding approaches the referent". According to Skaggs, there are only two ways to propitiate signification: through affective and conceptual semantic registers. The affective register can be divided into presence and expression which are related to feeling and emotional properties; and on the other hand, the conceptual register can be divided into denotation and connotation and it is related to cognitive and intellectual characteristics.

2.2 Graphic Design Systems

According to several authors (Ruder 1967; Woodbury 2010; Llop 2014) visual communication projects should be approached from a systemic strategy that simplifies the design process and brings coherence to the parties. Gerstner (1979) adds that a graphic design system permits to arrive at graphic solutions that otherwise would not have been achieved. All the authors mentioned above agree that a graphic design system is composed of elements (graphic objects), the attributes that these can acquire, the modifications that can be made from variables, and the relationships, based on combination rules (principles of design), that are established between them. Gerstner (1979) and Kenna (2012) developed a morphological box (with elements, parameters and principles of design), in order to design graphic solutions from combinations of their components. In both cases the relational logic is very similar: first, the elements are chosen; then these elements are given some parameters; and finally a concatenation function based in one or more principles of design is used to relate

[1] Skaggs (2017) calls sign what it has been previously defined as representamen.

[2] Skaggs (2017) calls referent what it has been previously defined as object.

each of the parts of the system. In case the result is not exactly the expected one, Gerstner (1979) proposes to apply a multiplication factor to determine how much the attribute to be modified should vary its valuable.

Moreover, Llop (2014) highlights the need to create a structure that allows an open and adaptable selection for each communicative need. A balance has to be found between an abstract system, which embraces different typologies of projects, and a concrete system that allows for practical application.

2.3 *Interaction Design*

Human-Computer Interaction (HCI) is a field of study focused on the interactive process between users and computer systems, with the aim of providing the basis for the design and evaluation of interactive products. The variables involved in this interactive process are very diverse, so as Hartson (1998) indicates, the HCI is cross-disciplinary in its conduct and multidisciplinary in its roots.

Although traditionally Human-Computer Interaction has focused its study on the user's skills and cognitive processes, according to Norman (2002), emotional aspects play a fundamental role, since they affect the cognitive processes. In other words, the users' affective states influence how they solve their problems. Besides the causes, another important aspect in interaction design is the process-related consequences. According to Hassan and Martín (2003), the design of a product can evoke emotions explicitly, expressing *affection*; or implicitly, through its aesthetics. According to the authors, the most effective mechanism to emulate affective states by a computer system is through the personification of the system (e.g. voice assistants). The authors also point out that when we talk about aesthetics in interactive products, we are not only referring to the visual appearance of the product, but to the aesthetics of the interaction, where appearance is a part.

In the book *Interaction Design: Beyond Human–Computer Interaction*, Rogers et al. (2011) state that "one main aim of interaction design is to reduce the negative aspects of the user experience while enhancing the positives ones".

2.4 *Graphic and Natural Interfaces (GUI, NUI)*

In the book *User Interface design and evaluation* Stone et al. (2005) explain that "a user interface is simply the part of a system that enables interaction and serves as a bridge between the users and the system, in order to fulfill their tasks and achieve their goals". The authors highlight that the user interface and the ways of interacting with systems are different for each system, and point out that to users the interface often is the system (Constantine and Lockwood 1999).

As far as the analysis of human-computer interactions is concerned, there are four types of User Interfaces (UI) (Liu 2010), namely: Batch Interface (BI), Command Line Interface (CLI), Graphical User Interface (GUI) and Natural User Interfaces (NUI). BIs are non-interactive user interfaces, where the user specifies all the details of the batch job in advance, and receives the output when all the processing is done. On the other hand, CLIs prompt the user to provide input by typing a command string with the computer keyboard and respond by outputting text to the computer monitor. Especially relevant for this research are the GUIs and the NUIs. A GUI is a hierarchical, graphical front-end to a software system that accepts as input user-generated and system-generated events from a fixed set of events and produces deterministic graphical output (Memon et al. 2003). The term NUI stands for the ways of interaction with a device based on methods that would be as natural and intuitive for a human being as possible. Therefore, such interfaces can be based e.g. on voice, touch or image and movement detection and interpretation (Glonek and Pietruszka 2012). In other words, when we interact with a computer system by speaking to it, tapping or swiping, gesturing in the air, or using a digital pen to write on a screen, we are using a NUI (De los Reyes 2008).

The basis of GUIs has been sustained throughout their development around desktop metaphors. Rieder (2013) points out that "most NUI interfaces with which we interact look like GUIs, but, as NUIs mature, the ways in which we control a computational environment will have less to do with on-screen metaphors, icons and buttons, and more to do with an ethos that we perform". The author, based on the previous work of Selfe and Selfe (1994), concludes that by contributing to the development of new interfaces, we will change the ways in which we experience data flows, and thus be able to elevate the role and value of our creations to serve new purposes in today's brave new NUI worlds (Wigdor and Wixon 2011).

2.5 *Variable Fonts*

On September 14, 2016, variable fonts were presented to the public through the release of the Opentype 1.8 specification, at the ATypI 2016 conference. The work was the result of a joint effort by several major technology companies: Google, Microsoft, Apple and Adobe. The main objective was to reduce the space and bandwidth consumption of typography on the web. However, variable fonts hide behaviours that could completely transform the role of typography in visual communication by becoming a dynamic and interactive element. The novelty of variable fonts is its ability to generate new glyphs from interpolation between two or more masters. The advantage is that we only need a single file to create multiple styles of a typeface.

Nevertheless, the creation of fonts from parameters has both analog and digital predecessors. The most direct references from which both theoretical and technological concepts have been recycled are PostScript Type 1 Multiple Master (Rickner 2016) and TrueType GX (Phinney 2018).

In the following lines we proceed to define the concepts that make up the variable fonts with the purpose of facilitating the subsequent explanation of the model.

2.5.1 Axes

Variable fonts are defined by the axes along which the typeface is modified. An axis is a parameter determined by the font designer that is used to create different styles within a type family. When axes are declared, they must have a maximum and a minimum value between which they are interpolated. (Constable and Jacobs 2018). Variable fonts can contain multiple axes, there being no specific limit. It is possible to vary the font from a single axis as we can see on Fig. 1.

Or the variation can affect several axes as we can see in the Fig. 2.

Note that a glyph does not have to be modified for each of the axes and the variations need not only affect the contours of the glyph. According to Willis (2016):

Fig. 1 Example of one axis. Own elaboration

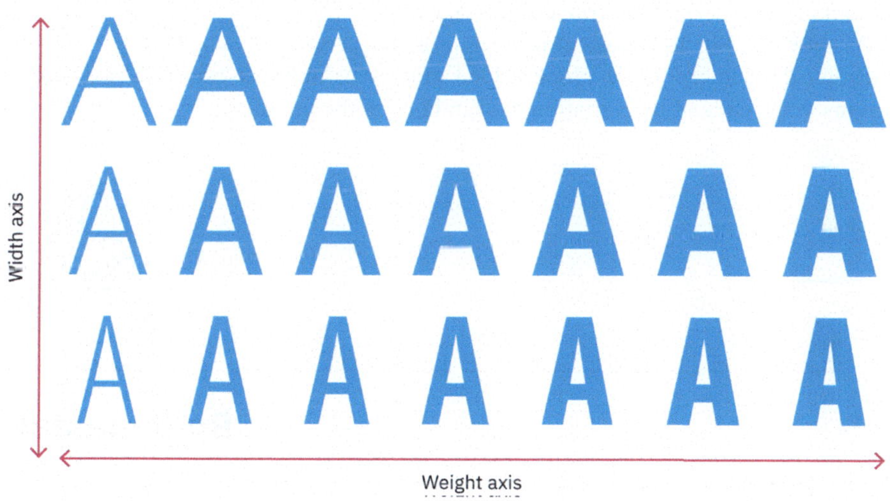

Fig. 2 Example of two axes. Own elaboration

> The variations can affect not just glyph outlines, but font metrics, too: widths, font-wide ascent and descent values, left and right side bearings, horizontal and vertical kerning, and so on. Variations can also affect OpenType layout rules—for instance, by substituting simpler versions of a glyph at small optical sizes or at extremely heavy weights, or by adjusting the positioning rules used in complex scripts like Indic and Arabic.

One of the most important aspects for technological advances to end up being incorporated is the compatibility with existing systems through a common language. To this end, the OpenType 1.8 specification provides a definite semantics for the axes. The objective is that the user obtains a result in accordance with the expectations of, for example, selecting a bold style. The axes tags are recorded in the *fvar* and *STAT* tables. (Constable and Jacobs 2018). There are five default registered axes: weight, width, optical size, slant and italic and the designers can also create custom axes to add other kind of variations.

2.5.2 Master

A master is a set of nodes with coordinates specified beforehand by the designer in the design space, that form the contour of a glyph. From the information in these glyphs, delta values can be varied to generate new instances. For each glyph a variable font can contain one, two or more masters, which allow the typeface to vary from an interpolation between each of these. For example, as Fig. 3 shows, a font can contain one master that would correspond to the light style and another one to the bold style, and the user can select any weight in between (Poizat 2017). The usual practice is to create two masters, one at each the ends of the axis, and from these, they are interpolated. It is essential that they contain the same number of nodes and contours for the correct interpolation to take place.

As shown in Fig. 4, the use of three or more masters can also be used to facilitate and control the interpolation process. One strategy would be to establish two master designs at the ends of the variation axis and one in the middle.

Fig. 3 Two master designs. Own elaboration

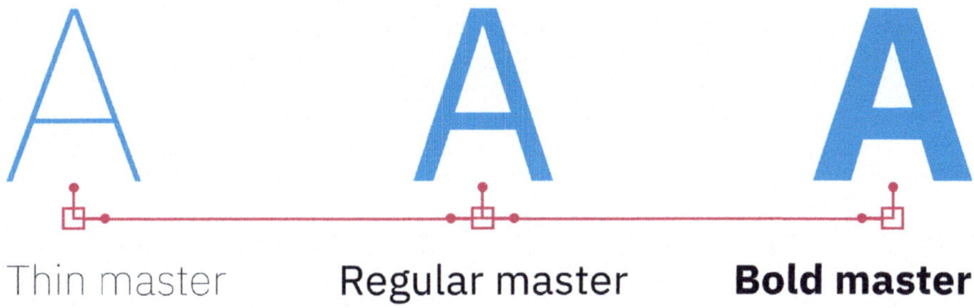

Fig. 4 Three master designs. Own elaboration

2.5.3 Deltas

Deltas are numerical values that determine the variation in the X and Y position of master nodes. These delta values (see Fig. 5) are stored in tables which describe how glyphs outlines change across the font's variation space. If the glyphs are defined by

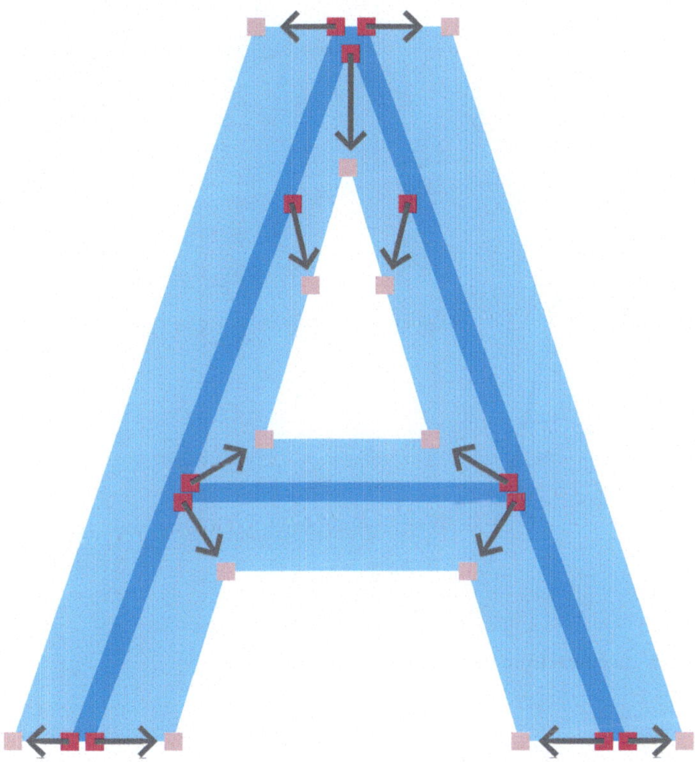

Fig. 5 Simulation of deltas creation from a master. Own elaboration

TrueType curves, delta values are stored in the *gvar* table or if the curves are based on OpenType CFF, in the *CFF2* table (Constable and Jacobs 2018).

2.5.4 Instances

An instance is any glyph generated from interpolation between one or more axes. From the master designs, the source interpolates to generate new instances that have not been previously defined by the designer (see Fig. 6).

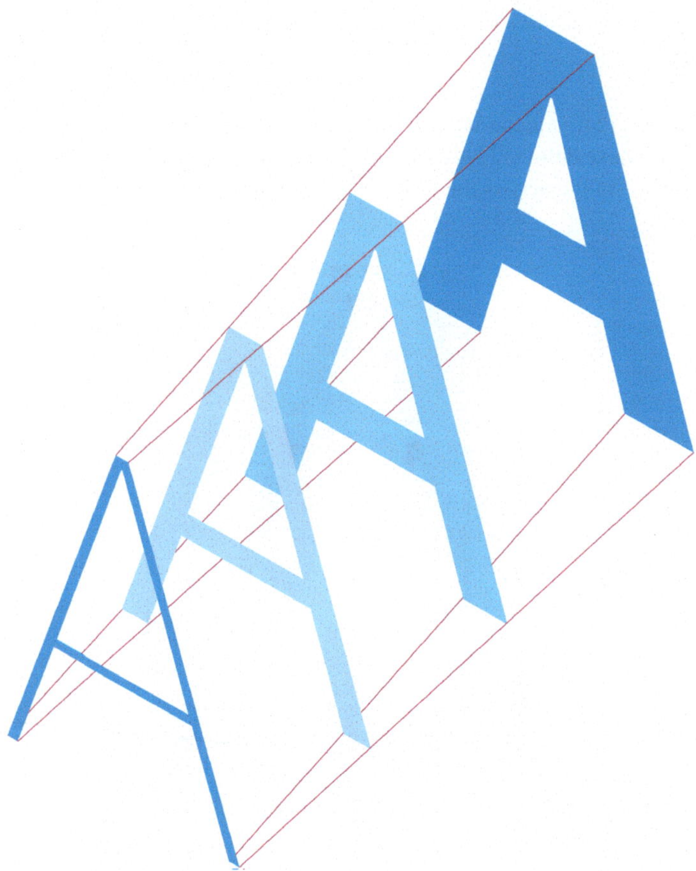

Fig. 6 Instances generated from two masters. Own elaboration

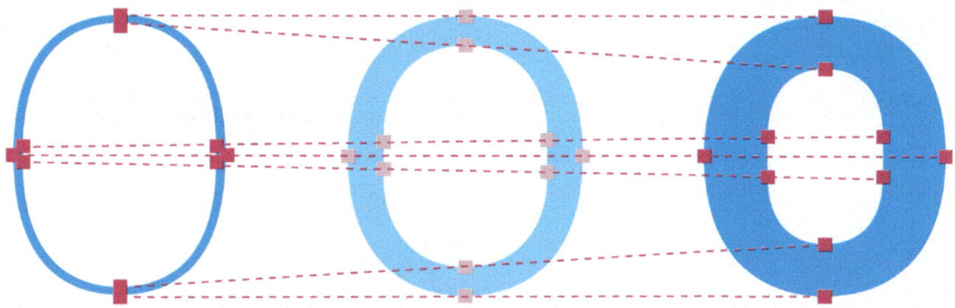

Fig. 7 Simulation of interpolation between two masters. Own elaboration

2.5.5 Interpolation

Interpolation is the mathematical function used by variable fonts to generate instances from master. Specifically, a linear interpolation is used to generate a straight line between two pairs of nodes. New nodes can be created at the intersection points of the generated lines to configure the instances. That is why the position of the nodes is crucial so that the shapes do not overlap when interpolating (see Fig. 7).

The problem with Opentype 1.8 supporting only line interpolations is that in many cases it limits the drawing possibilities of the glyphs or requires more planning for the placement of the nodes. The Underware Foundry (2018) has been exploring applying cubic curves to variable fonts interpolation. They have named this type of interpolation *Higher Order Interpolation.*

2.5.6 Design Space

Once the elements of a variable font have been described, it is time to define the design space concept, which is the most important idea to understand the logic behind variable fonts. This is a virtual multidimensional space in which the font is developed. This space is built from the axes included in the font and determines the range of variability of the font. It can be understood as the framework in which the font is developed. A basic example of a two multidimensional design space can be seen in Fig. 8.

3 Sensor Variable Font

Once the concepts of signification, graphic design systems, interaction design, GUI, NUI and variable fonts have been defined, we proceed to introduce the proposed model. The Sensor Variable Font model objective is to improve the process of

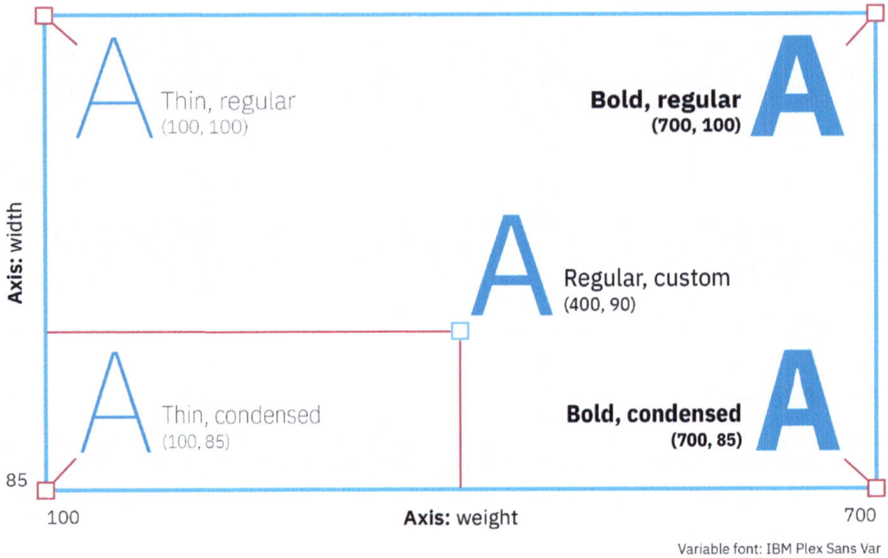

Fig. 8 Design space consisting of two axes and one interpolated instance. Own elaboration based on Constable and Jacobs (2018) and RoboFont (2018)

signification of graphic interfaces through variable fonts, establishing a relationship between typography and the data collected by different sensors, resulting in more satisfactory user experiences.

First off, the model requirements are identified. Then, the architecture model is explained, including its components and the architecture flow. Finally, advanced applications of the model are presented.

3.1 Model Requirements

In accordance with the need stated in the *Introduction* of this document, the model must conform to the following criteria:

- Improve the process of signification. The model has to transmit a certain communicative intention which improves the process of signification.
- Communicate through typography. The means to improve the user experience must be the axes of variable fonts. Please note that when we refer to typefaces, we must not limit ourselves only to the creation or use of alphanumeric glyphs, but it can also involve any graphic form into the font.
- Flexible and specific. The model must have parts of a higher level of abstraction that allow it to be applied to interactive projects of different nature and obtain multiple results each time. At the same time the results must be specific enough to

be used in the designs. The types of data that are used as input can be numerical, textual, and boolean.

- Easy to apply. The model has to be simple enough so that it can be applied. Firstly, the technological implementation must be simple so that designers without great technological knowledge can use it. And secondly, in relation to the definition of the expression to improve the process of signification.

3.2 *Architecture Model*

Taking into account the requirements described above, a basic model has been proposed. As we can observe in Fig. 9, the data collected by the sensor are the input for the model. From this information the *Normalizing function* normalizes the sensor value to its corresponding axis value of the font, and the *Signification function* modifies the values to meet the proposed communicative intent. Finally, the output of the system is the axis of the font transformed.

3.2.1 Sensor

The sensor is in charge of detecting a certain phenomenon and return it in the form of data. The frequency and type of data will depend on each type of sensor and the nature of the phenomenon.

3.2.2 Variable Font

The variable font is the communicative medium through which the process of signification is enhanced, either through the representation of the sensor data or other content that is modified by reacting to the data it receives.

3.2.3 Normalizing Function

The *Normalizing function* establishes an equivalence between two ranges of values: the minimum and maximum values selected for the sensor and the ones for the

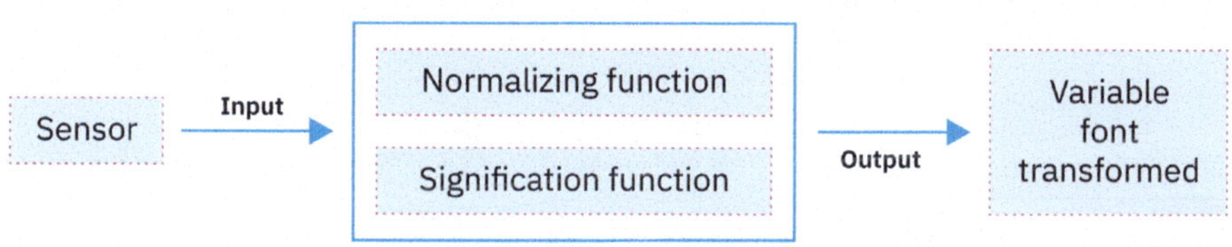

Fig. 9 Architecture model, Sensor Variable Font. Own elaboration

Fig. 10 Basic example of the model improving the signification of the wind speed and direction representation through the slant axis of the variable font. Own elaboration

axis. The function transforms the data collected by the sensor (input model) into the equivalent of the axis. For instance, if the sensor has registered a value of 60 cm of distance between itself and a person, this could be equivalent to a value of 400 of the weight axis.

3.2.4 Signification Function

The *Signification function* is in charge of giving semantic value to the graphic interface to meet the communicative objective by improving the process of signification. For this purpose, the designer must define expressions capable of relating the signification intent to the values of the axes and those registered by the sensor. In order to undertake this action, the designer can rely on design principles such as balance, contrast, repetition or randomness, among others[3] to transform the normalized data received by the sensor.

For example, we can imagine an application that shows wind speed and direction. We want to create a symmetrical relationship, on the one hand, between the wind direction and the direction of inclination of the slant axis of the font; and on the other hand, between the wind speed and the degree of inclination of the slant axis of the font. The higher the speed, the higher the degree of inclination. To do this, we can establish the following relationship through the sentence:

Slant axis value = Standardized wind speed (Value transformed by the *Normalizing function*) * (±1) (To modify the direction of the slant variation axis).

If the value registered by the sensor is that the wind comes from the east, it applies a negative value on the slant axis: Slant axis value = (0.8) * (−1) = −0.8.

Note that in this case two variables applied to a single axis have been used: wind direction and speed. For a more reliable representation the slant axis should be replaced by one that contemplates a range from 0 to 360. Figure 10 shows a graphic representation of the example.

[3]Concerning the design principles that govern the relationship between the elements of a graphic design system, Dondis (1992), Wong (2001) or von Engelhardt (2002) can be taken as a reference contrasting authors.

3.3 Architecture Flow

In this section we will go further in defining the proposed model. Figure 11 shows an extended version of the architecture flow. As the figure shows, the data collected by a sensor is taken as an input to modify the axis of a font through a normalization process (*Normalizing function* of the model), in which minimum and maximum values must be selected for the sensor and the axis. These values have to be contained within the predefined range for the sensor and the axis, and it is the designer's decision to make them coincide with these default values or to establish others to reflect the communicative intent. Without a specific order of execution, the *Signification function* is defined with the objective of transforming the values of the axis by means of operators, expressions and/or sentences based on design principles that obey the proposed communicative intention. The reason why the *Normalizing* and *Signification function* are at the same level is because in many cases the *Signification function* will condition the design of the normalizer or vice versa. Finally, it is decided whether the value of the axis, now transformed into an instrument with greater semantic capacity, will be applied to all glyphs or only to specific ones.

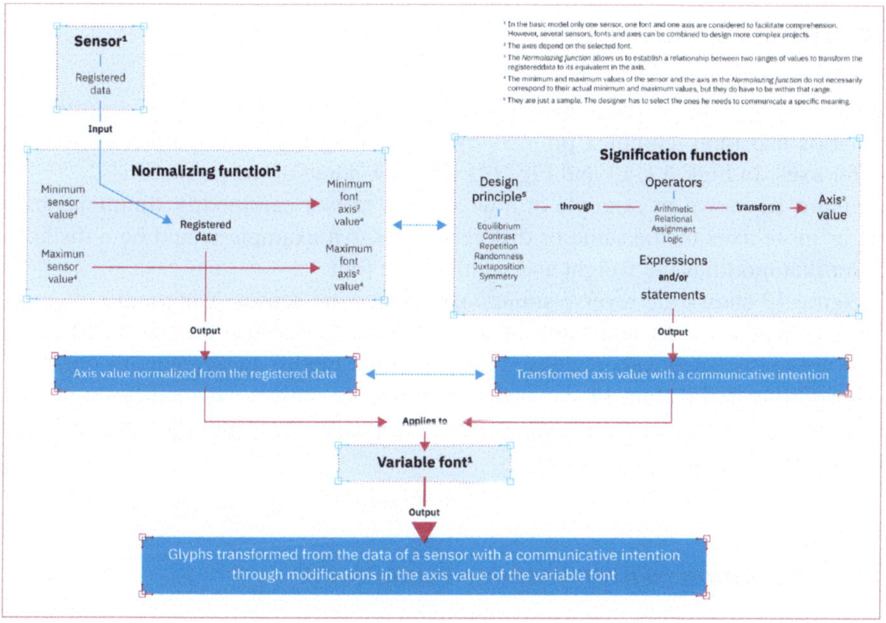

Fig. 11 Architecture flow of the Sensor Variable Font model. Own elaboration

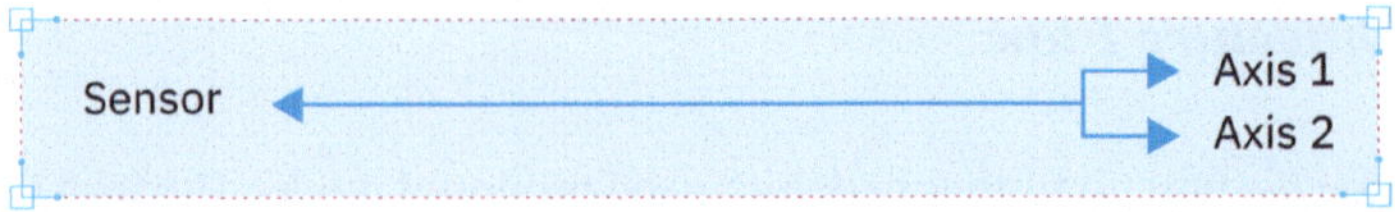

Fig. 12 Advanced model case with one sensor and two or more axes. Own elaboration

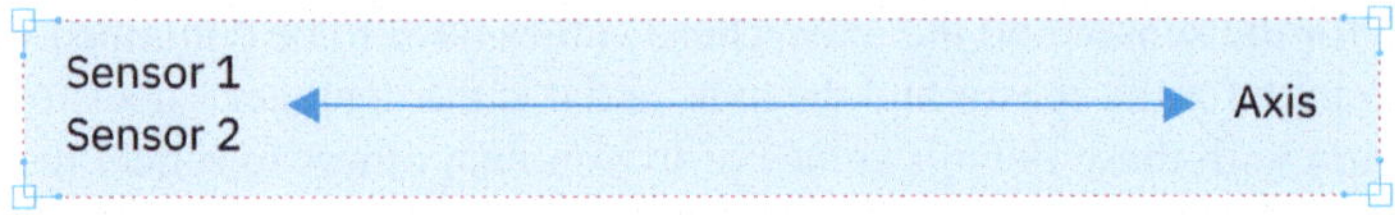

Fig. 13 Advanced model case with two or more sensors and one axis. Own elaboration

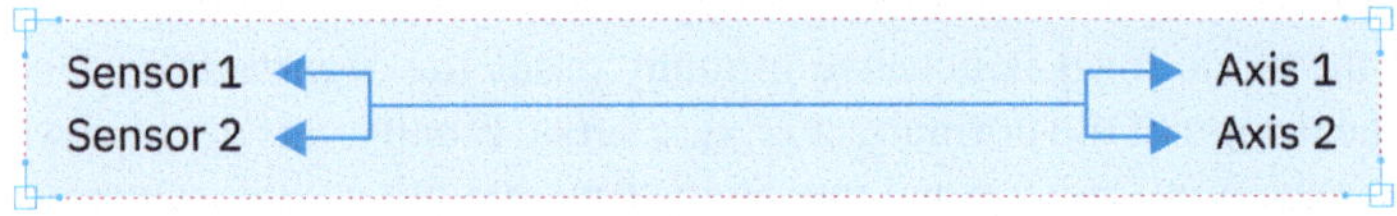

Fig. 14 Advanced model case with two or more sensors and two or more axes. Own elaboration

3.4 Advanced Model Cases

The flexibility of the proposed model makes it suitable for adaptation to very different scenarios and more complex projects by introducing a greater number of sensors and/or axes. In Figs. 12, 13 and Fig. 14) we show some of the possibilities.

Figure 12 shows an example of how a single sensor can modify simultaneously two or more axes of the same or different fonts. An example would be a distance sensor that modifies the weight and width of the font.

Figure 13 shows the reverse situation, two or more sensors can modify a single axis. In this case we could think of a temperature sensor on the one hand and a humidity sensor on the other, whose values together modify the weight of a typeface.

In addition to this, Fig. 14 shows that two or more sensors can modify simultaneously two or more axes. For example a presence sensor activates the italic axis and another speed sensor the slant axis.

3.5 Evaluation Sensor Variable Font Model

A first model evaluation process has been carried out through the development of some prototypes. These prototypes have made it possible to test and reflect on the suitability of the model. In the words of George E. P. Box (Box et al. 2009):

> All models are approximations. Assumptions, whether implied or clearly stated, are never exactly true. All models are wrong, but some models are useful. So the question you need to

ask is not "Is the model true?" (it never is) but "Is the model good enough for this particular application?".

3.5.1 Evaluation Methodology

The methodology used has been *practice-led research* defined by Candy (2006):

> If the research leads primarily to new understandings about practice, it is Practice-led. Practice-led Research is concerned with the nature of practice and leads to new knowledge that has operational significance for that practice. […] The primary focus of the research is to advance knowledge about practice, or to advance knowledge within practice. Such research includes practice as an integral part of its method and often falls within the general area of action research.

Therefore, the knowledge that emerges during the creation of these prototypes and their subsequent reflection will be more important than the prototype itself. Along the same lines, according to Leavy (2015) and Carrillo (2015), a primary aspect of *practice-led Research* is its self-reflectivity. This aspect reconfigures the traditional relationship between the research subject and the object of study because it means that the former requires involving themselves in the process, working on projects that reflect both critical and subjective perspectives. This does not detract from the quality of the research results, but rather reveals aspects that could not be revealed otherwise. Moreover, the prototypes developed serve the function of facilitating the understanding of the model.

3.5.2 Model Implementation

The following lines detail the implementation of the model and the characteristics of the prototypes. We need a technological scenario to implement the model in which all the components of the model have a place: sensor, *Normalizing function*, *Signification function* and variable font. As shown in Fig. 15, we have used Arduino (https://www.arduino.cc/) to collect data from the sensors, a microcontroller on which sensors can be connected to interact with the physical environment. In order to link the microcontroller with the *Normalizing function* that will normalize the data received by the sensors, a server-side application has been created with node.js (https://nodejs.org/es/), express.js (https://expressjs.com/es/) and socket.io (https://socket.io/).

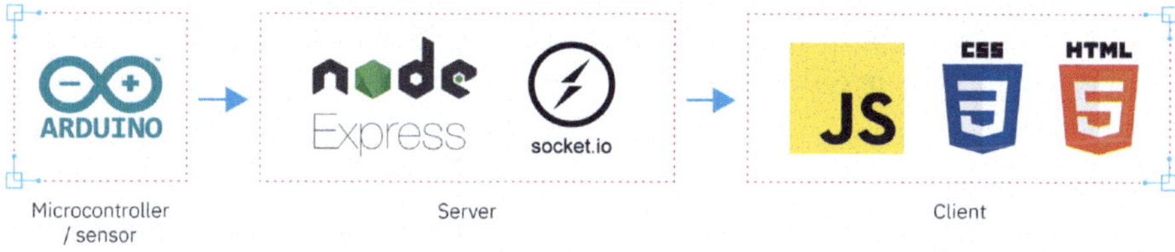

Fig. 15 Technological implementation of the Sensor Variable Font model. Own elaboration

Finally, we have been used the standards HTML, CSS and JS (W3C 2016) for the development of a client-side application that will improve signification and render, both the data and the selected variable font.

3.5.3 Prototype Development

On-Board Computer Car Application

We have considered for the first prototype the interface of an on-board computer car as a possible case of use (see Fig. 16). Specifically we want to draw the driver's attention to a possible collision due to proximity of another car, object or person through the axis weight of the font. To this end, a *Signification function* is defined, with the intention of providing a semantic value to the graphical interface, through the principle of juxtaposition. That is, if the collision distance decreases, the weight of the font increases.

The variable font selected for the prototype was Kairos Sans[4] and its weight axis, which has a minimum value of 250 and a maximum of 900. The data receiver is a distance sensor whose capacity is fixed in a range of 4 cm as minimum and 40 cm as maximum. The *Normalizing function* is used to establish the relationship between the minimum and maximum values of the sensor and the axis. In this case, as a result of the *Signification function* defined above (if the collision distance decreases, the weight of the font increases), an inverse relationship is established by assigning the distance 4 cm to the weight 900, and the distance 40 cm to the weight 250. The result we obtain is the corresponding value of the weight axis, normalized to the distance detected by the sensor, and transformed according to the communicative intention.

Branding Application

In order to show different contexts of model use, the next prototype is based in a branding approach (see Fig. 17). Certainly, in the next few years we will see variable fonts apply to branding design. The case of use that we have designed is to alter the logo on a display, every time a person is about to enter the store. The defined *Signification function* is based on the principle of randomness: each time a customer is detected by the presence sensor, each letter of the logo will randomly modify its axis of rotation.

In this case the variable font used has been designed specifically for the prototype. We have started from the Open Source font, Public Sans,[5] adding an axis that we have named *Rotate*, with a minimum value of 0 and a maximum of 360. The variation consists of the rotation of the glyphs on themselves from a central axis. The axis contains five masters in order to further control the rotation during the interpolation process.

---

[4] Available at https://github.com/Monotype/Monotype_prototype_variable_fonts/tree/master/KairosSans.

[5] Available at https://github.com/uswds/public-sans.

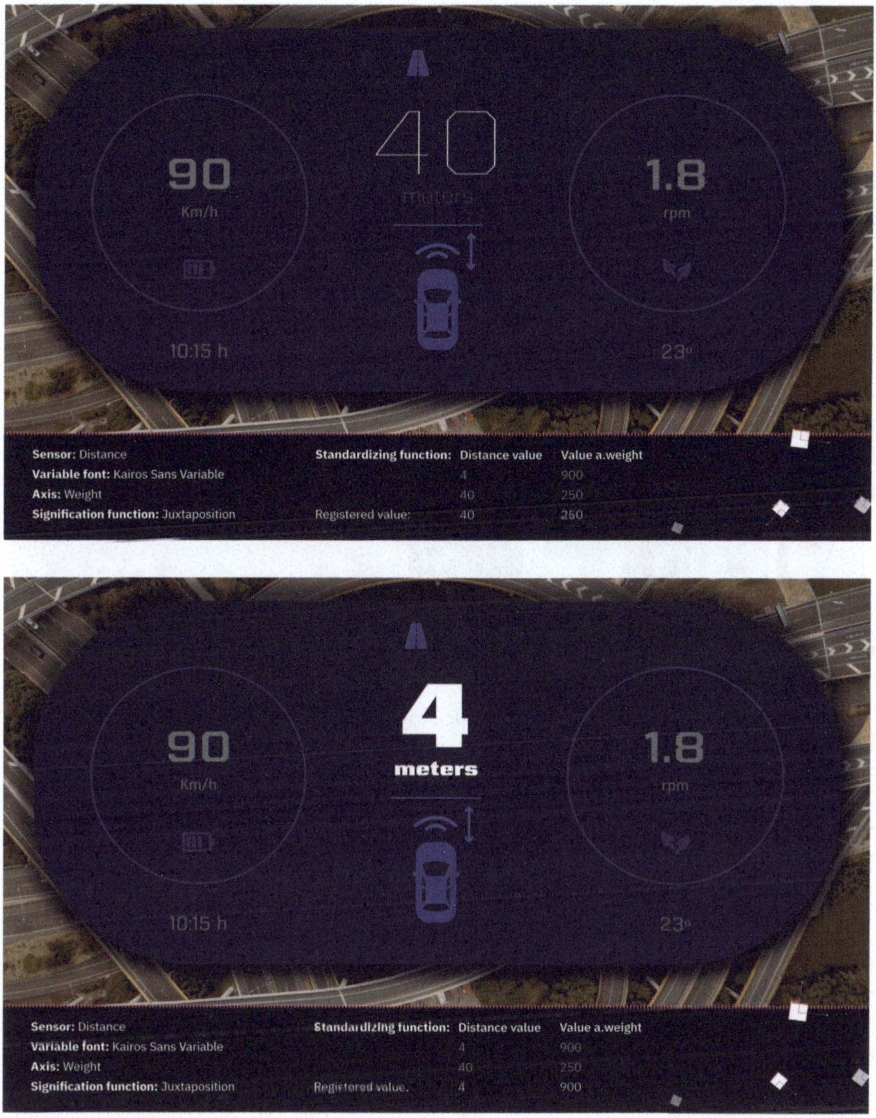

Fig. 16 View of the prototype (distance sensor on an on-board computer car) with two different recorded values. Own elaboration

As mentioned above, a presence sensor would be used. The criteria for selecting this sensor has been that it returns binary values, thus being able to exemplify the use of the model with data of a different nature. The values of the sensor are 0 and 1. In this prototype the *Normalizing function* transforms the 1 value into a value between 0 and 360 in a random way. The result is that every time a user enters the store, the

Fig. 17 Brand identity application of the model with a random principle and binary data. Own elaboration from Brian Kraus image

sensor triggers the variation of the logo reproduced in the graphical interface to meet the branding campaign.

Chat Application

In order to show the possibilities defined in the requirements of the model, in which it is specified that other types of data such as textual ones and non-alphanumeric typefaces can be used, we have designed a prototype that shows the emotions of messages through the axes of a variable font (see Fig. 18). The defined *Signification function* wants to improve the signification process by creating a symmetrical relationship between the content of the message and the shape of the glyph. For example, if the content of the message has a great deal of joy in it, the font (in this case the emoticon font) will vary to a smiling face. One application of this prototype could be in chat services or application products by modifying the shape of the avatars according to the conversation.

To identify the emotions we have made use of the Tone Analyzer application[6] developed by IBM. This service "uses linguistic analysis to detect joy, fear, sadness, anger, analytical, confident and tentative tones found in text". On the other hand,

[6]Available at https://www.ibm.com/watson/services/tone-analyzer/.

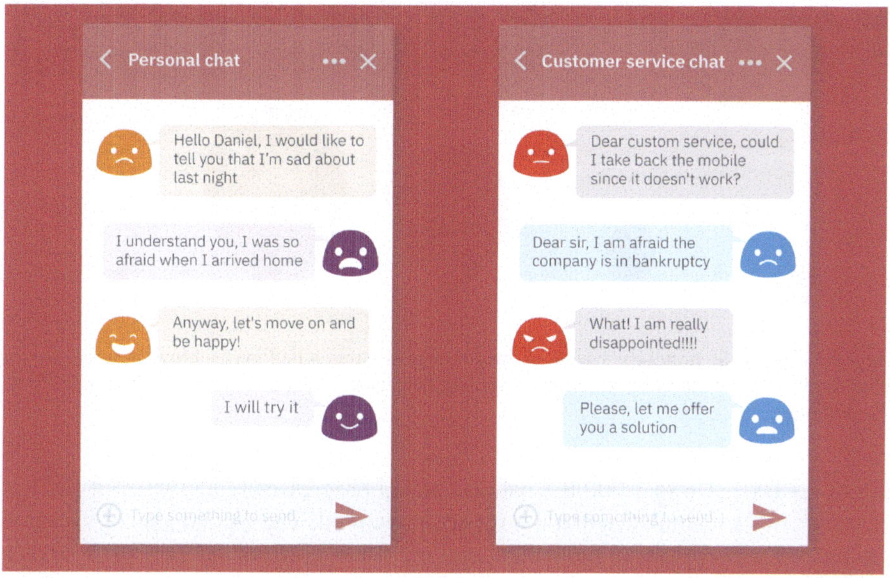

Fig. 18 Application of the model simulating a chat app with textual data and a non-alphanumeric font (note that the variable font designed is the one which represents the emoticons). Own elaboration

to represent the data returned by the application we have specifically designed a font (based on Noto Emoji[7]) which has a single axis with five masters, one for each emotion: anger, sadness, neutral, fear and joy (for the purposes of the prototype, we haven't represented all the emotions). The value of the axis varies between −100 to 100 which allows different degrees of each emotion to be represented. For example from −100 to −50 the different degrees of anger are represented. For this purpose, the *Normalizing function* transforms the value calculated by the Tone Analyzer application and generates its equivalent from the source variation axis.

Blow Balloon Game

The last prototype included in this chapter shows the application of the model from another non-alphanumeric typeface. In this case, we have devised an interactive application of a playful nature in which you have to blow through a sensor to inflate a balloon as much as possible before it gets pricked by the cactus and pops (see Fig. 19). The defined *Signification function* is based on the principle of contrast and play. The harder you blow, the more the balloon will inflate, but if you overdo it, you will pop it and lose. In addition, while you inflate the balloon you can move it left and right with a tilt sensor.

The variable font has been designed in an express way for this prototype. The character contained in the balloon is the lower case *a*. The typeface has two axes called Inflate and Move. The first one simulates the balloon swelling. Its values go

[7]Available at https://www.google.com/get/noto/#emoji-zsye.

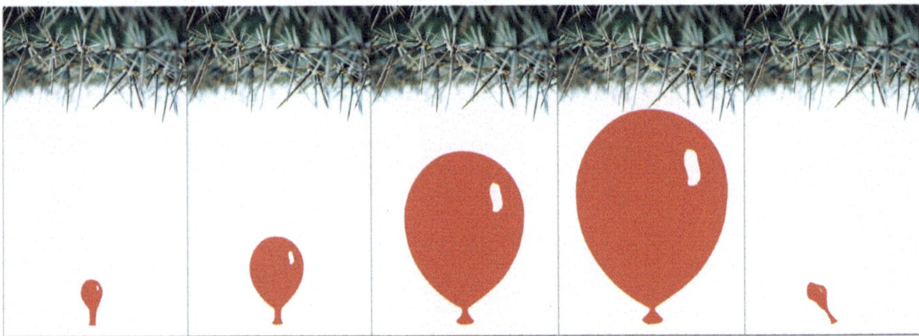

Fig. 19 View of the prototype based on the game of inflating a balloon by blowing into a sensor which makes use of a non-alphanumeric font and two sensors that affect two different axes. Own elaboration

from 0 to 1001. Up to 1.000 the balloon grows progressively and when it reaches the value 1.001 it simulates that it has been punctured. The second axis of variation simulates a lateral shaking movement and its values go from −1 (left) to 1 (right), being 0 the vertical position. Regarding the sensors, a sound sensor has been used to simulate blowing and a tilt sensor to simulate shaking. The values defined in the *Normalizing function* range from 10 to 500 for the sound sensor and in the case of the tilt sensor the sensor returns only three values: up, down and hold.

The development of this and other prototypes can be consulted on the website: www.sensorvariablefont.com.

4 Conclusions

Once the implementation of the model has been carried out, it can be stated that the model proposed improves the process of signification of graphic interfaces through the use of variable fonts modified from data collected by sensors.

In addition, thanks to the development of the prototypes several improvements to the model have been made. Firstly, the architectural flow has been modified by detecting that the *Significant function* is not always executed once the values have been normalized, but sometimes occurs earlier. It has also been observed that if the graphic results obtained must to be adjusted, transformation constants can be used in the *Signification function* or limit the range of values in the *Normalizing function* in order to communicate the proposed intention.

We have also been able to verify through the proposal of more advanced scenarios that it is capable of supporting the collection of data of different nature from an indeterminate number of sensors, as well as the use of an indeterminate number of axes of the font.

Finally, we can confirm that the model has been created with enough level of abstraction and sufficient flexibility, thanks to the implementation of different types of prototypes which guarantee the application of the proposed model to multiple interactive projects in fields such as IoT, games, data visualization or branding. These are just a few cases of using the model to improve the process of signification, however the options are infinite and it is up to the designer to apply the model for his or her purposes.

5 Limitations

During the development and evaluation of the model we have found some limitations mainly related to the technological barrier that users may have and to the system of interpolation of the fonts.

Regarding the technological barrier that the users of the model may have, this mainly refers to the problems related to the implementation of the model. The latter requires a basic knowledge of web programming languages, such as HTML, CSS or JavaScript.

Futhermore, with regard to the system of font interpolation, in the design of glyphs we find the limitation that the system of linear interpolation significantly limits the variations that can be implemented in the axes of the fonts.

6 Future Research

Future research should further validate the model with different user profiles through workshops with student and professional designers and through interviews with experts in typography and interaction.

Concerning the development of the model, one of the proposals is to investigate how to improve the process of signification by further defining the design principles along with their corresponding expressions, which could make it easier for the designer to implement it. However, a balance has to be found so as not to limit the flexibility of the model. Another approach could be to investigate how to facilitate the technological implementation of the model or expand it to other platforms.

Finally, future work could continue to explore the application of the model to more specific use cases, such as application with more complex interfaces as a data visualization dashboard that displays temperature, wind, speed, air pollution, noise levels, etc. Another field of application could be digital accessibility in order to respond to the different needs of profiles. In addition, these findings could provide additional information about how to go deeper into the characteristics that a typeface must have, in order to improve the process of signification, and resulting in better user experiences.

References

ATypI (2016) Special OpenType Session. [Video]. Retrieved from https://www.youtube.com/watch?v=6kizDePhcFU

Box GEP, Luceño A, Paniagua-Quiñones MDC (2009) Statistical control by monitoring and adjustment, 2nd ed. Wiley, New York

Candy L (2006) Practice based research: a guide. (Creativity and Cognition Studios, 1). University of Technology, Sydney. http://research.it.uts.edu.au/creative/eae/intart/pdfs/PBR%20Guide-1.1-2006.pdf

Carrillo P (2015) La investigación basada en la práctica de las artes y los medios audiovisuales [Practice-based research in the arts and media]. Revista Mexicana de Investigación Educativa 20, 64:219–240. http://www.redalyc.org/articulo.oa?id=14032722011

Chandler D (2007) Semiotics: The basics (Second edition). Routledge

Childers TL, Jass J (2002) All dressed up with something to say: effects of typeface semantic associations on brand perceptions and consumer memory. J Consum Psychol 12:93–106. https://doi.org/10.1207/S15327663JCP1202_03

Cisco (2016) Internet of things. (Research Report). Retrieved from https://www.cisco.com/c/dam/en/us/products/collateral/se/internet-of-things/at-a-glance-c45-731471.pdf

Constable P, Jacobs M (2018) OpenType font variations overview. Retrieved from https://docs.microsoft.com/en-us/typography/opentype/spec/otvaroverview

Constantine LL, Lockwood LA (1999) Software for use: a practical guide to the models and methods of usage-centered design. Addison Wesley, New York

De los Reyes A (2008) Predicting the past. In: Web Directions South 2008. Sydney Convention Centre, Australia, 25 Sept

Doyle JR, Bottomley PA (2004) Font appropriateness and brand choice. J Bus Res 57:873–880. https://doi.org/10.1016/S0148-2963(02)00487-3

Doyle JR, Bottomley PA (2009) The massage in the medium: transfer of connotative meaning from typeface to names and products. Appl Cogn Psychol 23:396–409. https://doi.org/10.1002/acp.1468

Dondis DA (1992) La sintaxis de la imagen. Introducción al alfabeto visual [A Primer of Visual Literacy]. Gustavo Gili

Gerstner K (1979) Diseñar programas [Designing Programmes]. Gustavo Gili

Glonek G, Pietruszka M (2012) Natural user interfaces (NUI): review. J Appl Comput Sci 20(2):27–45. Retrieved from https://pdfs.semanticscholar.org/e633/64072c292f7a3a1b526c6aee92843ed33a94.pdf

Grayson K (1998) The icons of consumer research: Using signs to represent consumers' reality. In: Stern BB (ed) Representing consumers: voices, views and visions. Routledge, pp 27–43

Hartson HR (1998) Human–computer interaction: Interdisciplinary roots and trends. J Syst Softw 43(2):103–118. https://doi.org/10.1016/S0164-1212(98)10026-2

Hassan Montero Y, Martín Fernández FJ (2003) Más allá de la Usabilidad: Interfaces' afectivas'. No solo usabilidad 2

Jeong B, Kim S-I, Hah S (2017) The analysis of the impact on the interface design for mobile device in relation with brand preference. In: Chung W, Shin CS (eds) Advances in affective and pleasurable design. Springer, Berlin, pp 483, 695–714. https://doi.org/10.1007/978-3-319-41661-8_67

Kahn P, Lenk K (1998) Design: principles of typography for user interface design. Interactions 5(6):15. https://doi.org/10.1145/287821.287825

Kenna H (2012) A practice-led study of design principles for screen typography—with reference to the teachings of Emil Ruder. Doctoral dissertation. Retrieved from http://ualresearchonline.arts.ac.uk/6051/1/HKenna_PhD_Thesis_LCC.pdf

Leavy P (2015) Method meets art: arts-based research practice (Second edition). The Guilford Press

Lee S, van Zyl I, Ralarala M (2019) Typographic shifts arising from the connection between the user. User interface and typographic layout. in: 8th International DEFSA Conference. https://www.defsa.org.za/sites/default/files/downloads/2017conference/14Typographic.pdf

Liu W (2010) Natural user interface- next mainstream product user interface. In: 2010 IEEE 11th international conference on computer-aided industrial design & conceptual design, vol 1, pp 203–205. https://doi.org/10.1109/CAIDCD.2010.5681374

Llop R (2014) Un sistema gráfico para las cubiertas de libros. Hacia un lenguaje de parámetros [A graphic system for book covers. Towards a language of parameters]. Gustavo Gili

Memon AM, Banerjee I, Nagarajan A (2003) GUI ripping: reverse engineering of graphical user interfaces for testing. In: 10th working conference on reverse engineering 2003 (WCRE 2003), pp 260–269. https://doi.org/10.1109/WCRE.2003.1287256

Naciones Unidas (2018) 68% of the world population projected to live in urban areas by 2050, says UN. [Blog post], 16 May. Retrieved from https://www.un.org/development/desa/en/news/population/2018-revision-of-world-urbanization-prospects.html

Norman DA (2002) Emotion and design: attractive things work better. Interactions 9(4):36–42. https://doi.org/10.1145/543434.543435

Nørgaard N (2009) The semiotics of typography in literary texts. A multimodal approach. Orbis Litterarum 64(2):141–160. https://doi.org/10.1111/j.1600-0730.2008.00949.x

Peirce CS, Hartshorne C, Weiss P (1998) Collected papers of Charles Sanders Peirce. Thoemmes Press

Phinney T (2018, January 27). Why variable fonts will succeed. [Blog post]. Retrieved from https://www.thomasphinney.com/2018/01/why-variable-fonts-will-succeed/

Poiza F (2017). How New Font Technologies Will Improve The Web. [Blog post], 18 Sept. Retrieved from https://www.smashingmagazine.com/2017/09/new-font-technologies-improve-web/

Portugali, J. (2000). *Self-Organization and the City.* Spinger

Rath KA (2015) The rhetoric of type: an exploration of the experiential and iconic nature of letterforms. Thesis, Retrieved from https://repository.up.ac.za/handle/2263/53461

Rickner T (2016, November 29) Part 1: from truetype GX to variable fonts. [Blog post]. Retrieved from https://www.monotype.com/resources/articles/part-1-from-truetype-gx-to-variable-fonts

Rieder DM (2013) From GUI to NUI: Microsoft's Kinect and the politics of the (body as) interface. Present Tense J Rhetoric in Soc 3(1). Retrieved from http://www.presenttensejournal.org/wp-content/uploads/2013/09/Rieder.pdf

RoboFont (2018). Creating variable fonts, 10 Sept. Retrieved from https://robofont.com/documentation/how-tos/creating-variable-fonts/

Rocha IT (1993) A metaphysical and linguistic approach to type design and typography. Thesis, Retrieved from https://scholarworks.rit.edu/cgi/viewcontent.cgi?article=4840&context=theses

Rogers Y, Sharp H, Preece J (2011) Interaction design: beyond human-computer interaction, 3rd edn. Wiley, New York

Ruder E (1967) Typography: a manual of design: a textbook of design. Arthur Niggli

Salminen V (2016) Typography for user interfaces. [Blog post], 21 June. Retrieved from https://viljamis.com/2016/typography-for-user-interfaces/

Selfe CL, Selfe RJ (1994) The politics of the interface: power and its exercise in electronic contact zones. College Compos Commun 45(4):480–504. https://doi.org/10.2307/358761

Serafini F, Clausen J (2012) Typography as semiotic resource. J Vis Literacy 31(2):1–16. https://doi.org/10.1080/23796529.2012.11674697

Skaggs S (2017) FireSigns: a semiotic theory for graphic design. The MIT Press

Stone D, Jarrett C, Woodroffe M, Minocha S (2005) User interface design and evaluation. Burlington, Elsevier

Underware Foundry (2018). Case study: Hhigher order interpolation for variable fonts. [Blog post]. Retrieved from http://underware.nl/case-studies/hoi/

Vincens G, Hornus J (2017) Typography: writing the future city. 3 Perspectives on new urban experiences [White paper]. Retrieved from website Black[Foundry]: https://black-foundry.com/wp-content/uploads/2017/12/WhitePaper_TypographyWritingTheFutureCity.pdf von Engelhardt J (2002) The language of graphics. A framework for the analysis of syntax and meaning in maps, charts and diagrams. Doctoral dissertation. Retrieved from https://dare.uva.nl/search?identifier=c136c6f0-b987-4264-aeef-db053ea56a61

Wigdor D, Wixon D (2011) Brave NUI world: designing natural user interfaces for touch and gesture. Morgan Kaufmann, Burlington

Willis N (2016) Variations fonts and OpenType 1.8. [Blog post], 21 Sept. Retrieved from https://lwn.net/Articles/701158/

Wong W (2001) Fundamentos del diseño [Design Basics]. Gustavo Gili

Woodbury R (2010) Elements of parametric design. Routledge, London

W3C (2016) Web design and applications. Retrieved from https://www.w3.org/standards/webdesign/

Yee J (2006) Developing a practice-led framework to promote the practise and understanding of typography across different media. Doctoral dissertation. https://doi.org/10.13140/2.1.5140.3040

Dynamic Visual Identities: Exploring Variation Mechanisms to Achieve Flexibility

João Miguel Cunha, Tiago Martins, Pedro Matos Chaves, João Bicker, and Penousal Machado

Abstract Dynamic visual identities differ from the conventional ones by the occurrence of variation in at least one of the elements of their visual system. The type of dynamism depends on the variation mechanisms used, which may confer different features to the visual identity. Flexibility is one of these features and consists in the ability to adapt to different content and formats. We focus on the study of how flexibility can be achieved using different variation mechanisms by conducting practical experiments.

Keywords Dynamic visual identity · Flexibility · Graphic design · Visual identity · Logos

1 Introduction

In recent years, a movement towards variability has been observed in the visual identities (VIs) adopted by entities, such as institutions, museums and even places. These identities are characterised by context-relatedness, processuality, performativity, and non-linearity (Felsing 2010). Despite this sense of novelty, dynamism has been present in visual identities for quite a while. An early example of a graphic mark with multiple variations is the one used by the publishing house Alfred A. Knopf.

J. M. Cunha (✉) · T. Martins · P. Matos Chaves · J. Bicker · P. Machado
Department of Informatics Engineering, CISUC, University of Coimbra, Coimbra, Portugal
e-mail: jmacunha@dei.uc.pt

T. Martins
e-mail: tiagofm@dei.uc.pt

P. Matos Chaves
e-mail: pchaves@student.dei.uc.pt

J. Bicker
e-mail: bicker@dei.uc.pt

P. Machado
e-mail: machado@dei.uc.pt

N. Martins et al. (eds.), *Perspectives on Design and Digital Communication*,
Springer Series in Design and Innovation 8, https://doi.org/10.1007/978-3-030-49647-0_6

Since its foundation in 1915, Alfred A. Knopf uses a graphic mark based on a borzoi dog that changes with nearly every book published, depending on the needs and preferences of the book jacket designer. Many variations exist, ranging from more minimalistic to more ornate, however, each one is immediately recognised as the graphic mark of Alfred A. Knopf.

In the late 1950s, the Swiss graphic designer Karl Gerstner introduced the concept of flexibility in the design of VIs with the identity for the *Boîte à Musique*, a record shop in Basel (Hollington 2011:9; Hewitt 2008). Gerstner, who was interested in geometry, mathematics and computer systems, developed this identity as a program, capable of simultaneously adapting to functional requirements, e.g. proportion, and maintaining its overall style and personality (Hewitt 2008). The result was an identity that operated with its personality rather than simple consistency, allowing it to vary its appearance while being easily recognised (Hewitt 2008).

In the early 1980s, when television was being established as a ubiquitous medium, the collective Manhattan Design designed the graphic mark for MTV channel. It revolutionised the design of VIs as it showed that graphic marks could be adaptive and work as content (Hewitt 2008). Similarly to the aforementioned dynamic visual identities (DVIs), it challenged the notions that graphic marks should be presented in a static way. However, MTV did not change for functional reasons as *Boîte à Musique* did, as it only adapted on a stylistic level to feature the latest graphic trends (Hewitt 2008). The possibilities created by the television medium have allowed the graphic mark to adapt and change its look in each iteration, being regularly animated and decorated in numerous ways.

At the beginning of the new millennium, more variable VIs emerged. For example, the VI for the Lovebytes 2007 festival, which was designed by the collective Universal Everything and the designer Karsten Schmidt using a generative process. Based on the theme of the festival in that year, which was "process", they designed and developed a generative process in which a seed spreads its genes to create over 20.000 unique furry creatures representing the festival. Each creature has individual features: body colour and shape, hair colour and length, eye shape, and name. In addition to this, the logotype is also dynamic as its shape changes.

There has been a shift towards designing graphic marks as living organisms (van Nes 2012: 6; Pearson 2013: 26; Guida 2014:122; Leitão 2014: 29,112; Kopp 2015:118–119). Technological advancements have given the opportunity to VIs to be more variable, unpredictable, personalised, and closer to their target audience (Allen and Simmons 2010:146 cited in Leitão 2014: 31; Armstrong and Stojmirovic 2011; van Nes 2012: 6; Leitão 2014: 26; Leitão 2014: 99,153). Designers are now exploring new possibilities in the design of VIs that were not possible a generation ago due to technical limitations (Kreutz 2007: 12; Evamy 2012: 8).

Regarding research on the topic, several authors have addressed the categorisation of DVIs. Despite being able to group existing DVIs according to several criteria, most existing categorisations are of little help when it comes to designing a visual identity system. In order to address this issue, Martins et al. (2019) developed a model based on how dynamism is achieved using specific graphic-based techniques—referred to as variation mechanisms (e.g. scaling)—identifying the characteristics conferred to the VI (e.g. adaptation to formats). We build upon this model, which we believe may provide clues that can be used when designing a VI and conduct experimentation with the goal of further analysing the impact of variation mechanisms on the developed VI.

2 Background

Dynamic visual identities (DVIs) are defined by the existence of variation in one or more of the elements of its visual system. In these identities, some elements provide diversity while others contribute to a sense of visual coherence (Oliveira and Raposo 2016). The dynamism of a visual identity varies according to how the variation occurs. Several authors have addressed the categorisation of DVIs, e.g. de Kreutz (2001), Felsing (2010), Hollington (2011), van Nes (2012), Jochum (2013), Pearson (2013), Murdock (2016) and Silva and Martins (2018). A thorough analysis of these perspectives is conducted by Martins et al. (2019), who identified two main issues: (i) there is no agreement in terms of terminology, and (ii) the existing perspectives are somehow redundant or incomplete.

In addition to the approaches analysed by Martins et al. (2019), two works are worth mentioning as they address the topic. The first is the book "On the Road to Variable: The Flexible Future of Typography" (Victionary 2019), which addresses the topic variable typography. The authors of the book state that variable typography encompasses several aspects of communication design in which there is an observed evolution from static to flexible, including liquid/fluid/dynamic visual identities. The structure adopted is based on the variation of position, width, height, styles and through transformation. In addition to not being focused on DVIs, this work seems to be aligned with the group described by Martins et al. (2019) as "not specific enough", as the topic "through transformation" includes too many types of variation. The second work that we would like to mention is a thesis produced by Lorenz (2016), who conducted a thorough analysis of dynamic visual identities and proposed an analysis model. Despite being similar to the work developed by Martins et al. (2019) by focusing on visual attributes, the two models differ in several aspects. For example, Lorenz (2016) includes in his model a topic related to elements and their attributes, in which he identifies the following items: Line, Form, Volume, Typeface, Logo and Copy. Such level of detail is not addressed by Martins et al. (2019).

2.1 A Model of Features and Mechanisms

As previously stated, our work builds upon the model proposed by Martins et al. (2019), which is based on how variation visually occurs. For ease of understanding of our work, we briefly explain the model presented by Martins et al. (2019), to which we refer the reader for a more thorough description. This model proposed by Martins et al. (2019) considers three aspects: (i) identity focus, (ii) variation mechanisms, and (iii) features. The identity focus identifies where variation occurs—in the graphic mark and/or in the system. The model also distinguishes between how the variation is implemented—variation mechanisms (VMs)—and which features are achieved. The VMs identified by Martins et al. (2019) are colour variation, combination, content variation, positioning, repetition, rotation, scaling and shape transformation. The VMs can be used separately or in combination. The features proposed are flexible, fluid, generated, informative, participatory, reactive and unlimited. The features are oriented towards client needs and requirements, for example, a flexible DVI is characterised by its ability to adapt to different contents, formats or media. Some illustrative examples of DVIs analysed in terms of VMs used can be observed in Fig. 1. For a more detailed description of the model, we refer the reader to the work by Martins et al. (2019).

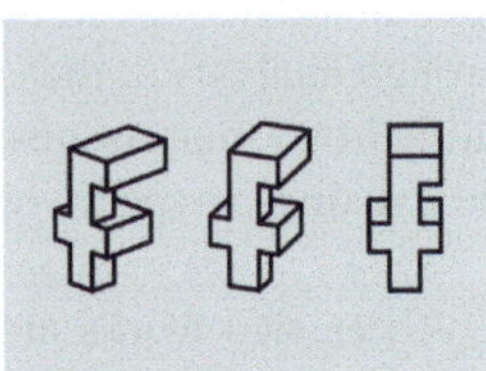

Rotation
Fórum do Futuro visual identity
R2

Positioning
Provisório visual identity
Desisto

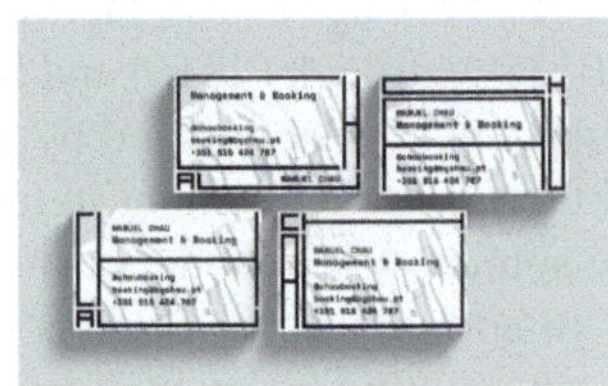

Scaling
Chau visual identity
Divisa

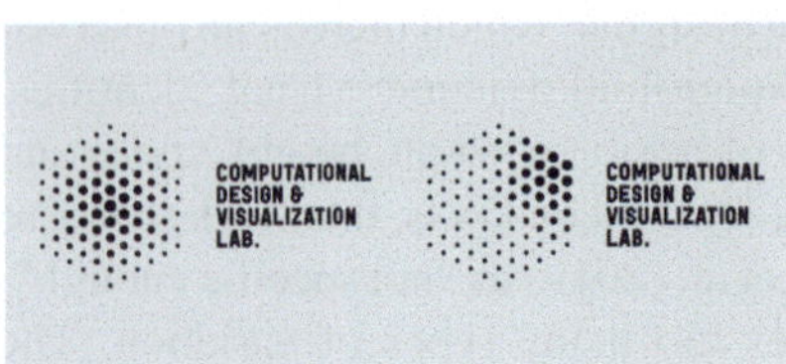

Shape transformation
CDV Lab. visual identity
José Maria Cunha, João Miguel Cunha and Tiago Martins

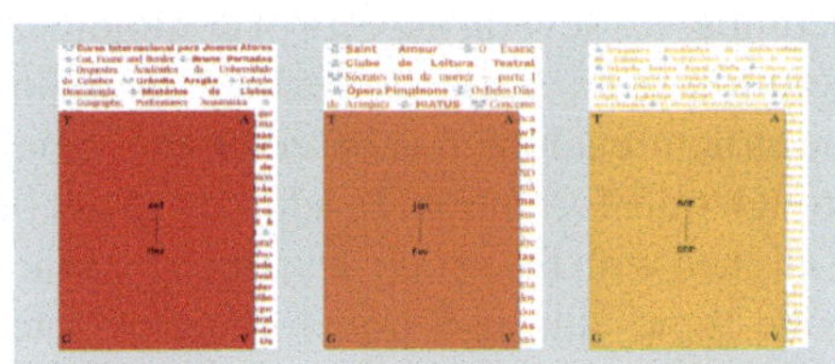

Colour variation
TAVG visual identity
Bürocratik

Combination
Cucurico visual identity
Pacifica

Content variation
Teatrão visual identity
Paul Hardman

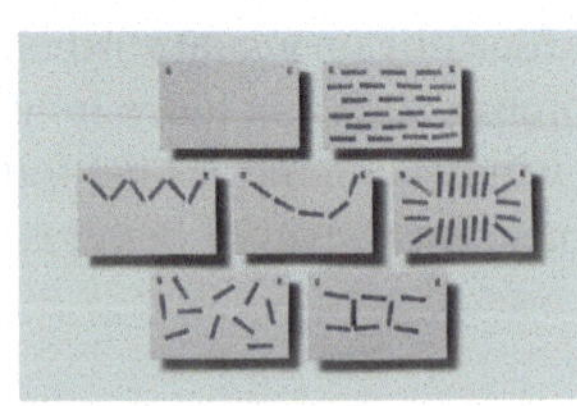

Repetition
S-E visual identity
Studio Degrau

Fig. 1 Examples of visual identities that use a variation mechanism

3 Experimentation

In the last two decades, technological evolution has changed the way visual identities are developed. In order to better represent the entity that they stand for, visual identities are now often required to adapt to constantly changing environments (van Nes 2012). Moreover, different media should be considered when designing visual identities, making them suitable not only for printed materials but also for digital ones (Shaughnessy and Bierut 2009). These aspects make flexible DVIs increasingly relevant, due to their adaptability to new content and media/formats (Martins et al. 2019). In addition, the results presented by Martins et al. (2019) indicate that the flexible feature is one of the most recurrent in the analysed set of DVIs. Despite this, few studies exist on this subject. We conduct experimentation focused on the study of the flexibility in DVIs, addressing its advantages and conducting practical experimentation to study how it can be achieved using different variation mechanisms. A possible approach to test the model of DVI categorisation consists in applying it to existing visual identities. However, this type of experimentation was already explored by Martins et al. (2019), who report the results of an application of the model to a set of DVIs. Moreover, the examples that illustrate some of the VMs using existing DVIs are also aligned with this kind of approach (Fig. 1). For this reason, for our experimentation, we followed a different approach, which consists in identifying two possible client types and developing solutions for DVIs to be adopted by them. As such, the experimentation is performed using two case studies: a theatre and a television channel.

3.1 Methodology

Previous research work identified flexibility as one of the most frequent characteristics in DVIs (Martins et al. 2019) and one that is mostly related to specific needs of the client—the requirement of adapting to different content or media. We focus on experimenting with VMs with the goal of identifying different ways in which they can be used to achieve flexibility. First of all, it is important to mention that the goal of our experimentation is not to create VIs, but instead to better understand the advantages of each VM in terms of adaptability to different content, formats and media.

In our experimentation, we follow a client-oriented approach. Firstly, we identify clients with needs related to flexibility by assessing in which sectors flexibility is mostly used. According to Martins et al. (2019), flexible DVIs are most used in the sector of Art and Museums. Theatres are a type of client that belongs to this sector and can have several necessities related to flexibility, for example, the adaptation to new content (e.g. new events) or to different media for advertising purposes (e.g. print and digital). For these reasons, the first case study (CS1) is a theatre. After producing a list of possible candidates, we selected the Diogo Bernardes Theatre,

Fig. 2 The current graphic marks (on the left) and developed proposals (on the right) of the first case study (top row) and second case study (bottom row). The second case study has two proposals (A and B)

located at Ponte de Lima, Portugal. Given its current static visual identity (Fig. 2), we consider it suitable for investigating the advantages of introducing dynamism to address flexibility-related needs.

Flexibility is also useful in digital media, e.g. a television channel, due to its likely high variability of content and constant need for change. For this reason, a television channel can profit from a VI with a flexible character, allowing easy adaptation. Similarly to the process of choosing CS1, we also produced a list of possible candidates from which we chose as the second case study (CS2) the Portuguese television network SIC, later focusing on the SIC Radical for the experimentation. Our choice is based on the fact that SIC currently has a static VI that can be used for comparison purposes, and also due to its multi-channel structure, which is useful to conduct experimentation on the informative feature (Fig. 2).

To guide the experimentation process, we defined a methodology composed of the three main tasks described below. The first one involves the creation of the base visual identity to be used as a skeleton from which mutations may occur (de Kreutz 2012). For CS1, we designed a base VI inspired by the current VI of the theatre (Fig. 2). For CS2, we made two different proposals to increase the number of possibilities to achieve flexibility, using different visual elements in the experiments. The first proposal (version A) is capable of maintaining some coherence between the channels and at the same time allowing for their clear distinction, representing them in a faithful way to their specificities (A in Fig. 2).

On the other hand, the second proposal (version B) allows to maintain a greater coherence between the channels graphic marks (B in Fig. 2). Both proposals achieve the informative feature, as the VI is capable to represent each channel and at the same time being recognisable as making part of SIC group. For the experimentation described here, we focused on the SIC Radical channel.

The second task consists in experimenting with individual VMs. We conducted experiments to identify the advantages of each VM in achieving flexibility. For each VM, we use the elements of the base VI system (e.g. a circle and a plus sign in CS1) and applied variation both in the graphic mark and in the visual system, having content and format adaptation as a goal.

The third task concerns the experimentation with a combination of different VMs in order to identify possible advantages in comparison to VM individual usage.

3.2 *Results and Discussion*

In this section, we present experiments with each individual VM and with a combination of two VMs, analysing how they work and identifying advantages.

Rotation: there is a graphic element that is rotated (Martins et al. 2019). Our results show that rotation alone is not an efficient way to achieve flexibility. During the experimentation, the square in CS1 (left in Fig. 3), the arrow and the "R" symbol in CS2 (right in Fig. 3) were rotated and used in different rotation angles. Regarding adaptation to content, rotation is not suitable as it only works with a small number of events—differences would only be perceptible to a certain point. It may be employed to distinguish between event types, provided that they are small in number—i.e. using different rotation angles for different types of event. This codified correspondence between angle and type of event is not easily perceivable, which makes it an unsuitable choice for adaptation to content. Moreover, rotation alone is not able to make elements to adapt to different formats.

Positioning: there is a graphic element that is positioned in different ways (Martins et al. 2019). In this experimentation, the circle (CS1), the arrow (CS2) and the "R" symbol (CS2) were placed in different positions in relation to the logotype (Fig. 4). Similarly to rotation, using it for content adaptation relies on a codified correspondence. For this reason, even though it allows the distinction between a small number of events, it is not recommended to use it for that purpose. As far as format adaptation is concerned, positioning allows the same elements to fit in different formats, often resulting in only showing part of the element (Fig. 4).

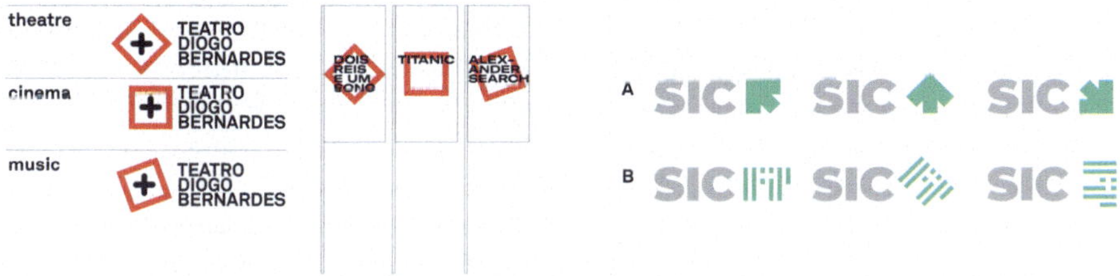

Fig. 3 The use of rotation in CS1 (left) and CS2 (right)

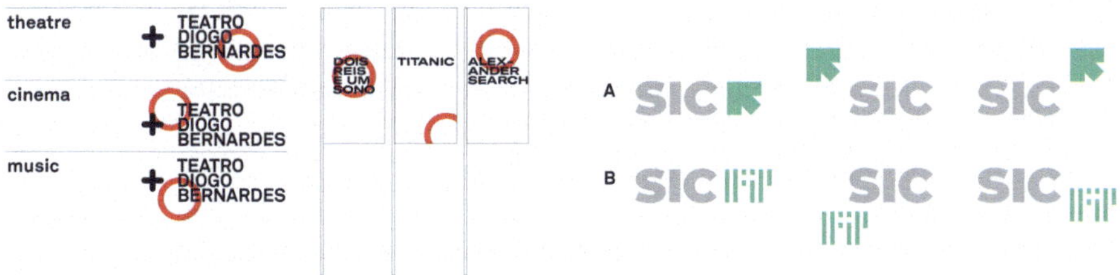

Fig. 4 The use of positioning in CS1 (left) and CS2 (right)

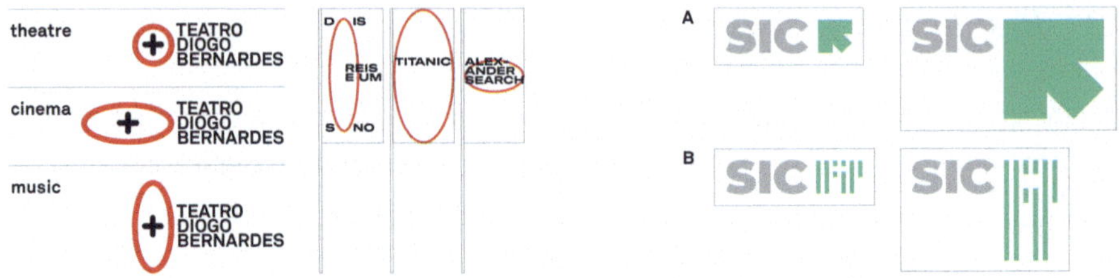

Fig. 5 The use of scaling in CS1 (left) and CS2 (right)

Scaling: there is a graphic element that changes in size (Martins et al. 2019). In CS1, the circle was stretched in different ways to adapt to different formats and to different content (left in Fig. 5). In CS2, the two versions were experimented with: in version A, the arrow increased and decreased in size, without changing its proportions so that the VI did not lose its consistency; in version B, the lists that make the "R" symbol were stretched and shrunk, vertically (right in Fig. 5). These three situations serve to show the importance of the characteristics of the element in which the variation mechanism is being used—the circle in CS1 allows a uniform scaling, the arrow in CS2 requires uniform scaling to maintain the arrow shape and the striped "R" allows a vertical scaling by scaling individual stripes.

During our experimentation, scaling did not show any indication of being a good solution for adaptation to different content. The only way of being used in such a way would be to map certain sizes to different contents. This is similar to what occurs in rotation and positioning—a codified correspondence that only works with a small number of events or event types. Moreover, the fact that the proportions of the arrow in version A of CS2 cannot be altered makes it hard to distinguish different contents—even though the arrow size changes, its shape remains the same. In version B, even though R's with different heights could be used to codify different contents, we do not consider it as an ideal way to achieve content adaptation (Fig. 5).

When experimenting with CS1 (circle shape) we identified scaling as one of the most indicated VMs to adapt to different formats, working well in the graphic mark and in the system (Fig. 5). On the other hand, the experiments done with CS2 did not show good results, mostly due to the shapes used in the VI—version A only allows the filling of some areas and the version B only allows the adaptation to vertical formats, without distorting the stripes (Fig. 5).

Shape transformation: there is a graphic element that changes in shape (Martins et al. 2019). The fact that shape transformation has no defined limits makes it capable of adapting to different contents and formats. Regarding content adaptability, one approach is to transform the shape into something that represents what it stands for (e.g. a letter representing the event type, as seen for CS1, left in Fig. 6). Another approach relies on a codified mapping between event and shape, which works best with small numbers (e.g. few event types). For example, the shape of the circle was changed to represent different types of events (the banners for CS1 in Fig. 6). A third approach consists in changing the shape to resemble a certain object related to the

Fig. 6 The use of shape transformation in CS1 (left) and CS2 (right)

content being represented, making it adaptable to a large number of contents. This was done by creating graphic elements that represent each television show, e.g. a *shuriken* ("ninja star") for "American Ninja Warrior" in Fig. 6.

The distinction between the VMs shape transformation and content variation can be hard to perceive. Nonetheless, the difference relies on the fact that in shape transformations the changes applied to the shape of the element should always guarantee that a certain degree of similarity, to make the resulting shape be perceived as the same element, which does not happen in content variation. Based on this, we consider that changing the "R" symbol into a *shuriken* (Fig. 6) crosses the boundary between shape transformation and content variation. Regarding adaptation to format, shape transformation can be used to make an element fit different sizes, provided the similarity requirement is fulfilled (e.g. maintaining the perception of the symbol as an arrow in CS2, as seen in Fig. 6).

Colour variation: there is a graphic element that changes in colour (Martins et al. 2019). According to the experimentation, colour variation allows the distinction between a small number of event types (e.g. theatre, cinema, etc.), as observed in Fig. 7. On the other hand, despite allowing the distinction between different contents (e.g. using a different colour for each theatre play as seen in the banners of CS1 in Fig. 7), it is not a good way of clearly identifying each content – beyond a certain number of variations the colours become too similar. Moreover, this VM has no effect on format adaptation as colour change is not able to make elements to adapt to different formats.

Fig. 7 The use of colour variation in CS1 (left) and CS2 (right)

Fig. 8 The use of combination in CS1 (left) and CS2 (right)

Combination: different graphic elements from the VI system are used in combination (Martins et al. 2019). Briefly, combination may lead to some degree of flexibility but it is not an efficient method to achieve it. For CS1, a system of three symbols was created (left in Fig. 8) and each pair of symbols represents different content. According to the experimentation, combination is not appropriate for content adaptation (e.g. using a different combination for each theatre play) as it relies on a codified use of a set of different elements, which may even be seen as mere ornaments. However, when used with a small number of content instances (e.g. event types), it may allow distinction between them.

On the other hand, in CS2, we created different pictograms using the rectangular module from version B of the VI (right in Fig. 8), which can be used in combination. This approach shows potential for content adaptation, by using the pictograms to represent different types of shows. Furthermore, combination does not allow the adaptability to different formats as it has no effect on it.

Content variation: there is an area or space where different imagery is placed (Martins et al. 2019). For CS1, we set the inside of the circle of the graphic mark as the area for content variation to (left in Fig. 9). For CS2, the content variation was made through the use of images placed inside the arrow and the "R" symbol (right in Fig. 9). Due to the limitless in terms of what can be used as imagery, this VM allows the VI to adapt to any content (e.g. using images of each theatre play). Regarding adaptation to formats, there is not a direct relation but it may be possible in certain situations if the dimensions of the imagery are taken into account in its selection.

Fig. 9 The use of content variation in CS1 (left) and CS2 (right)

Fig. 10 The use of repetition in CS1 (left) and CS2 (right)

Repetition: repeated placement of the same graphic element (Martins et al. 2019). The use of this VM can go from pure element repetition to complex composition with the goal of producing new elements (e.g. letters). Regarding adaptation to content, the VI can adapt to all kinds of content using the repetition of elements (e.g. circle) to write the event information (e.g. title), as in CS1 in Fig. 10 (left). Moreover, this method can also be used to represent different event types, e.g. creating the initials of each type of event (left in Fig. 10) or the type of show (repeating the lines of the "R" in the version B of CS2, on the right in Fig. 10). Repetition can also be used to encode different types of shows (e.g. different number of arrows in the version A of CS2, Fig. 10).

Repetition also allows the adaptation to different formats, by increasing or reducing the number of repeated elements and the way they are arranged. This shows that repetition is a good VM to use in order to achieve flexibility.

Content variation and Scaling: After concluding the experiment on each VM individually, it was observed that, with the exception of repetition, none of them could achieve the adaptability to content and to format at the same time. However, VMs are normally used in combination. For this reason, we decided to experiment with VM combination in order to assess how the combined use could lead to higher flexibility. In this experiment, we chose to combine content variation and scaling because they are the VMs in which we observed the best results—content variation was the best VM in content adaptation and scaling was the best VM for adaptation to format.

Content variation and scaling, when used together, offer the sum of their individual advantages, allowing the adaptation to different content and format at the same time. In CS1 (observed on the left in Fig. 11), the content adaptation is achieved by using

Fig. 11 The use of content variation and scaling in CS1 (left) and CS2 (right)

images that represent the events and format adaptation is achieved by resizing the circle, which is used as content area, to fit in different layouts.

Regarding CS2, we only experimented with version A of the graphic mark, using the arrow shape as content area (right in Fig. 11). Similar to what happens in CS1, the VI could achieve content adaptation by using different images to represent the different shows. As in the experimentation of scaling, the adaptation to different formats was achieved with limitations, as the proportions of the arrow could not be changed. The best solution that scaling offered, in this case, was to allow the arrow to fill larger or smaller sizes that had their proportions, or to increase and decrease its size proportionally so that it could fit in any format.

4 Final Remarks

We build upon the model for categorisation of Dynamic Visual Identities proposed by Martins et al. (2019) and study how different variation mechanisms can be used to achieve flexibility.

In summary, all the VMs are capable of achieving some degree of flexibility but the majority of them are not efficient. In fact, only repetition (with the creation of patterns) and content variation were capable of adapting to different content in a perceptible way, the latter being the only one capable of doing it without limitations. Regarding format adaptability, the only VMs that achieved it in a consistent way were repetition—with the creation of different patterns—and the scaling and shape transformation, which are the only VMs capable of doing it without any kind of constraint. With the exception of repetition, all VMs have problems in simultaneously adapting to content and format. Even though we had stated in (Chaves et al. 2019) that scaling and shape transformation were capable of achieving format adaptability without any kind of constraint, the experimentation with a second case study (CS2) made it possible to conclude that the advantages that VMs offer to achieve flexibility depend on the visual elements that are used (e.g. circle in CS1 works differently from the arrow shape in CS2). Therefore, in the process of creating a flexible DVI, the choice of VMs must be made in accordance not only with the needs of the VI, but also with the elements created for it.

Moreover, the sets of VMs seem to only offer the sum of their individual advantages. A good example of this is the combination of the VMs content variation and scaling, which achieved full adaptation to content and formats in CS1 (theatre) due to the advantages of each of the two VMs. Therefore, there is a factor to be taken into account when choosing the VMs set to use when creating a VI. Based on our experimentation, the most suitable solutions to achieve full flexibility (content and format adaptation) are repetition or a combined use of content variation and scaling. The other VMs can be used as a complement to achieve flexibility but should not be used as the main mechanism to do it.

Even though the main objective was to study flexibility, we partially addressed the informative feature, i.e. conveying information to the audience, by analysing how different content or data can be distinguished. Other authors focus on this topic, e.g. (Parente et al. 2018). However, the fact that a visual identity is flexible does not mean that it is also informative. Although each case is different, this process allowed us to see the real advantages of each VM in achieving flexibility. Nonetheless, further experimentation is required on the subject, in particular regarding different combinations of two or more VMs.

Acknowledgements The authors would like to thank the designers and design studios—Bürocratik,[1] Pacifica,[2] Paul Hardman,[3] Desisto,[4] Studio Degrau,[5] R2,[6] Divisa,[7] CDV Lab[8] and José Maria Cunha[9]—who provided us with images of the projects shown in the beginning of this article.

This research is partially funded by Fundação para a Ciência e Tecnologia (FCT), Portugal, under the grant SFRH/BD/120905/2016.

References

Armstrong H, Stojmirovic Z (2011) Participate: designing with user-generated content. Princeton Architectural Press, New York.

Chaves PM, Cunha JM, Martins T, Bicker J (2019) Flexibility in dynamic visual identities: exploring variation mechanisms to achieve flexibility. In: Proceedings of the third international conference on design and digital conference (DIGICOM), Barcelos, Portugal, 15–16 Nov 2019

Evamy M (2012) Logotype. Laurence King, London, United Kingdom.

Felsing U (2010) Dynamic identities in cultural and public contexts. In: Design2context (ed). Lars Müller Publishers

Guida FE (2014) Generative visual identities. New scenarios in corporate identity. In: Soddu C, Colabella E (eds) GA2014 – XVII Generative art Conference. Domus Argenia, pp 121–132

Hewitt, J. (2008). Flexible consistency, consistent flexibility

Hollington S (2011) Flexible visual identity systems. MA in Communication Design, Kingston University

Jochum E (2013) dynamic branding: how flexible design systems turn brands into dynamic visual identities. Zurich University of the Arts, Zurich, Switzerland

Kopp R (2015) Changeable graphic design for hypermodern brands. Comunicação, Mídia e Consumo, 12(34):117–137

Kreutz EA (2001) As principais estratégias de construção da identidade visual corporativa. Universidade Católica do Rio Grande do Sul, Porto Alegre

Kreutz EA (2007). Identidade visual corporativa mutante: uma estratégia comunicacional contemporânea. In: XXX Congresso Brasileiro de Ciências da Comunicação

[1]https://www.burocratik.com/.

[2]http://thisispacifica.com/.

[3]http://andpaul.net.

[4]http://desisto.pt/.

[5]https://www.studiodegrau.com.

[6]https://www.r2design.pt.

[7]https://divisa.pt.

[8]http://cdv.dei.uc.pt.

[9]http://www.josemariacunha.com.

Kreutz EA (2012) Construindo marcas mutantes. Chasqui. Revista Latinoamericana de Comunicación 119:61–65
Leitão S (2014). Princípios estruturantes e orientadores da identidade visual de marcas em ambientes multimeios. PhD thesis, Departamento de Comunicação e Arte, Universidade de Aveiro.
Lorenz M (2016) Sistemas visuales en identidades dinámicas. Universitat de Barcelona
Martins T, Cunha JM, Bicker J, Machado P (2019) Dynamic visual identities: from a survey of the state-of-the-art to a model of features and mechanisms. Visible Language 53(2):4–35
Murdock J (2016) Fluid identity: history & practice of dynamic visual identity design. College of Communication and Information of Kent State University
Oliveira F, Raposo D (2016). Metamorfosis. dynamics of graphic behaviour on contemporary brands. In: Primer Congreso de Diseño Gráfico: Marcas gráficas de identidad corporativa, pp 161–168
Parente J, Martins T, Bicker J (2018) Data-driven logotype design. In: 2018 22nd international conference information visualisation (IV). IEEE, pp 64–70
Pearson L (2013) Fluid marks 2.0: Protecting a dynamic brand. Managing intellectual property, 26–30 May
Shaughnessy A, Bierut M (2009) Graphic design: a user's manual. Laurence King Publishers
Silva R, Martins N (2018) A identidade Dinâmica do MIT media Lab. In: Proceedings of the 2nd international conference on digital design & communication
van Nes I (2012) Dynamic identities: how to create a living brand. BIS Publishers, Amsterdam
Victionary (2019) On the road to variable: the flexible future of typography. Editors: TwoPoints.net

Transmedia Storytelling: A Case Study with Alice's Adventures in Wonderland

Patrícia Ferreira

Abstract School cannot ignore the fact that the expansion of technology has changed the way we interact with other people. This reality and the use of technology to motivate the students, causing them to become producers of their own learning, makes them more confident. One of the tools that can contribute to this paradigm is Transmedia Storytelling. Technology can be an important tool in increasing students' motivation in classroom context. In this way, in the face of the mobility associated with digital technology, learning does not have to stop at the end of class. It is possible to students to have a greater freedom, through the use of several platforms, so they can access activities proposed by teachers. This new paradigm, which includes technology in the context of the classroom, can contribute to improve pedagogical practices. A case study was carried out in order to verify the true impact of a Transmedia path in classroom environment, where Transmedia Storytelling potentialities were explored by students with reading and pedagogical activities.

Keywords Transmedia storytelling · Education · Motivation

1 Introduction

The emergence of mobile devices and social networks has changed the way social interactions take place. Education cannot ignore this reality, as the mobility that is associated with digital technology brings numerous advantages to school, allowing students to use different educational platforms.

Transmedia narratives, for the most part, are based on not only individual characters or on specific plots, but in complex worlds of fiction that can sustain multiple interrelated characters and their stories. The human being is attracted by the mastery of what can be known about a world that expands beyond our reach. This is a pleasure very different than the one we associate with the end found in the most classically constructed narratives.

P. Ferreira (✉)
Instituto Politécnico de Tomar, Tomar, Portugal
e-mail: aluno20581@ipt.pt

N. Martins et al. (eds.), *Perspectives on Design and Digital Communication*, Springer Series in Design and Innovation 8, https://doi.org/10.1007/978-3-030-49647-0_7

Transmedia Storytelling not only develops the creativity of people, but it helps them to be more critical, to understand in a more detailed way what is presented to them and achieve and address problem solving in a faster way.

Creating reading experiences with Transmedia Storytelling can contribute to enhance students' motivation by allowing them to explore, create and recreate stories and be part of them.

> Our students have changed radically. Today's students are no longer the people our educational system was designed to teach. (Prensky 2001, p. 1)

Transmedia Storytelling, as an educational resource, can be used in order to create the necessary adequacy of pedagogical practices, and should be used as a complement to the methodologies used, reinforcing the way classes can be taught using technology and the media to motivate students and to turn them into producers of their own learning, having the possibility to use digital tools and develop their cooperative learning, work together in groups, discuss problems and evaluate results.

> Transmedia Storytelling exemplifies learning in the twenty-first century by merging the concept of storytelling with that of the listener-learner and the resulting emotional engagement with the pervasiveness of media. We might define Transmedia learning as: the application of storytelling techniques combined with the use of multiple platforms to create an immersive learning landscape which enables multivarious entry and exit points for learning and teaching. (Fleming 2013, p. 371)

It is possible to reinforce different strategies in classroom context while using technology, this will increase students' motivation and their learning capability while becoming knowledge producers, developing learning capabilities, working in groups, discussing different problems and evaluating results, using digital tools and different platforms.

2 Transmedia Storytelling in Educational Context

The concept of Transmedia Storytelling was promoted through Henry Jenkins who mentions that Transmedia Storytelling represents a process in which elements that make up a fiction are dispersed systematically through multiple distribution channels with the goal of creating an entertainment experience unified and coordinated where each of these channels makes its contribution to the unfolding of the story (Jenkins 2007). Henry Jenkins is a professor of Communication, Journalism, Art Cinematography and Education at the University of California South (United States of America).

Jenkins (2007) defines Transmedia Storytelling as a process in which elements of a fiction are dispersed through various distribution channels in order to create a unified and coordinated entertainment experience where each of these channels makes its contribution to the development of the story.

Jenkins (2007) defined seven basic principles of Transmedia Storytelling—Spreadability versus Drillability, Continuity versus Multiplicity, Immersion versus

Extraction, Extractability, World Building, Seriality, Subjectivity, Performance, which are presented below.

Spreadability refers to a process of dispersal—to scanning across the media landscape in search of meaningful bits of data. Drillability refers to the ability to dig deeper into something which interests us. […]

Continuity versus Multiplicity The media industry often talks about continuity in terms of canons—that is, information which has been authorized, accepted as part of the definitive version of a particular story. Education has often dealt in the range of canon—not only the canon of western literature which deems some books as more worth reading than others but also the structures of disciplines and standards which determine what is worth knowing and how we should know it. Multiplicity, by contrast, encourages us to think about multiple version—possible alternatives to the established canon. […]

Immersion versus Extraction In terms of immersion, we might think about the potential educational value of virtual worlds. I don't mean simply having classes in Second Life which look like virtual versions of the classes we would have in First Life except with far less human expressivity. I mean the idea of moving through a virtual environment which replicates key aspects of a historical or geographical environment. […] Extractability captures another principle which has long been part of education—the idea of meaningful props and artifacts in the classroom. […]

World Building comes out of thinking of the space of a story as a fictional geography. […] But world building also depends on cultural geography—our sense of the peoples, their norms and rituals, their dress and speech, their everyday experiences, which is also often the pleasure of reading a fantasy or science fiction narrative. But it is also part of the pleasure of reading historical fiction and a teacher can use the activity of mapping and interpreting a fictional world as a way of opening up a historical period to their students. […]

Seriality […] At its heart, seriality has to do with the meaningful chunking and dispersal of story-related information. It is about breaking things down into chapters which are satisfying on their own terms but which motivate us to keep coming back for more. […]

Subjectivity At heart, subjectivity refers to looking at the same events from multiple points of view. […]

Performance In speaking about entertainment, I discuss performance in terms of a structure of cultural attractors and activators. The attractors draw the audience, the activators give them something to do. In the case of the classroom, there are a range of institutional factors which insure that you have a group of students sitting in front of you. […] (Jenkins 2007)

Bidarra and Rodrigues (2018) refer that Transmedia Storytelling entails the development of characters, the story, worldbuilding and audience.

Transmedia Storytelling not only provides information, but also roles and goles that the audience can take while recreating the story, that is why it can bring great benefits to students and teachers.

> Technologies are bridges that open the classroom to the world, which they represent, mediate our knowledge of the world.
>
> They are different ways of representing reality, in a more abstract or concrete way, more static or dynamic, more linear or parallel, but all of them, combined, integrated, allow a better understanding of reality and the development of all potentialities of the student, different types of intelligence, skills and attitudes. [...] Technologies allow showing various ways of capturing and showing the same object, representing it from different angles and means: through movements, scenarios, sounds, integrating the rational and the affective, the deductive and the inductive, the space and time, concrete and abstract. (Moran 2007)

It is necessary to understand that "Students, no longer want to just listen to the teacher, they want to speak, they want to be heard, they want to be more participative." (Santos, as mentioned in Morales and Alves 2016) School must be a place for learning, a space for innovation. Keeping the educational curriculum as it is unsustainable and students are in need of a change of these methodologies, it is necessary to integrate digital in classroom context.

> A Transmedia pedagogy uses technology in an integrated way that allows learners and content to flow seamlessly across media platforms. Education across multiple media allows for great continuity in learning. Every piece of the puzzle works to engage the learner. Transmedia techniques, when responsibly and effectively applied in an educational context, immerse students in their own learning and, as a happy corollary, advance media literacy education for all. (Fleming 2013, p. 371)

When applied to education, Transmedia Storytelling can bring numerous advantages and new forms of creative expression. Students will be able to learn how to develop work on multiple platforms, reinforcing educational methodologies with the use of technology and media and creating video, audio or text content. It is, therefore, essential to encourage the use, in class, of digital platforms (Cruz et al. 2016).

> Students are so involved in the media that the traditional school model no longer catches their attention and they prefer to pay attention to what is happening in the world of their cell phones than in class. Instead of removing the student's platform, the school should adapt to these platforms, drawing his attention and inviting him to interact with him. (Cruz et al. 2016)

Most students feel great resistance to devote a substantial part of their time to studies. In fact, picking up books or notebooks becomes more and more a demotivation, as students prefer to use their time on their phone or tablet. Against this, the educational concept must be able to bring students' attention back to the classroom and will not be able to continue with the old-fashioned concept of expository classes, it is necessary to insert, in classes, digital platforms and look for new ways to fit into the daily lives of the students.

According to Costa (cited by Rodrigues and Bidarra 2014), p. 4:

> The use of ICT in education is still insufficient and derives from inadequate preparation for teacher training in relation to exploring and using the pedagogical potential of technologies in learning, as well as other factors, such as the current format of the offer of training actions, punctual and limited over time, with a more technical focus, without addressing the issues related to the curricular integration of technologies.

Young people are increasingly focused on social interaction through digital platforms, so why not bring this new paradigm into the classroom and benefit students and teachers, making students feel more motivated, as they have the opportunity to work with something that accompanies them on a daily basis.

It is also possible to promote mobility, which means that learning doesn't have to finish at the end of the class. When there is greater freedom in implementing contents, using different platforms, students can access the proposed activities by teachers wherever they are.

It is possible to make students content producers, making them use technology to develop attractive projects, making them more confident and more critical, improving their writing and exhibition skills, while working alone or in groups.

> Teachers can use digital resources in education, mainly the Internet, as support for research, for carrying out student activities, for communication with students and students among themselves, for integration between groups inside and outside the class, for publishing web pages, blogs, videos, for participation in social networks, among many other possibilities. (Moran 2013)

3 Methodology

The aim of this investigation was to describe how Transmedia can contribute to increase students' motivation, thus contributing to the improvement of teaching practices. For this, a case study was chosen. To that extent, observation sessions were used, opinion questionnaires addressed to students and teachers and documentary analysis of documents related to the School.

In this investigation, the potential of Transmedia Storytelling was explored when applied in the classroom context, in classes with the 7th year of schooling. For the application, in the class context, physical and digital media were created that served as support to the activities developed during the classes.

In this sense, this research explores the potentialities of Transmedia Storytelling when applied in classroom context from the study of an autonomous reading work—Alice's Adventures in Wonderland, by Lewis Carroll.

For the application in the context of the classroom, physical and digital media were created, by the researcher to support the activities provided during the classes.

They were:

1—A book that contained the story of Alice's Adventures in Wonderland with one QR code per chapter, giving access to an excerpt from the Alice movie that matched the text.

2—A website on the Wordpress platform (created by the researcher and available at https://transmediapt.wordpress.com), which provided students and teachers with various resources, including the ebook, educational games about the story, and creative writing.

The study took place at Vila Nova da Barquinha School Group. The choice of the school where the study was carried out was based on two main criteria: the location, which was favourable to the researcher because it is close to her workplace, and the degree of innovation, as it is one of the few National group that implemented the Pedagogical Innovation Pilot Project.

The choice of the 7th grade was since the book "Alice's Adventures in Wonderland" is one of the books proposed for this level of education, for autonomous reading. The choice of the teachers was on the subjects where this study could be applied. Since it is a literary work, it made sense that it should be applied in Portuguese class.

4 Study Description

In carrying out this investigation, it was necessary to resort to the construction of activities on different platforms, with different media, for students to experience a Transmedia experience.

These means were:

- a printed book with the story of Alice's Adventures in Wonderland with a QR (Quick Response) code per chapter. The QR code transports the user from the physical media to digital, having an application and a camera to read the code, the QR Code application was installed on all tablets and, students, when scanning the code, with the tablet's camera, had the opportunity to view an excerpt from Alice's film that corresponded to the excerpt of the text they were reading.
- a website on the Wordpress platform (created by the researcher) that had available to students and teachers various activities (reading/downloading the ebook, games, creative writing, podcast, questionnaires, facts about the author and illustrator, videos and other sites of interest).
- an ebook where students had the possibility to choose alternative paths in the story, choosing the route that Alice took in the course of the story. Since Alice's world is completely absurd, it was decided to develop this methodology for the ebook: make Alice "jump" between chapters, according to students' choices to, having only the first and the last chapter in common and, at the end of the reading, be allowed a new moment of large group discussion about the chapters that each group had read. Since time was extremely limited, the decision that reading the ebook had to be limited time, that is, students could not browse the book, choosing Alice's steps, freely. Thus, the choice was made each group would only read four chapters of the story and could not go back in the story.
- educational games about the story, available on the website, games made on Educaplay platform where students had the opportunity to test their knowledge of the story.
- an area, on the website, where they still had the possibility to create small texts (creative writing). Here, the students were able to let their imagination run free and create short texts about each chapter story, creating an alternative version of happenings in Wonderland.

- questionnaires that were given to students and teachers on the applicability of Transmedia Storytelling in class context.

5 Study Results

The study took place in the academic year 2018/2019, during 3 sessions. During the sessions it was possible to observe how the students interacted with the provided material.

This project was implemented in four phases:

1—Handling of the printed book and reading QR codes to access extracts from the Disney movie, Alice in Wonderland. Character identification of each chapter.
2—Read the ebook with the story Alice's Adventures in Wonderland with paths that allow students to change the sequence of the story without changing its meaning.
3—Access to the Transmedia Storytelling Site (https://transmediapt.wordpress.com) where students had the opportunity to: Play; Obtain information about the author's life and work; Access the illustrator image gallery-John Tenniel; Recreate the story with creative writing proposals; Access links to sites of interest about the story; Listen to the podcast of the story (hosted on the Anchor website).
4—Respond to questionnaires about the importance of Transmedia products in education.

At the beginning of the session, the class was divided into groups, the printed book was distributed and given a chapter of the story to each group. The book had one QR code per chapter, and when students scanned the code, they had the opportunity to view an excerpt from the Alice's Adventures in Wonderland movie that matched the text they were reading.

The integration of technology into traditional media has proceeded smoothly, students have read their chapters using technology without any difficulty.

Then the students used the tablets to access Mentimeter, which allowed them to create a word cloud, as they were asked to write down the names of all the characters they found in the chapter they were reading in order to create a moment in large group discussion.

Then they were asked to read the ebook. At this point, the students' willingness to read the story was remarkable in all sessions, the room was silent, and the students read the story quite quietly.

After reading the ebook, students were able to access the website and test the educational games that were created for the activity about the story (created on Educaplay), a tool that combined a moment of teaching with leisure.

Feedback from students and teachers was unanimous regarding the importance Transmedia narratives can play in motivating students. All were satisfied and even asked to repeat classes like this with the literary works that they were currently working in the Portuguese subject, request reinforced by the teachers, who commented that it was with this type of projects that they could reach students, because students would feel more motivated when using tablets and computers.

In the teachers' questionnaire, the question was asked "Is this story captivating? And can it make learning more effective?" The teachers' answers were very positive, one of the answers was "Yes. Students are more interested and participative."

In the first question of the student questionnaire, "I seek in different media (traditional and digital) to deepen my knowledge about my favourite books" it was found that 87.2% of students agree or completely agree. Using the media, students seek to deepen their knowledge about their favourite books.

In the second question of the student questionnaire, "I like linear narratives—with beginning, middle and end—even when stories are told through different media.", It was found that 77% of students answered either agree or completely agree, which shows that students enjoy reading a narrative using different platforms. After applying the project, it was found that students naturally changed the narrative platform, using all the tools with extreme ease.

In the third question in the student questionnaire, "I like stories that have alternate versions of the characters and their universes, offering new perspectives." 92.3% of the answers focus on agree to completely agree. Students find it very interesting to know more about certain characters or even about the universes of the stories.

On the question "I like to get different perspectives on a fiction story, through secondary characters or through websites or books." 84.7% of students agree or totally agree with the statement. Students like to explore more about their favorite stories and have mentioned that they like to know more about the characters.

In the fourth question in the student questionnaire, "I like to share social media content related to my favorite fiction content." There was a scattering of responses. 25.6% of respondents say they do not agree with the statement and 74.4% agree. This may be due to the kind of sharing students like to do on their social networks. According to Sampaio [9] young people use mobile phones to communicate with colleagues and friends and to access social networks.

In the fifth question of the student questionnaire, "I like to buy elements related to my favorite stories, such as miniatures of characters, props and costumes and merchandising (pens, posters, etc.)." It was found that 84.7% of respondents answered that they agreed with the statement. When asked about this kind of purchase, some students mentioned that they often buy the miniatures of the characters from their favorite stories.

In the question "I value fiction content (books, series or films) that allows me to participate in the narrative", 89.8% of the students agreed with the statement. This type of interaction with the public has immense advantages, namely the fact that it is possible to interact with the narrative motivating students through interactivity.

In the end, the students participated in a creative writing activity using the tablets to create a story-related text. The proposals concerned the opening chapter they had read. The interaction of the groups was very interesting to observe, the students worked in harmony and were always interested.

In the teacher's questionnaires it was asked "Can students create story extensions to give additional educational value?" And the answers were all positive, but one answer was "Yes be creative, and create new situations." (teacher 1)

In fact, feedback from students and teachers was unanimous the importance that Transmedia narratives can assume in the motivation of the students, as seen in the sessions streamlined in this study. The students were always available and interested, made everything they were asked, and, in the end, they were motivated.

In one of the sessions, Teacher 2 even commented with the researcher who thought it was with these types of projects that students were able to reach, as they ended up feeling more motivated when using tablets and computers.

After analyzing the questionnaires, it is verifiable that there is a high level of receptivity on the part of the students, regarding the implementation of Transmedia narratives in an educational context. Young people try to learn a little more about their favorite stories in order to learn more about the characters and the universes of the stories.

Currently, we are no longer able to dissociate young people from technology, because the use of mobile devices—computer, mobile phone or tablet—something they use continuously and continued on a daily basis, for the most different purposes, playful, school/professional, personal. Transmedia narratives can bring this reality to life in classroom, leading students to use something from their daily lives in the classroom.

As Prensky (2001) points out, students have changed radically, today's students are no longer the people for whom the system of teaching has been designed and school must find ways to reduce this gap that exists between what is the interests and needs of the students, and what the evolution of society demands and allows.

During the sessions, it was possible to observe the way in which students interacted with the material provided by the researcher. The fact that they have the possibility to interact with the tablet during the class was a reason for great satisfaction on the part of these students.

During the sessions, the researcher had the possibility to observe some constraint regarding the use of the internet, the students were not able to view the excerpts of the film when photographing the QR code, being necessary the researcher to go through the groups, with the mobile phone and read, using mobile data. This constraint was also felt when it was necessary to view the site, some students had great difficulty in accessing it.

The fact that you cannot access the internet quickly, delayed the entire session process, leaving very little time for other activities. Not all students had the opportunity possibility to try the games created for the session. Lack of time also limited creative writing activity; some students even stated that they wanted more time to be able to write everything they liked to write about the story.

6 Conclusions

The results obtained in this investigation are quite satisfactory, although it is a very small sample of the Portuguese school system.

There is great potential in the application of Transmedia narratives in educational context, there is acceptance by teachers and enormous satisfaction on the part of students to use technology in the classroom.

This new reality, of technologies in classroom context, may prove to be a challenge for teachers, who may not be prepared for a new reality where the technology meets traditional teaching.

Education on different platforms can allow a continuity in the learning of young people, they are involved in their own learning. We are in a virtually digital age and it is necessary to improve the educational methodology in to include technology in an educational context. Moran (2000) states that students have the possibility to use these tools in order to develop their cooperative learning, interacting effectively, which can contribute significantly to improve the quality of learning.

It was intended that the various platforms would create new experiences to students, to take them from moment to moment a combination of the story told, and the experience involved. In this experience, with this project, students had the possibility of using new platforms during class.

Moments much appreciated by the students, who felt motivated, and by teachers who demonstrated that it would be beneficial that there were more works to be treated in this way.

Despite the constraints, education on various platforms can allow continuity in the learning of young people, because, in this way, they are involved in their learning.

References

Bidarra J, Rodrigues P (2018) Design of a transmedia project targeted to language learning. Consultado em 6 maio 2019, em: https://www.researchgate.net/publication/273773346_Design_of_a_Transmedia_Project_targeted_to_Language_Learning

Cruz T, Porto C, Benia R (s.d.) (2019) Narrativas Transmídia Aplicadas à Educação: O Uso da Gamificação e da Criação de Fanfictions Para Estimular a Aprendizagem. Consultado em 28 abril 2019, em: https://pt.scribd.com/document/342523958/Narrativas-Transmidia-Aplicadas-a-Educacao-O-Uso-da-Gamificacao-e-da-Criacao–de-Fanfictions-Para-Estimular-a-Aprendizagem

Fleming L (2013) Expanding learning opportunities with transmedia practices: inanimate Alice as an exemplar. DigitalCommons@URI. Consultado em 12 maio 2019, em: https://digitalcommons.uri.edu/jmle/vol5/iss2/3/

Jenkins H (2007) Transmedia storytelling 101. Consultado em 6 abril 2019, em: http://henryjenkins.org/2007/03/transmedia_storytelling_101.html

Morales M, Alves F (2016) O Desinteresse dos Alunos pela Aprendizagem. Consultado em 11 maio 2019, em: http://www.diaadiaeducacao.pr.gov.br/portals/cadernospde/pdebusca/producoes_pde/2016/2016_artigo_ped_unioeste_marciadelourdesmorales.pdf

Moran J (2000) Mudar a forma de ensinar e de aprender. Consultado em 12 maio 2019, em: http://www.eca.usp.br/prof/moran/site/textos/tecnologias_eduacacao/uber.pdf

Moran J (2007) As mídias na educação. Consultado em 12 maio 2019, em: http://www.eca.usp.br/prof/moran/site/textos/tecnologias_eduacacao/midias_educ.pdf

Moran J (2013) Educar o educador. Consultado em 12 maio 2019, em: http://www.eca.usp.br/prof/moran/site/textos/tecnologias_eduacacao/educar.pdf

Prensky M (2001) Digital natives, digital immigrants part 1, on the Horizon, vol. 9, Issue: 5, pp 1–6. Consultado em 5 abril 2019, em: https://doi.org/10.1108/10748120110424816

Rodrigues P, Bidarra J (2014) Transmedia storytelling and the creation of a converging space of educational practices. Int J Emerg Technol Learn. Consultado em 21 abril 2019, em: https://www.online-journals.org/index.php/i-jet/article/view/4134

Narrative Objects in Virtual Reality

Rafael Silva and Daniel Brandão

Abstract This chapter questions what differentiates interactive narratives in virtual reality, proposing spatial storytelling as a dimension natural to the medium. We analyze Offland, a project which consisted in the creation of a fictional world and a virtual reality experience, to explore this medium's immersion and storytelling. The lessons taken from user testing help understanding how goals, exploration, linearity and interactivity relate to the fictional immersion and experience. From there we look at the structure of space and narratives as constructed by virtual objects with narrative value. It is clear that interactive storytelling is based on modularity (Miller in Digital storytelling : a creator's guide to interactive entertainment. CRC Press 2014; Murray in Hamlet on the holodeck: the future of narrative in cyberspace. The Mit Press, Cambridge, Massachusetts 2017), and when looking at the spaces, events and action points, objects are what sustain these modules. Objects can be essential to the intended narrative, can add secondary value to the experience or can be decorative, giving spatial context and immersion. Through details an object can indicate a much larger fictional world and allow immersion in it (Pacat in Fantasy worldbuilding: the power of detail. WQ. writers in their landscapes. Queensland Writers Centre 2017). Objects can engage in the narrative, through indicating different atmospheres, pacing, tension and goals. With interactivity, the user can create or alter virtual objects, adding their own contribution to the narrative. Objects connect the physical and the virtual, being that they can act as a visual interface or a controller, to interact with the virtual environment. The use of objects is natural form of interaction and narrative, as it presents virtual reality as we are used to, from the mental schemas built from our natural lives in physical reality.

Keywords Virtual reality · Interactive storytelling · Immersion · Storyworlds · Participatory narratives

R. Silva (✉)
Instituto Politécnico do Cávado e do Ave, Braga, Portugal
e-mail: rafsilva@outlook.pt

D. Brandão
University of Minho / CECS, Braga, Portugal
e-mail: daniel.c.brandao@gmail.com

N. Martins et al. (eds.), *Perspectives on Design and Digital Communication*, Springer Series in Design and Innovation 8, https://doi.org/10.1007/978-3-030-49647-0_8

1 Interactive Storytelling

1.1 Traditional, Interactive and Virtual Reality Storytelling

Humans have an innate impulse to connect the past, present and future by constructing narratives (Miller 2014). This allows us to predict the future based on the past, giving the opportunity to strategize, while helping people understand each other and forming a community.

Based on Abbott's (2011) definitions we consider narrative as the representation of stories, a story being a series of events over time, and events considered the actions and reactions of entities. An entity (character or not) usually exists within a setting or story world. In the digital setting we call objects to the constructing units of a digital environment (Manovich 2001), which can appear in different scales and with different properties. A parallel can be created between the fictional world's entities and the virtual environment's objects.

For Abbott conflict is what structures a narrative. The typical narrative structure is based on the Greek three act structure, and as McKee (1997) explains usually involves five events: Inciting Incident, Progressive Complications, Crisis, Climax and Resolution. Conflict can relate both to the structure, setting or characters, happening in three levels: Inner Conflicts, Personal Conflicts and Extrapersonal Conflicts. Conflict leads to closure, which is a play on expectations and answers that can result in frustration or satisfaction for the audience (Barthes as cited in Abbott 2011). Interaction and relations between different digital objects are what structure a virtual environment and define both the space and the experience.

For Miller (2014) transmedia, change and evolution are a certainty in digital narratives, as they can be: nonlinear, with different outcomes, experienced actively through agency and the user becoming a co-creator through participation, reflecting Manovich's (2001) definition of digital media. Digital narratives inherit characteristics from the digital that are defined by the digital objects (see Table 1).

Table 1 Comparison between traditional storytelling, digital storytelling and digital objects

Traditional stories	Digital storytelling	Digital objects
Preconstructed, story elements cannot be changed	Are malleable; not fixed in advance	Can change their properties
Have a linear plot; usually told in linear fashion	Are nonlinear, non-chronological	Can be rearranged in space and time
Author/writer is sole creator	The user co-creates the story	Can be created by the user
Are experienced passively	Are experienced actively	Can be interacted with by the user
Have one unchangeable ending	Different endings are possible	React to other objects and systems and cause reactions

The use of digital medium to tell stories presents some clear advantages:

- Higher engagement and attention;
- Audiovisual content causes a great retention;
- Easily edit and adapt content to different audiences;
- Greater immersion;
- Digital channels such as online communities also allow for the perpetuation of fictional universes.

It is important for creators to understand the potential and weakness of any medium. The cinema industry invests a great sum of money translating stories told in books to screenplay adaptations. In interactive medium like mobile applications and console games there is original content exploring forms of interactive storytelling, but adaptations of linear stories remain simple, not using digital medium to their potential (Clarke and Mitchell 2001), perhaps due to fear of damaging the original story's integrity or simply because of the additional work involved. When we talk about virtual reality (VR) a different problem occurs: the lack of a storytelling model and best practices.

Miller (2014) and Alexander (2017) write about how narratives are told in the digital, giving practical guidance for the process, Hamlet on the Holodeck (Murray 2017) focuses on the relation between narratives and technology, touching the fields of video games, VR and mass participation. However, traditional storytelling in VR has been criticized by Bailenson (2016) who uses the terms: "…Failed from a narrative point of view…", as in many experiences people look straight without guidance, missing the action, or there is no freedom to choose where to look at. Because of the sensorial immersion, our instinct is to naturally interact with the environment, which can distract from the storyteller's intended story and focus points.

For Bielskyte (2016), in VR, storytelling is not the focus, the focus is to create story experiences, and for this, the production model that typically prioritizes plot and characters through the director, must also give authority to production designers (or "world builders"), technology specialists and user experience designers. McDowell (2019) also points toward a deeply collaborative and nonlinear methodology with the human at the center, which will pave the way for new practices concerning stories.

With VR, the space, virtual objects, virtual characters, and the system become the story, according to Damiani (2018b) we shift from linearity to semi or non-linearity and participatory narrative. This exploration of how narratives, immersion and interactivity work in VR, is the goal of our project, Offland, which consisted of creating and testing a fictional universe and the corresponding VR experience.

1.2 Creating a Virtual Reality Experience

The project consisted in building a fiction world and creating a VR experience, exploring the potential of this medium for immersion and storytelling. An original fiction world was used: Offland, which is a fantasy approach to the western genre, centered around an inhospitable wasteland (Fig. 1). The project is based on McDowell's methodology (2019), in which the design of a world precedes the telling of a story.

The VR experience is about ten minutes long and portrays one specific scenario of an illusion inducing oasis, centering the experience in exploration, survival and altered states of mind such as hallucinations (Fig. 2). The virtual environment serves us as a sandbox to test different moments and experiences, to answer in what ways fiction storytelling can be enhanced by VR's interactivity. We interpreted Brett Leonard's concept of Storyworlding (as quoted in Bailenson 2016) through short narratives distributed through space, in which the user participates naturally through interaction with the environment. The virtual experience also explores user participation, allowing for users to leave voice recordings for the next users, and creating a more collective narrative.

Through user testing we found that the experience should start with a goal to guide exploration, balancing linearity and nonlinearity allows for a narrative that's both comprehensive and engaging, the lack of characters or their representation causes little emotion and empathy, details make the fictional world more discernible, and participation should feel simple to the user and not be forced.

A big part of the production was focused on translating aspects of a fictional universe to a narrative told through virtual space and represented essentially by virtual objects, as virtual space is perhaps VR's natural language of storytelling.

Fig. 1 Design for the title screen of the experience

Fig. 2 Screenshot of the oasis of Illusions, in which the narrative is based

1.3 Narratives Through Space

Manovich (2001) presents a duality between games, which were seen as more explorative and movies, which were seen as linear narratives. But this separation assumes the narrative as self-contained instead of seeing the interaction of the game as a new form of transmedia storytelling, as Jenkins (2002) explains calling game designers "narrative architects". For Brown (2017), the natural language of storytelling in video games might even be the story conveyed by the gameplay and interaction itself.

In a highly presential medium such as VR, constructing the space is a need, and for a fictional world to hold a believable immersion, world building is essential (Anders 2013).

VR is gaining popularity (Metry 2017) and hardware is improving (Durham 2017). As for content, we are still learning the language of the media, there are efforts to create rules and guidelines for user interfaces like Alger's manifesto and research (2015), but they do not cover the complexity of immersion, composition and narratives. As Milk (2016) puts it, before learning the language of storytelling in VR, we are still learning its grammar through experimentation.

In virtual environments, space becomes the story as Fraga (2017) points out:

> Space has been designed to tell that story—a story that embodies a specific philosophy about the human natural habitat—a story of which the participant is a character, participant, and agent.

Brett Leonard (as quoted by Bailenson 2016) uses the term *Storyworlding*, as the stories are not told but lived, and the creators build worlds from which the stories emerge. For stories to emerge from worlds, McDowell (2019) suggest starting with an origin story, which can be a simple first question, then moving onto contextual questions: “Where are you?” or “When are you?”, and then ask what is driving the world with high level provocations: “What if?” and “Why not?”. As he states: “The more questions you ask, the more narrative details start to emerge, raising questions in themselves… it becomes more and more robust, at multiple scales … simultaneously”.

Seeing the virtual environment as a game environment, Danskey (as cited in Qin et al. 2009) believes that what happens in a game is the heart of its narrative, and unique stories can emerge from the interactions between autonomous characters and systems within a simulated story world (Ryan et al. 2015) resulting in endless possibilities of events not scripted by the original authors. The narrative is perceived by the user but not imposed, as our brains project stories where they don’t exist (Heider-Simmel as cited in Damiani 2018a). Any of these approaches to storytelling require for narratives to be well defined and structured.

1.4 Structuring Narrative in Space

The structure in digital storytelling (Miller 2014) is similar to traditional structures but is based on modularity, being that the building blocks are decisions and action points. Nonlinearity assumes the existence of different triggers and conditions that allow for branching structures. A narrative with too many outcomes might become an unneeded production effort, being that the user will only experience a small part of them. For this, designers can create a critical story path, consisting of what events are essential for the user to make sense of the story. Roach (as cited by Miller 2014) explains that this structure can be supported by worlds (or spaces), that allow for the user to interact freely, but for the story to advance, the player must successfully perform certain tasks. In this setting, called “string of pearls”, there are:

- Tasks or goals which can be acquiring objects or information, encountering characters or experiencing an event, which advance the story;
- Interactions that enrich the story and experience but are not critical to the narrative;
- Triggers that can change the mood, narrative branches, character attitudes, environments or experience.

Miller (2014) and Murray (2017) present a variety of structural models for interactive storytelling, that differ mostly on navigation, linearity, freedom to explore, sequence, hierarchy and perspective. Choosing the right structure for a project depends on the media, audience, production capacity and intent of the narrative.

Interactivity can also break the cohesiveness of a narrative (Miller 2014), and the challenge is in tying the various elements to supply momentum. For Roach (as cited in Miller 2014), narrative in interactive medium is broken into small information pieces: characters, atmosphere, action. But if there are too many pieces and the user is inputting constantly, there are no opportunities for story. He suggests the balance between linear narratives and narrative pieces.

Jenkins (2002) mentions the use of micro narratives to shape the user's emotional experiences, the narrative is not viewed as linear plot list, but the focus is in the environment's narrative value, through pre-existing narrative associations, embedded information or providing resources for narratives to happen.

Time, which is a basic structural unit of the film medium, becomes optional as a structural construct. It can be used in interactivity for higher engagement or to represent aspects of the story world (Brown 2019), but space is essential to an interactive narrative, as users will be able to experience the narrative at their own pace, through exploration. Space is composed of the environment and objects. Some objects can be interacted with and trigger reactions in other objects, environments or systems. While some effects might be for amusement (e.g., trying different tools in a virtual environment), others will be perceived as plot progression and move the user forward in the narrative structure.

2 Narrative Objects

2.1 Objects with Narrative Value

A narrative object in VR is essentially a virtual object which contains narrative value. Existing within the virtual environment, an object will naturally have spatial properties: position, scale, rotation, shape and material. An object is considered dynamic if it's properties can change over time or with interaction. We might also consider complex objects, which can have no spatial representation and can be composed of other objects or events. However, for narrative value to be understood, context is necessary, as narrative is not inherently present in singular objects, but instead is a construct by which we view the world (Lotto 2016; Douglas and Hargadon 2000). A virtual object will be perceived as part of a narrative according to how much it informs, it's emotional implications (Tolkien 1947), it's influence on behavior (Kaplan et al. 2016) and how coherent it is with the remaining objects, environment and already perceived narrative.

Roach (as cited in Miller 2014) divides narrative points into essential and secondary, and a similar structure makes sense for object classification. We can divide narrative objects into those which are essential, secondary and decorative. Essential narrative objects must be experienced for the intended narrative to make sense, they will define the critical story path, and they should have more focus in production. Secondary objects provide details or allow the user to do enjoyable actions which will add to the richness of the experience but are not critical for the narrative success. Decorative objects exist to sustain the space on which the narrative happens, they are most likely structural or decorative, with the function of creating spatial context and immersion.

Opposition or tension is what makes story events be perceived as narrative (McKee 1997) and a correct balance of pacing makes the story engaging (Murray 2017; Troeth

2015). These tension events occur to characters in spaces, through their relation with other characters, their inner selves, objects and the space itself. Narrative objects ought to reflect this, evoking characters, mental states, ideas, emotions, actions, other objects, events, environments and spaces. Details in virtual objects can indicate many aspects of the story and point towards a much bigger fictional world (Pacat 2017).

2.2 *Details and the Fictional World*

The virtual object can be a representation of something that exists fictionally, for example, a sword prop in the virtual environment is a digital object with properties (position, scale, color, length, etc.) that might change upon interaction (moving it will cause the position to change, fighting enemies might make it change colors and textures, to indicate dirt, etc.), and react to functions and conditions (if the sword is moved at a high speed it will damage other objects it encounters). But when speaking about the dramatic and fictional aspect, we perceive it as a sword because of its shape, sounds and maneuverability, the existence of a sword might indicate hidden truths about the fictional world: what kind of weapons nearby civilizations use, what kind of technology do they got, the story might be in a medieval setting, etc. And it might contain additional information related to the object itself: did the sword belong to another character, perhaps a friend or an enemy? Are there engravings that can tell a story? Is the sword one-of-a-kind, perhaps a legendary weapon like the Excalibur? These kinds of abstract relations made by the user when interacting with the virtual object will trigger his cognitive processes and emotions.

According to Pacat (2017), details are what makes fiction interesting and compelling, designers need to have special attention to transfer details of the fictional world into the experience. In Offland we went through a process of world building focused on the project and many of the aspects of the fictional world were not directly included in the experience but small details made the users question the existence of huts in the desert and the corresponding civilizations who built and dwell in them. Using equipment with fictional brands (Fig. 3) indicates the existence of commerce, craftsmanship and societies. Using references to a fictional mythology (Fig. 4) indicates the existence of history, religions, cultures and communities. Our test participants had difficulty understanding all the aspects of the fictional world, but even so reported to feel like they were in another place, and manifested interest in gaining deeper knowledge about that fictional world. In an experience with more length and freedom to explore, this kind of imaginary immersion is likely to happen.

Objects in the virtual environment can be considered part of the interface as they present information about the virtual environment and are means to control it. Virtual objects are a sensorial representation (usually visual) of objects that exist within a fictional world. They are represented throughout virtual space or graphical user interfaces.

Fig. 3 Screenshots from Offland. A fictional brand is applied to multiple technological equipment

Fig. 4 Screenshots from Offland. Statues related to the fictional mythology

2.3 *Objects as Interface Elements*

Sensorial feedback is something from the natural world that is to be expected in the digital world. We are used to interacting and feeling the results (e.g., while touching a flower, we feel its texture, humidity and smell it is fragrance). Nielsen (1994) states that "the system should always keep users informed about what is going on, through appropriate feedback within reasonable time.", and this is crucial from an interactive narrative point of view, as the user needs to be informed of his goals and their completion (Ryan et al. 2015). As Boag (2012) explains: "The lack of positive feedback leaves the user with a less pleasurable experience".

Feedback is related to multisensorial input and perception, being that general VR devices support visual, audio, haptics and time (in order to create motion). Audio and visual interfaces can be categorized based on their diegesis (being part of the virtual/fictional world) and relation to virtual space (See Table 2; Andrews 2009; Stonehouse 2014; Fagerholt and Lorentzon 2009):

- Diegetic interfaces: The user interface elements exist within the virtual and fictional world, information is passed through virtual objects or environment, making the experience seamless, without additional layers of abstraction.
- Non-diegetic interfaces: The interface is layered on top of the experience, usually represented in an independent space within the user's point of view (in a 2D plane or small depth range). It is informative, without a connection to the fictional world. While creating a possible distraction, it is also more immediate to convey information.
- Spatial interfaces: The interface elements do not exist within the fictional world but are represented in the virtual world in perspective, making them an abstract layer that seems like part of the world. They are used to provide more immediate information preserving the immersion.
- Meta-Diegetic interface: Like non diegetic interfaces, they are relative to the user's point of view, however, they are representations of elements that exist in the fictional world, and the controlled avatar would have access to (e.g., using car velocimeter fixed to the heads up display, the user can look around while keeping track of speed, without actually looking at the virtual dashboard). It is useful for presenting information valuable to the action, without distracting from it, while maintaining a connection to the fictional world.

Through stereoscopy and headtracking, VR brings the dimension of depth to non-spatial interfaces, this can be to convey importance, keeping in mind that interface elements at distances lower than 0.5 m can become hard to perceive, and distances higher than the headset's limit become imperceivable (20 m in Alger's VR setting, 2015). Edward T. Hall's work on proxemics (as explained in Jahnke 2019), limits the general intimate space to 0.45 m, and according to Alger this is discomforting for visual interfaces. He suggests the placement of VR elements at about 1.3 m from the user, which is close to Hall's limit between personal space and social space (Table 3). Alger predicts the use of non-diegetic interfaces in a space independent of the virtual

Table 2 Diegesis in user interfaces (Andrews 2009)

		Is the representation existing in 3D virtual space?	
		No	Yes
Is the representation existing in the fictional world?	**No**	Non-diegetic representation	Spatial representation
	Yes	Meta representations	Diegetic Representation

Table 3 Proxemics and distance ranges. (Jahnke 2019)

Intimate space	Personal space	Social space	Public space
<0.45 m	0.45–1.2 m	1.2–3.7 m	3.7–7.6 m

space, however, these notions of proxemics can also be applied to other virtual avatars or objects, which can serve as an interface, and according to their proximity, will influence our perception, ease of use, and emotions towards them (Marks 2017).

Human perception uses pattern recognition to quickly identify something that is different in the environment, this is a survival trait that will make an element stand out through contrast, scale, shape, color and other properties (Alger 2015). Perception depends on the sensory intensity of each element (e.g., in a setting where everything is dark, the white will stand out, and the reverse happens). Each element presents multiple sensorial dimensions and intensities. But if every element is presented in high intensity, sensory overload will happen, the user will have difficulty focusing on a singular object and might be distracted from the intended content or narrative immersion. In reverse when the user is deeply immersed he will become less aware of the interface, when the user has a solid mental schema of the interface he will interact with it without being distracted from the content, maintaining immersion (Douglas and Hargadon 2000).

For presenting objects as interface elements, it is important to understand how can interfaces result in positive experiences:

- Creators should prototype often, adjusting scale, proximity, controls to best suit the user (Slevin 2017);
- The user should be guided towards the intended points of viewing (Gardner 2016);
- Interface information can be used to tell the user more about the world, stimulating and satisfying curiosity (Slevin 2017);
- It might be important to use familiar visual cues, not only for assisting narrative but also for signaling points of interaction (Unity 3D 2019);
- When a sensory is not available to be represented, use sensory substitution (e.g., touch can be represented visually through a highlight in the object) (Jerald 2017);
- The design should be minimalist. Every extra unit of information, increases the cognitive load, competing with relevant units of information and diminishes their relative visibility (Nielsen 1994);
- Interface should follow real world conventions, unique terminology will increase the cognitive load (Nielsen 1994; Joyce 2019);
- The user's memory load should be minimized, by making objects, actions and options, visible or easily retrievable whenever appropriate (Nielsen 1994);
- The interface will strengthen the experience by using terms (linguist or aesthetical) that point towards the fictional world (Joyce 2019);
- Interface should be consistent, and each type of element, state and action should be represented differently (Nielsen 1994);
- Account for both inexperienced and experienced users, being that there can be more advanced and efficient ways of doing the same actions (Nielsen 1994).

The virtual object, as any other interface element must be clear and engaging to the user, according to the importance of the said element to the narrative. Engagement is the first step of immersion (Brown and Cairns 2004). The user needs primarily to have access and interest, and only then will he invest time, effort and attention, becoming engrossed by the medium. This comes with the challenge of continuously creating interest and comprehension of the narrative.

2.4 Narrative and Object Engagement

For both books and film, narrative hooks are used to introduce an interesting idea and capture attention (Epstein 2002). In traditional media, the objective for a hook is to pitch a concept or to attract the reader within the first pages. In VR a narrative hook could be what Leonard (as cited in Bailenson 2016) calls narrative magnets, which are cues that call the attention of the user and make him engage into a new narrative. The narrative magnets can work through perception cues, which can appeal to a determined sense without disrupting immersion, and through psychological cues, where the user will start to perceive the premise and conflict of a story through context and the environment, which will gradually involve him in the intended narrative experience (Shepard 2014).

The narrative events must be perceived as a story by the user, and this proposes the challenge of presenting exposition, tension, surprise and resolution through space exploration. The early prototypes of our project Offland, presented a non-conventional story, with only objects spread across the space, each with narrative value. Upon testing it, we concluded that generally it lacked consistency, context and purpose. The addition of a starting event with tension and goals to the experience helped guide the rest of the narrative, helping the user to make sense of every event until the ending (Figs. 5, 6 and 7). The String of Pearls approach breaks the narrative into scenarios and each scenario into objects, events and interactions. This method helped in the organization and coherence of the story. Besides having the same starting and ending point, the journey of each user is still different, being its own story.

When there are multiple narrative paths, it is important to accept that not all users will experience all possible narratives, and thus defining a critical story path (Miller 2014) is important to ensure that the user is directed to the intended point of view and that there is a continuity between points and objects. This can be done with objects, which can acquire multiple functions relating to the critical story path:

- Give the user a new goal (e.g., a letter mentioning a buried treasure). It is important for tasks to be simplified into hierarchical steps, and that the completion criteria is understood (Jerald 2017);
- Guide towards the goal (e.g., a compass);
- Guide towards a space (e.g., directional signage);

Fig. 5 Screenshot from Offland. The narrative begins with a moment of tension

Fig. 6 Screenshot from Offland. The directional movement guides the eye of the viewer to the next goal

- Remind the user of the goal. Jerald (2017) suggests the explanation of the goal should be present and accessible (e.g., repeated audio);
- Inform about the completion of the goal (e.g., objects which contain meters that will fill according to the objective);
- Provide a joyful reward or catharsis upon the completion of the goal (e.g. a trophy or a unique tool with new capacities);

Fig. 7 Screenshot from Offland. The use of narrative objects to provide goals and guide the user

- Act as clues, revealing something that was previously unknown to the user (e.g., finding the weapon of the crime can reveal multiple information about the criminal);
- Give information about how to perform a certain task. Brown (2015) gives the example of Half-Life 2's tutorials which explain how to defeat certain enemies solely through the environment and arrangement of objects.

Another challenge in digital storytelling is providing the user with motivation to spend time working through the narrative, Roach (as cited in Miller 2014) taps on the user's tendency to solve problems. For Douglas and Hargadon (2000), engagement is about interest, experimentation, shifting perspectives, dramatic changes, and uncertainty. The uncertainty presents likely suspicions, encouragement to keep guessing and a twist at the end. Brown and Cairns (2004) suggest keeping rewarding their efforts accordingly. For Salen and Zimmerman (2004) goals, conflict and uncertainty is what allows players to understand a game narrative completely.

Murray (2017) reminds of the importance of opposition to provide energy and interest, which can be present even in abstract games like Tetris. For Troeth (2015), these variations in energy/tension/pace over time are essential for a good narrative. Conflict should not be so overbearing that the user feels tempted to give up or too unchallenging that users will lose interest. Antagonists should have an understandable motive, being that the level of motivation makes a more dramatic story. The opposition should be personal to the user or user's character (Fullerton 2014). Objects can be used to characterize antagonistic forces or the user's character, revealing their motivations, objectives, origins, plans, dreams, fears, virtues and flaws.

Objects can make or break the tension, as they can contribute to the environment and atmosphere of a scene. This can be through subtle hints that danger is nearby in a thriller setting (e.g., a knife with blood in the floor) or that the user reached a secure place (e.g., a closed door in a safehouse or a light in a dark setting).

In video games, generally, there are playable moments with action and cutscenes with exposition. In VR it is hoped that interactivity and shifts in pacing are more natural and do not risk breaking the mediatic illusion. Interactivity in a scene is given by objects which act as the control interfaces to affect other elements of the virtual space. These objects might work as tools to use in playful activities and see change in the world, as the user will feel more immersed if the environment reacts to his actions (Heeter 1992). Objects used for creation (e.g., paint brushes or musical instruments) will allow for artistic expression and a sense of authorship. Pieces of puzzle can create uncertainty, challenge and eventually lead to resolution. Containers can create a fast feedback of uncertainty and reward. Weapons can bring forward the user's survival instincts and induce him into skill-based challenges. Other types of objects can create different types of energy depending on the context and plot.

For guiding the user to a determined object (for narrative or interaction reasons), multiple sensory cues might be used. Non-diegetic visual cues can be more immediate (e.g., highlighting the object or the use of a graphical interface compass pointing toward the object), but there are also many ways to make a virtual object stand out:

- The object should be designed with a visual shaped that indicates its interactivity or function, creators will benefit from knowledge of product design (Norman 2013);
- The object's disposition in relation to other objects will change its interpretation (through proximity, similarity and general composition as seen in the Gestalt theory, as explained by Alger 2015);
- It is important for the most recurrent interactable objects to be placed on comfort zones. The user might ignore objects that are too hard to reach (Alger 2015);
- The user assumes nearby objects as important and interactable (Marks 2017);
- The object's size conveys more intense meanings than in other digital media. According to the user's profile, big might mean scary and small might mean cute. (Marks 2017);
- Lightning can be used to guide the eye of the viewer to the intended object;
- Additional perception cues might increase the sense of it being interactive, and might be essential in some experiences or narratives (Unity 3D 2019);
- Use other senses such as haptics and sound to give realism to the object (Beasley 2017);
- More properties, functions and conditions will make it more possible for stories to emerge from the system. (Brown 2015);
- Details increase the possibilities of fiction (Pacat 2017);
- Interactive characters, objects and environments that react to the user's behavior adds to sense of presence (Slevin 2017; Heeter 1992; Marks 2017).

The object can acquire multiple functions that guide toward the intended narrative, and present interactivity that will balance the interest and tension in an experience. Through creating engaging objects, creators can gain control over the user's narrative path and ensure that the narrative always remains appealing. Interactive objectives add multiple possibilities and is where the potential of interactive storytelling in VR can be explored.

2.5 Interactive Objects

Interaction is the exchange of actions between two objects. In human-computer interaction (HCI) this means a "dialogue": a communication loop between a user and an object, though an interface (See Fig. 8).

There is a continuous stream of commands and feedback between the user and the interface. The interface acts as a boundary and door to the digital/virtual world, being able to change the properties of the digital objects and to receive updates to present to the user as feedback.

Commands refers to the actions inputted by the user through multiple interfaces, while feedback refers to the sensory signals sent by the interface to the user.

The interactive object is in its essence digital but can be representative of anything in the abstract dimension (Fullerton 2014). The object doesn't interact solely with a user, but can interact with the system, environment and other objects of the virtual world.

For Miller (2014) the purpose of interaction in a narrative is for stimulus and response, navigation in the virtual environment, control over objects, communication, exchange of information and acquisition. In VR the illusion of non-mediation is created, and these natural interactions become intuitive to the user.

Interaction with virtual objects should be seamless, through intuitive manipulation and controls that mimic actions the user is used to do in reality, perhaps the most natural are touching and grabbing which is what we learn since babyhood (Gribetz 2016).

In Offland we felt the importance of the user understanding the objective, how to interact, and the success of his interaction. Many participants in our tests were confused by the lack of instructions and feedback. In the parts where it was clear what to do and how to do it, they showed more confidence and engagement. Each interaction should be accessible and should consider a balance between effort and reward. In our experience we had multiple narrative objects spread across the space, we noticed that many participants only interacted with those that were near and easy to access. It's important to stimulate the desire to explore through good placement of objects, clear user goals and rewards.

When manipulating an object, the inputs given by the player will update the object's properties over time and result in effects through functions and conditions. The object is in continuous communication with the interface, and any changes that occur in it might be represented through the interface if it is relevant to the experience. An interactive object usually does not exist alone and is surrounded by an ecosystem of other interactive objects, some directly affected by the user, others

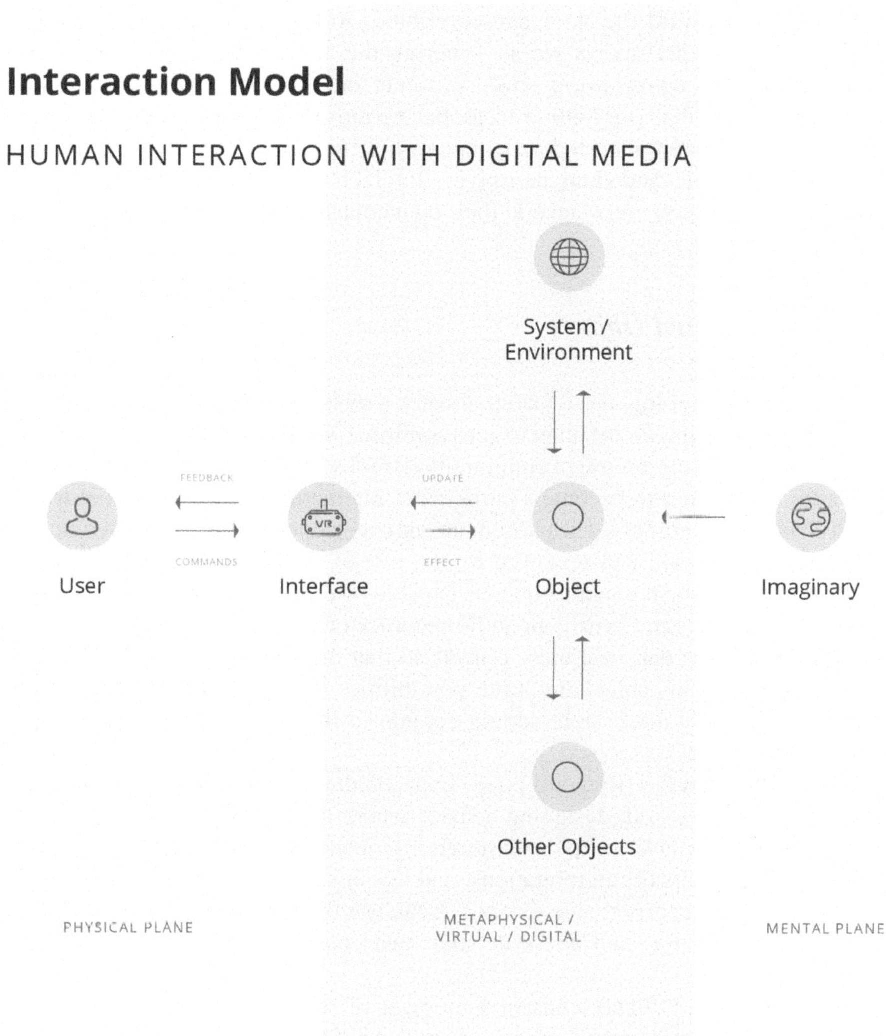

Fig. 8 Interaction model representation

through interaction with the system and other objects. The object affects the environment and system continuously. Until its properties change (through interaction or not) it is perceived as a seamless part of the environment.

The objective of interaction in VR immersive storytelling becomes one different than pure simulations, games or movies, the goal is to create the illusion of a non-mediated experience, in which every aspect: the actions, commands and user interfaces point toward the story and contributes to the immersion. With interactivity, McDowell (2019) says we are entering the "post-cinematic" era of storytelling, where the entire world space presents multiple narrative opportunities. We moved from tribal storytelling to global narrative, making sense of the world through multiple interconnected experiences, holistic and collaborative knowledge that support organic and fluid narratives. Interactivity creates the possibility of participation, in which users can add their own contribution to a global narrative.

2.6 User Created Objects

In traditional storytelling, participation creates a relationship between the teller and the audience, allowing for the teller to get a confirmation on his story and adapt it to the listener, while creating a sense of community (Brooks 2003; Miller 2014). The digital allows for the listener to become a participant, interacting with the fictional world, which changes accordingly. The participant can even create and share his own stories, which can be assessed and reviewed by the rest of the digital community. When the virtual environment contains objects capable of producing other objects (e.g., a polaroid camera, a paint brush, an audio recorder or any interface that instantiates objects), the system can save these objects so that the next users will find them in their experience. This creates multiple possibilities such as collaborative problem solving, community discussion, adding content to the narrative or the creation of new narratives.

Where Thoughts Go (Rizzotto 2018) expands the notion of VR narrative to the creation of a story world, designing a space where the narratives unfold naturally. In the experience, players explore through a sequential narrative arc, by receiving other players answers or interpretations, and leaving their own. As Rizzotto puts it: "The point is that the experience serves as a catalyst for your own personal narrative, allowing you to reflect and arrive at your own conclusions about the world and yourself".

Our experience, Offland, ends in a moment of reflection, asking the player to leave a public testimony of what was experienced, by his own words (Fig. 9). This allows for the virtual world to become a medium from which the narratives emerge according to interaction, instead of imposing narratives. The last moment allows for a player to listen to all the previously recorded stories of other players and complement his experience with the shared stories of others (Fig. 10). During testing, we noticed players felt that the testimony recording was a little sudden, most of them were surprised and didn't know exactly what to say. There are difficulties in forced participation as most players may lack the spontaneity to make relevant contributions, and the act of participating itself is not always stimulating or rewarding. Users might be inclined to participate and engage in a community if they are interested and understand the underlying cultures of the fictional world and of the community. Participation should also be rewarding, not only upon conclusion, but the means of participating should provide fun.

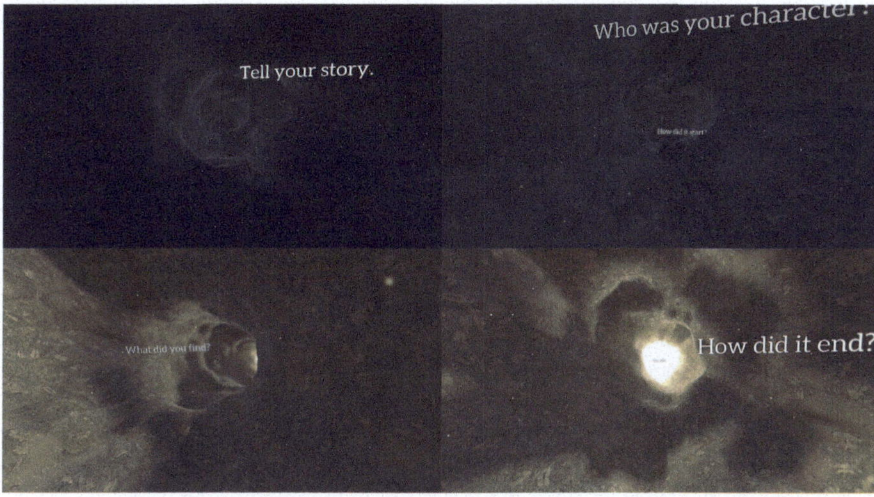

Fig. 9 Screenshot from Offland. Motion sequence for recording user testimonies

Fig. 10 User interface design for listening to the testimonies of other players

In general, the participative approach to storytelling creates a very unique experience, where the collaborative narratives are presented through the space and the user is able to leave his own imprint into the virtual world and environment for future users, making him a co-creator of the story.

3 Conclusions

Storytelling presents new challenges with interactivity and VR, but many of the structures of more traditional media serve as base for exploring the language of storytelling in VR. The process itself of creating narratives for this medium is becoming more human-centered and focused on collaboration between creatives, artists, designers and technology specialists (McDowell 2019).

Our project, Offland, hopefully presents some insights into narratives told through space in VR, through the opinions of those who experimented. The sense of spatial presence is natural in VR and as such, space becomes more important than time in structuring narratives, shifting from the linearity found in film to exploration and non-linearity. The best narrative structure is relative to multiple factors, but it is important for creators to consider the critical story path and focus the production on this intended narrative. Research comparing the different interactive narrative structures in VR and the results of each one with different audiences would allow to reach more conclusions.

Non-linearity assumes modularity, as is natural in the digital (Manovich 2001).The building blocks of narratives might be action points spread through space, and the building blocks of space, objects, which can contain different levels of narrative value and interactivity.

Objects can represent and characterize elements found in traditional storytelling such as opposition, characters, spaces and actions. It is through details that deep information and the story world is made present in the mind of the user.

Objects that inform about the virtual environment can be considered interface elements. Interfaces can break or sustain the immersion, according to their diegesis, their position in the virtual space, and the sensorial intensity on which it is presented. It is indispensable that creators prototype often as VR is a highly presential medium. Interface should be clear and engaging, maintaining the immersion of the experience.

In interactive narratives it is important to captivate attention to the points that will trigger new narratives, being that, the narrative events must be comprehensible by the user, feeling consistent and with purpose. Objects can direct the user in a meaningful narrative, as they can give goals, guide towards location, guide the execution of tasks and serve as rewards for goals. Tension and interest of the narrative should be balanced, creating a good pacing of exposition and interactivity, or challenge and difficulty. Different narrative objects can be used to set up the atmosphere of a scene and interactive objects can be added to create different pacing.

Different techniques should be tested and compared, possibly adapting Qin et al. (2009) narrative immersion test to see the effectiveness of each technique. A more throughout classification of objects, related to their narrative value and interactivity could be created.

Interactivity also allows for the participation of users which can alter existing objects or create new objects in some scenes. In some contexts, this might mean new, deeper and more personal narratives, in other contexts it might mean the virtual environment as a collaborative continuous form of storytelling.

Objects are a big part of telling stories in virtual reality through space, but characters are also a pillar of storytelling, independently of the medium. With advancements in technology, VR agents will only become more relevant. VR agents might also be considered as highly complex interactive objects and part of the space. A VR agent is a character controlled by the system, if this VR agent reacts to both the environment and the player, it will create a presence reinforcement loop. As Marks (2017) explains: "Their social behavior is reinforcing that the world you're in, that's virtual, is actually more real… You start to believe they're actually here and this is all real because of this kind of reinforcement". In either case, research in virtual agents, their avatars, character design, artificial intelligence, and its effects on emerging narratives and immersion is relevant to interactive storytelling.

References

Abbott HP (2011) The Cambridge introduction to narrative. Cambridge University Press, Cambridge

Alexander B (2017) The new digital storytelling creating narratives with new media—revised and updated edition, 2nd edn. ABC-CLIO

Alger M (2015) Visual design methods for virtual reality. Retrieved October 5, 2019, from https://www.semanticscholar.org/paper/Visual-Design-Methods-for-Virtual-Reality-Alger/94d9115ffc204c4a904312d6cecaf3032101009c

Anders C (2013) 7 Deadly sins of worldbuilding. Retrieved 7 Oct 2019, from Gizmodo website: https://io9.gizmodo.com/7-deadly-sins-of-worldbuilding-998817537

Andrews M (2009) Gamasutra—game UI discoveries: what players want. Retrieved 5 Oct 2019, from Gamasutra.com website: https://www.gamasutra.com/view/feature/4286/game_ui_discoveries_what_players_.php?print=1

Bailenson J (2016) The trials and tribulations of narrative in VR: the Stanford Ocean Acidification Experience [YouTube Video]. Retrieved from https://www.youtube.com/watch?v=G6mmXcNE7co

Beasley C (2017) What *real* reality tells us about building virtual reality [YouTube Video]. Retrieved from https://www.youtube.com/watch?v=YreKeP4P_fc

Bielskyte M (2016) The new storytellers II: World-building: best practices for creating story worlds [YouTube Video]. Retrieved from https://www.youtube.com/watch?v=jtr0AZK64Do

Boag P (2012) Are you giving your users positive feedback?—smashing magazine. Retrieved 5 Oct 2019, from Smashing Magazine website: https://www.smashingmagazine.com/2012/07/are-giving-users-positive-feedback/

Brooks K (2003) There is nothing virtual about immersion: narrative immersion for VR and other interfaces. Alumni Media. MIT. Retrieved from http://alumni.media.mit.edu/~brooks/storybiz/immersiveNotVirtual.pdf

Brown E, Cairns P (2004) A grounded investigation of game immersion. In: Extended abstracts of the 2004 conference on human factors and computing systems—CHI'04, pp 1297–1300. https://doi.org/10.1145/985921.986048

Brown M (2015) Half-Life 2's invisible tutorial|teaching players [YouTube Video]. Retrieved from https://www.youtube.com/watch?v=MMggqenxuZc&t=1s

Brown M (2017) The last guardian and the language of games|game maker's toolkit [YouTube Video]. Retrieved from https://www.youtube.com/watch?v=Qot5_rMB8Jc

Brown M (2019) Clockwork games and time loops|game maker's toolkit [YouTube Video]. Retrieved from https://www.youtube.com/watch?v=CI-4cumMC-Y&t=6s

Clarke A, Mitchell G (2001) Film and the development of interactive narrative. Lect Note Comput Sci 81–89. https://doi.org/10.1007/3-540-45420-9_10

Damiani J (2018a) This vital storytelling principle is the key to producing great VR and AR content. Retrieved 31 May 2019, from Entrepreneur.com website: https://www.entrepreneur.com/amphtml/309476

Damiani J (2018b) AR and VR: living, breathing storytelling|loup ventures. Retrieved 31 May 2019, from Loup Ventures website: https://loupventures.com/ar-and-vr-living-breathing-storytelling/

Douglas Y, Hargadon A (2000) The pleasure principle: immersion, engagement, flow. In: Proceeding of the eleventh ACM on hypertext and hypermedia. Retrieved from http://ftp.cse.buffalo.edu/users/azhang/disc/disc01/cd1/out/papers/hypertext/p 153-douglas.pdf

Durham B (2017) Just when you thought VR couldn't get any better|Benjamin Durham|. Retrieved from https://www.youtube.com/watch?v=-0tsSU4APwI

Epstein A (2002) Crafty screenwriting—the hook. Retrieved 7 Oct 2019, from Craftyscreenwriting.com website: http://www.craftyscreenwriting.com/hook.html

Fagerholt E, Lorentzon M (2009) Beyond the HUD—user interfaces for increased player immersion in FPS games. Retrieved 5 Oct 2019, from https://www.semanticscholar.org/paper/Beyond-the-HUD-User-Interfaces-for-Increased-Player-Fagerholt-Lorentzon/16ee02a8839923752c6bc93f294bec67d73a586e

Fraga D (2017) Big ideas in VR: the space is the story—VRScout. Retrieved 28 May 2019, from VRScout website: https://vrscout.com/news/big-ideas-vr-space-story/

Fullerton T (2014) Game design workshop: a playcentric approach to creating innovative games. Taylor & Francis Group, Boca Raton

Gardner K (2016) Virtual reality storytelling. TEDxPrincetonU [YouTube Video]. Retrieved from https://www.youtube.com/watch?v=7LNEkmcR4BM

Gribetz M (2016) A glimpse of the future through an augmented reality headset. Retrieved 31 May 2019, from TED2016 website: https://www.ted.com/talks/meron_gribetz_a_glimpse_of_the_future_through_an_augmented_reality_headset/transcript#t-642171

Heeter C (1992) Being there: the subjective experience of presence. Presence Teleoperators Virtual Environ 1(2):262–271. https://doi.org/10.1162/pres.1992.1.2.262

Jahnke M (2019) Proxemics|interesting thing of the day. Retrieved 5 Oct 2019, from Itotd.com website: https://itotd.com/articles/6277/proxemics/

Jenkins H (2002) Game design as narrative architecture. Computer 44

Jerald J (2017) SIGGRAPH 2017 VR interactions [YouTube Video]. Retrieved from https://www.youtube.com/watch?v=RNypfiiyI8A

Joyce A (2019) 10 usability heuristics applied to video games. Retrieved 5 Oct 2019, from Nielsen Norman Group website: https://www.nngroup.com/articles/usability-heuristics-applied-video-games/

Kaplan JT, Gimbel SI, Dehghani M, Immordino-Yang MH, Sagae K, Wong JD, … Damasio A (2016) Processing narratives concerning protected values: a cross-cultural investigation of neural correlates. Cerebral Cortex, bhv325. https://doi.org/10.1093/cercor/bhv325

Lotto B (2016) The new storytellers II: World-building: best practices for creating story Worlds [YouTube Video]. Retrieved from https://www.youtube.com/watch?v=jtr0AZK64Do

Manovich L (2001) The language of new media. Mit Press, Cambridge, Mass

Marks R (2017) SIGGRAPH 2017 VR interactions [YouTube Video]. Retrieved from https://www.youtube.com/watch?v=RNypfiiyI8A

McDowell A (2019) Storytelling shapes the future. J Future Stud. https://doi.org/10.6531/JFS.201903_23(3).0009

McKee R (1997) Story: substance, structure, style. ReganBooks, New York

Metry M (2017) 21 stats you should know about virtual reality (VR) in 2017|VU dream. Retrieved 1 June 2019, from VU Dream website: http://www.vudream.com/21-stats-graphs-facts-you-should-know-virtual-reality-vr-in-2017/

Milk C (2016) The era of VR storytelling [YouTube Video]. Retrieved from https://www.youtube.com/watch?v=5CqPyT3G_SE

Miller C (2014) Digital storytelling : a creator's guide to interactive entertainment. CRC Press

Murray J (2017) Hamlet on the holodeck: the future of narrative in cyberspace, (Updated Edition).The Mit Press, Cambridge, Massachusetts

Nielsen J (1994) 10 heuristics for user interface design: article by Jakob Nielsen. Retrieved 5 Oct 2019, from Nielsen Norman Group website: https://www.nngroup.com/articles/ten-usability-heuristics/

Norman DA (2013) The design of everyday things: revised and expanded edition. Basic Books, New York

Pacat C (2017) Fantasy worldbuilding: the power of detail. WQ. writers in their landscapes. Queensland Writers Centre, (Issue 258). Retrieved from http://qldwriters.org.au/wp-content/uploads/2017/08/WQ-258.pdf

Qin H, Rau P-L, Salvendy G (2009) Measuring player immersion in the computer game narrative. Int J Hum-Comput Interact 25(2):107–133. Retrieved from https://www.researchgate.net/publication/220302079_Measuring_Player_Immersion_in_the_Computer_Game_Narrative

Rizzotto L (2018) Where thoughts go. Thought Co

Ryan J, Mateas M, Wardrip-Fruin N (2015) Open design challenges for interactive emergent narrative. ICIDS 2015. Retrieved from https://www.semanticscholar.org/paper/Open-Design-Challenges-for-Interactive-Emergent-Ryan-Mateas/cb330cfe820ae380deba9f5ef906b73508e701eb

Salen K, Zimmerman E (2004) Rules of play: game design fundamentals. Retrieved 7 Oct 2019, from MIT Press website: https://books.google.pt/books/about/Rules_of_Play.html?id=UM-xyczrZuQC&redir_esc=y

Shepard M (2014) Environmental storytelling. Retrieved 7 Oct 2019, from interactive storytelling—narrative techniques and methods in video games website: http://scalar.usc.edu/works/interactive-storytelling-narrative-techniques-and-methods-in-video-games/environmental-storytelling

Slevin C (2017) Oculus connect 4|explore the VR storytelling landscape [YouTube Video]. Retrieved from https://www.youtube.com/watch?v=vOVrcP6WMiE

Stonehouse A (2014) User interface design in video games. Retrieved 5 Oct 2019, from Gamasutra.com website: https://www.gamasutra.com/blogs/AnthonyStonehouse/20140227/211823/User_interface_design_in_video_games.php

Tolkien JRR (1947) On fairy/stories. Oxford University Press

Troeth S (2015) The hidden plot device—btconfBER2015 [YouTube Video]. Retrieved from https://www.youtube.com/watch?v=sLUml3NnQwM

Unity 3D (2019) Five tips to keep it comfy in VR—unity. Retrieved 5 Oct 2019, from Unity website: https://unity3d.com/how-to/design-and-develop-vr-game

Dimensions of the Transmedia Design

André Luiz Sens

Abstract The transmediality consists of products, practices, and processes involving stories expanded in various media, either through strategic market actions or spontaneously by his prosumers. It ranges from ARGs to the complex entertainment franchise systems. In this context, it is possible to perceive an expressive design role, facing complex interfacial instances, with their respective actors, platforms, and markets. Therefore, this work, derived from an exploratory investigation that resulted in the TRADE System's conceptual framework (Sens in Design transmídia: um sistema para análise e criação das interfaces de mundos narrativos multimidiáticos 2017), aims to present and discuss the different dimensions of transmedia design, as well as their components. The results point to a discussion about the design potentials and limitations in the analysis and creation of multimedia storyworlds.

Keywords Design · Transmedia · Multimedia · Storyworld

1 Introduction

The popularity of multimedia storyworlds as Star Wars, Mickey Mouse, Harry Potter shows a phenomenon treated by Kinder (1991) as "commercial supersystem of transmedia intertextuality", which encompass the stories that transcend the limits of a single platform, establishing connections with other texts in different media, whether developed by the institutions responsible for authorship, as well as those co-produced by the public, through decoding, remixing, sharing and content creation.

The concept of transmedia, from then on and especially after the expression "transmedia storytelling" developed by Jenkins (2001, 2003, 2006), begins to designate products, practices, and processes involving stories that are expanded through various media platforms, either through strategic market actions, or spontaneously

A. L. Sens (✉)
Universidade Federal de Santa Catarina / LAB DAT, Florianópolis, Brazil
e-mail: andrelsens@gmail.com

N. Martins et al. (eds.), *Perspectives on Design and Digital Communication*, Springer Series in Design and Innovation 8, https://doi.org/10.1007/978-3-030-49647-0_9

by consumers. They range from ARGs (alternate reality games), like The Beast (from 2001), to complex franchise systems, as Matrix (launched in 1999).

This transmediality, however, presents fields that transcend strictly technical or textual issues. It also involves the expressive design role, when dealing with different and complex interfacial instances, with its different actors, platforms, and markets. In the same way that it is possible to perceive that this performance is reconfigured, based on the redefinition of some conceptual paradigms that are deeply ingrained, such as the ubiquity of visuality, the hierarchical relationship of production and consumption and the existence of definitely finished results.

In this way, it is possible to define transmedia design as responsible for the analysis and creation of the interfaces that compose the systems of a multimedia storyworld, contributing its integration, interpretation, construction, and maintenance (Sens 2017).

This work, derived from an exploratory investigation that resulted in the TRADE System's conceptual framework (Sens 2017), aims to present and reflect on the different transmedia design approaches, as well as their associated components.

2 Dimensions of the Transmedia Design

As shown in the conceptual framework (Fig. 1), I identify three transmedia design dimensions:

- *Industrial and marketing dimension*: refers to the objective elements responsible for the technical and economic viability and sustainability of a transmedia project's consumption and production interactions;
- *Informational and communicational dimension*: considers the interface configurations that contribute to the informational and communicational quality of the connections and messages that constitute the storyworld, especially those related to the efficiency of the actors' navigation between the media spaces;
- *Aesthetic and experiential dimension*: deals with the aesthetic and multisensory opportunities and mechanisms present in the interface that define experiential possibilities related to the construction and perception of a storyworld.

To this extent, it is evident that the industrial and marketing dimension corresponds to the enabling aspects to be analyzed during the design process, while others refer to the resulting interfacial aspects. Besides, the intersections shown in the image emphasize the natural correlation between the areas.

The following sections deepen each of the transmedia design approaches, as well as the associated elements.

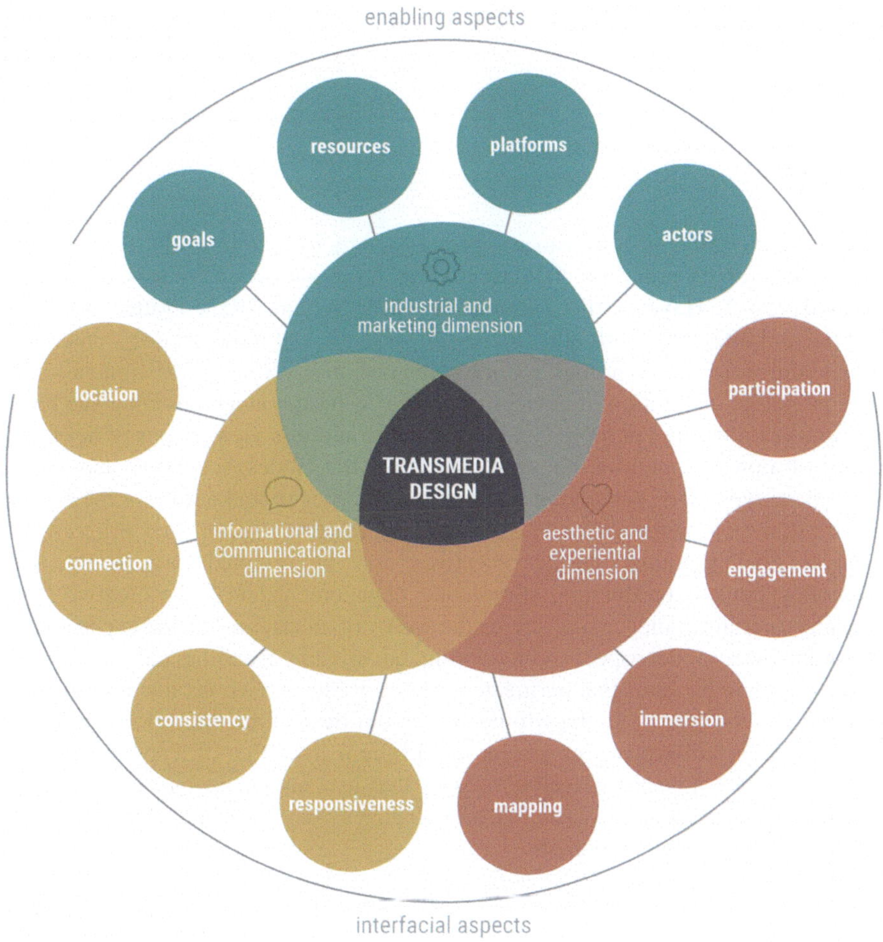

Fig. 1 Conceptual framework of transmedia design (TRADE System)

3 Industrial and Marketing Dimension

When designing a transmedia product, from an industrial-marketing perspective, it is necessary to consider the complex and dynamic nebulae associated with the production and consumption processes among the multiple media involved. About the design, these issues seem to pass basically through the analysis of objective elements (Bryson et al. 2004), that is, those that ensure the viability and technical and economic sustainability of a project.

In the case of a transmedia project, these elements are evidently associated with strategic, financial, social and technological issues that support the development of the interactions that occur between the systems of a multimedia storyworld.

Therefore, I identify the following design criteria: *goals*, *resources*, *platforms*, and *actors*.

3.1 Goals

Identifying the goals of a transmedia project seems to be one of the fundamental components for its progress. At least it is an issue addressed by several authors (Bernardo 2011; Hayes 2011; Gambarato 2013; Scolari 2013; Pratten 2015) as essential and integrated with other technical, strategic and financial decisions.

As Gambarato (2013) argues, a transmedia narrative does not constitute a juxtaposition, but an integration of devices or platforms based on a common goal. Thus, the identification of the purpose constitutes, in the author's view, as one of her foundations of a project, both in the sense of guiding the modes, scenarios, and agents involved, as well as of perceiving its function, in order to make it more interesting or relevant to your audience.

Hayes (2011) points out the objectives may be oriented towards the user (promoting content production, stimulating engagement, etc.), the creative team (reaching a certain audience, improving the ability of creatives, develop experiments, etc.) or business model aspects (entertaining, advertising, teaching, etc.).

In addition to the aims that permeate the storyworld as a whole, it is important to consider also the type of strategy to be carried out by each medium (Pratten 2015). The functions and purposes of a book are different from that of a social network, for example. So, it seems plausible to state that it is also necessary to design the specific objectives related to each platform, that contribute to the development of the transmedia project's general goals.

3.2 Resources

The construction of tangible and intangible resources is something widely recognized as fundamental for any organization, whether for its feasibility, as for the definition and implementation of competitive strategies in market situations (Barney et al. 2011). A logic that can be applied also in transmedia practices and products.

Osterwalder and Pigneur (2011) present four types of 'key resources' that must be evaluated to create and support business models: physical (equipment, buildings, etc.), intellectual (trademarks, patents, databases, etc.), human (employees, collaborators, etc.) and financial (money, lines of credit, etc.). A medium, as well as a business model, is configured inside on technological, social and economic arrangements. So, it is possible to relate it to all these different types of resources. A smartphone application, for example, has a headquarters (physical resource) with programmers, designers and other professionals (human resources) responsible for a system with codes, information and graphical interfaces (intellectual resources), sold in specialized virtual stores, from where profits come (financial resources).

Due to its multimedia nature, analyzing the resources of a transmedia project as a whole, especially the larger ones, may require a hard effort or become simply inefficient. For this reason, Hayes (2011) stresses that this assessment must be carried out from each platform. What seems more coherent, if we look at the different industrial logics of each medium, which are not necessarily integrated within the complex storyworld configurations. Besides, thinking about these narratives as a definitive whole disregards their organic and expandable character.

Although considering the pooling of all resources or investments for the total project viability does not seem to make much sense in this scenario, it seems interesting to think about how the resources generated by a medium can integrate with other compositions or even allow the creation of new ones. Profits from a literary bestseller, for example, can contribute to the production of a game belonging to the same universe. Or the fanfic author about a certain television series can be invited to script special episodes for the internet.

It is also worth noting that the current media business models offer a greater diversity of possibilities for creating and distributing content and intellectual properties. Other configurations emerge in addition to advertising, sponsorship, and sales, such as freemium models, crowdfunding, currency or virtual goods transactions, affiliate programs, among others (Anderson 2009; Hayes 2011; Scolari 2013).

Another issue that is possible to think about this equation is the intellectual and human resources coming from the collaboration and participation of the communities involved with a certain media or narrative arrangement. Constructions that are not necessarily the result of a concrete payment, but intangible satisfaction associated with a sense of contribution, self-promotion, prestige, among others (Anderson 2009).

3.3 *Platforms*

It is common for any design project to analyze and define the platforms on which the interactions with the developed artifacts or activities are carried out. In the transmedia context, this issue is amplified, particularly because it is generally associated as a multiplatform experience (Ytreberg 2009; Hayes 2011).

The concept of the platform is usually associated in the media field with a more technological inclination, as Pratten (2015), who uses the term to distinguish a printed book from an e-book, for example. However, this difference is not necessarily related only to tools, equipment and other physical and tangible components (hard technology). They also involve intellectual and intangible resources (soft technology), as well as the hardware/software correlation in the computational field (Rouse 2016). So, a book, a board game, and even a T-shirt can be considered platforms, composed of their respective hard technologies (pages, pieces, and fabric) and soft technologies (texts, signs, and prints).

The idea of a platform also depends on the media context to which it is submitted. A laptop and its software can be flagged as the platforms used to display hypermedia in an interactive museum gallery. Though in the case of a website, its platform is not restricted to just a specific computer and browser, but it expands to most mobile devices and systems with internet access.

It is also necessary to consider situations in which the same platform can subsidize different media, such as the individual applications present on the same smartphone, or possibly some specific resources within the same application (the feed and the stories of a social network, for example).

3.4 Actors

Bloggers, podcasters, vloggers, and youtubers are some new types of participation—and even profession—that emerge from new media configurations. Many of them present in the context of transmedia practices. Practitioners who are not necessarily consumers or users, as usually identified in design and marketing areas. They can also become producers and sharers, thus becoming partners, and not just customers, in the construction and consolidation of these multimedia storyworlds.

Terminologies such as 'prosumer' (Tofler 1980), 'produser' (Bruns 2006), 'wreaders' (Landow 1997) and 'VUP' (Dinehart 2011) seek to identify those subjects who present a behavior beyond passive consumption, participating directly in the creative and articulatory processes.

Faced with this varied and sophisticated participation, there is a designation that might serve as a generalization for the individuals of the transmedia ecosystem: *actors*, as Laurel (2013) makes it when compares the digital users to theater spectators that also assume the acting on cyberspace. Or when Solomon (2016) also uses the term to characterize the consumers, in order to highlight the different roles—buyers, users, influencers and others—played in each consumption experience.

However, the actor concept can also be linked beyond the dramaturgical issue. It can take the perspective on the social and economic agents—individuals and institutions—that perform activities, or else maintain relationships in a given territory (Sabourin, 2002). A perspective also assumed by Scolari (2013) about the companies, professionals, and users involved in the context of transmedia projects.

This definition also broadens the spectrum of participants within a project, who are usually treated in the literature as fans (Jenkins 2011). Although they are a very representative segment in this scenario, this association suggests the motivation that leads to transmedia practices is only related to devotion, passion or extreme enthusiasm for stories, brands or products, but can also be political, economic, educational, investigative, among many others.

4 Informational and Communicational Dimension

Faced with the complex circulation of messages and other informational materials inside a multimedia narrative ecosystem, it seems valuable to understand the design potential for navigation accessibility and usability through those spaces or their interconnections improvement, considering the storyworld prerogative. Thus, it was possible to identify the following related criteria: *location*, *connection*, *consistency*, and *responsiveness*.

4.1 Location

According to Jenkins (2009), in addition to the challenges of understanding what motivates the search for more information about a story, little is known about how it should be explained to indicate that they exist and where they are located. In this respect, the design could participate fundamentally, not only in investigating the best strategies but also in supporting the actors to understand where they are, what is available to be carried out and what directions to take.

In the need to establish a sense of orientation in these highly complex narrative spaces, information architecture can offer significant contributions. Widely consolidated in the human-computer interaction domain, this field involves the structural design of shared environments, with an emphasis on the analysis and definition of taxonomies and hierarchies (Rosenfeld et al. 2015). A very promising area not only in the information spaces of a single platform but also, as highlighted by Ding et al. (2017), in the strategic integration with other media.

In this sense, the concept of pervasive information architecture, developed by Resmini and Rosati (2011) gains relevance when addressing processes of the organization, labeling, navigation and search for content that transit or tend to propagate to other media, physical and virtual ones. Among the criteria pointed out by the authors is the placemaking, which deals with the procedures to reduce user disorientation between material, digital and hybrid environments, based on the constitution of a sense of place and the improvement of legibility and wayfinding.

Thus, in the transmedia context, the design could act in the analysis and development of resources and multisensory strategies (visual icons, sound indications, tactile cues, etc.) and verbal (labels, tags, taxonomies, etc.) that can inform the actors during their navigation between spaces. Without disregarding, however, the forms of representation and language of each medium involved.

4.2 Connection

A fundamental point regarding transmedia structures is the presence of hooks, bridges or links between the media involved (Long 2007; Ruppel 2009; Giovagnoli 2011; Beddows 2012). Elements very close to design scope, at least if we consider the creation and organization of links between texts and other content in the web field (Kalbach 2007).

Among the connection strategies usually associated with transmedia narratives are migratory clues and negative capacities. The migratory clues are tips present in the content of a medium that encourage the audience to address another, thus establishing a continuation or successive revelation of a story (Ruppel 2009). Negative capacities, on the other hand, are strategic gaps that produce in a story the sensation of mystery, uncertainty or doubt, thus provoking viewers or users to deepen their knowledge on a certain topic, leading to other expansions in the storyworld consequently (Long 2007).

Another associated concept is CTA (call-to-action), widely associated with the paths that lead users to move between media in the context of the internet, such as hyperlinks (buttons or images) that direct to a given landing page. Dena (2007), however, appropriates the term to deal precisely with multimedia spaces, like a rabbit hole in a film that leads players to a book, or a magazine QR code that gives additional related content via a mobile app.

However, all these types of connections, in general, are planned in a previously constituted scenario. They do not consider—or at least do not prioritize—the folksonomic potential of transmedia systems, that is, the possibility for the public to develop their categorizations and connections according to their repertoires, mainly in dynamic narrative structures that strongly suggest or involve the active contribution of all actors. For this reason, I propose the concept of *translink* (Sens and Palazzo 2016), which also considers the creative and organic processes inside a multimedia system. An example is hashtags. When an expression preceded by a hash is presented during the showing of a TV program and later replicated in discussions about attraction within a social network, it is established a link between media. Besides that, the hashtag emergence is not one-sided. It can be conceived by anyone in any media space, establishing communication and social around a theme, which can result in new storyworld extensions.

4.3 Consistency

Consistency (and other similar concepts like continuity and cohesion) is usually pointed out in the transmedia field (Long 2007; Scolari 2009; Giovagnoli 2011; Pratten 2015; Dowd et al. 2013) to emphasize an integration, logic or coherence between the informational components present in each storyworld medium.

However, this issue is a critical point, because of the multiplicity foundation (Jenkins 2011), which the various perspectives on a particular work that does not necessarily establish coherence with the universe thought or defended by its original authors. Not only due to the distinct narrative lines created by fans but also to the specific properties and languages of each medium. The characters in a live-action movie may not have the same characteristics as their representations in a graphic novel, even though they have similar physical and psychological attributes.

Despite the possible differences or contradictions, establishing some consistent elements seems to be something significant for keeping a world sense that allows its recognition among the actors. At least that is what Nielsen (2011) affirms about a need for maintaining a continuity relationship between the visual aspects, functions, data, and content between the different devices, in order to make a 'product family' feeling. Or according to Resmini and Rosati (2011), the definition of a logic throughout distinct media, environments and moments in which it operates.

These ideas can be intrinsically related to another transmedia basis, the seriality, which deals with the dispersion of information fragments related to the same storyworld throughout the various platforms (Jenkins 2011). This characteristic, also present in the television industry, involves, in addition to distribution, repetitiveness, that is, the reproduction of characters, scenic elements and narrative structures throughout the chapters, episodes and seasons (Zanetti 2009).

Besides this narrative resource, there are design solutions that can be applied as the use of a graphic brand and/or an identity system. In fact, Dena (2009) points out the visual identity as a recurring strategy among franchises in order to allow easy recognition of their products, even with possible formal, aesthetic or text variations among different media.

4.4 Responsiveness

Given the plurality of actors and information systems present in a storyworld, a transmedia project must provide alternatives to the varied possibilities of behavior and interaction. In design terms, it could be aligned with the responsiveness concept that reinforces the spaces' necessity of responding properly to different types of stimuli, uses, and functions.

The idea of responsive design (Marcotte 2010) emerges from the concept of responsive architecture developed by Fox and Kemp (2009), in which it presents the physical environments as a "multiple-loop" system where a continuous and constructive exchange of information is established. It deals with the structures and technologies that keep a 'dialogue' between environment and individuals, such as interfaces with motion sensors, which modify the physicality of spaces and/or the form of interaction with them.

Therefore, responsiveness goes beyond the page's adequacy in web design (Schade 2014) to deal with other issues also relevant to transmedia, related to the adaptation of the multiple narrative spaces, physical and virtual. Make them more resilient (Resmini and Rosati 2011) or malleable (Stackelberg 2011) to the needs, preferences, behaviors, strategies, and actors involved. In this sense, it is worth creating different opportunities for entering certain content, as well as making existing ones more accessible through customizations or modifications according to the personal preferences of readers, users, and other actors.

A way to make a narrative more responsive is, for example, the remodeling of audiovisual material in different media (TV, cinema, internet, etc.) and/or its modification (inclusion of subtitles, alternative languages, spaces for interaction, etc.) to meet various profiles and public behaviors.

However, responsiveness in this context does not only involve issues associated with the accessibility or usability of a system. They can function as a strategic and experiential tool in highly complex scenarios, as in the case of ARGs. As pointed out by Askwith (2006), these games have great difficulty in retaining audiences because they offer complicated narrative structures and require long-term involvement. Thus, they discuss the need to provide information resources at different stages of development of the narrative so that new people can be included, without conflicting with those that already exist.

5 Aesthetic and Experiential Dimension

Among the approaches presented here, the experiential one is of the most emphasized discussion about transmedia practices (Jenkins 2006; Norman 2010; Stackelberg 2011; Hayes 2011; Gambarato 2013; Pratten 2015). And perhaps the least accurate. In general, the experience is treated as an element that can be analyzed, designed or modeled (Hayes 2011; Pratten 2015). But, for Lopes (2012), it is just the result of interaction with the object. So, projecting it seems unviable due to the natural unpredictability of the individual subjectivity.

On the other hand, it is possible to identify in the transmediality specific cognitive, behavioral and emotional aspects that foster a sense of world and community. Thus, the experiential thing of transmedia design can focus on the analysis and creation of the opportunities and aesthetic mechanisms that contribute to it. So, I identify the criteria: *participation*, *engagement*, *immersion*, and *mapping*.

5.1 Participation

Participation is one of the central points in Jenkins' discourse (2006) and other authors (Evans 2011; Tenderich 2014; Pratten 2015) regarding transmedia practices, in which it reinforces a more active presence of the actors in the narrative development, mainly related to the act of creating, remixing and/or sharing content.

Nevertheless, the participation concept is not necessarily related to effective production. In its purest meaning, it is associated with the condition of doing or taking part in something (Cambridge Dictionary Press 2020). An idea that comes close to a broader sense of community, that suggests a plural contribution, from different profiles, as in transmedia storyworlds.

So, it seems important to verify the different participation possibilities. Hayes (2008) offers a relevant classification for that: the consumers are those who passively absorb content, the distributors send information considered interesting to their acquaintances, the critics make public comments, the editors mix and reframe the materials developed by others, and the creators are those responsible for the development of new content.

However, defining the participatory variety just by the quality or level of contribution seems limited. Among consumers, it is possible to distinguish significant behaviors according to medium specificities. Jenkins (2006), for example, classifies the TV viewer as zapper, casual, and loyal, as well Lawless and Schrader (2008) who defines the digital user as apathetic hypertext user, resource explorer, and knowledge seeker.

In a multimedia context, it makes the analysis even more complex. Pratten (2015) points out some significant participation opportunities, considering the kind of behavior in transmedia context: observing, exploring, gaming and role-playing. These actions are also associated by the author to the interaction type with other people: may be performed solo, in teams, in a community (in public by a participant, but shared or discussed with others), competitive (with people or characters), and collaborative (with the help of other ones, fictitious or not).

These activities may also vary according to the character of the community or multimedia structure involved. Askwith (2006), for example, describes the member profiles of an ARG in organizers, hunters, detectives, and lurkers. The organizers are responsible for mediating and moderating the clues and puzzles introduced during the game through blogs, databases, messaging systems and other resources and platforms used. Hunters look for information that can contribute to solving game problems and share them with the community. Detectives uncover clues and puzzles from information extracted by hunters and from discussions with other members. And lurkers passively watch the events that take place until the mystery is resolved.

Anyway, it is widely recognized that consumers, or those actors that participate passively on the storyworld, are the vast majority in transmedia projects (Dena 2009; Evans 2011; Pratten 2015), even with all possibilities of interaction and production available. Thus, I corroborate Davis (2013), who believes that the main challenge of a transmedia design product is enabling level variations of participation among the different narrative extensions.

A good way to investigate the possible roles and behaviors in each media interface, and maybe diversifying the participation in the storyworld, is through affordance theory (Gibson 1979; Gaver 1991; Norman 1999; Hartson 2003), which corresponds to the physical, logical and cultural conditions responsible for glimpsing the interaction possibilities of manners in the stories, whether related to navigation or construction of new texts (Laurel 2013). In design terms, a user not only perceives the shape of a pencil or a chair but the ways of writing and sitting. Specific to a media scenario, the characteristics of a platform may serve to indicate the type of action or participation of an actor. A QR code, for example, which appears on a television program indicates that there is extra information that can be accessed on the internet if the viewer positions the camera of its cell phone on the screen.

5.2 Engagement

As well as participation, engagement is identified as an important transmedia design criterion (Stackelberg 2011; Gambarato 2013), generally related to interactions or contributions with some cognitive and emotional bond.

However, the precision lack of this concept is notorious. Peters et al. (2009) emphasize the diversity of meaning contexts that the expression 'user engagement' is submitted, especially in the human-computer interaction field. It may be characterized as an experience, a process, a cognitive condition, an empathic connection or an interactive state.

They point out anyway an application predominance in situations where there is attention or emotion dedicated to something, as we can see on O'brien and Toms (2008), who define it as a quality of user experiences with technologies determined by a series of attributes, such as challenge, aesthetic appeal, feedback, novelty, interactivity, motivation, affection, among others. A concept close to the flow theory (Csikszentmihalyi 2008), used to describe experiences the participants reach a high level of concentration and fun.

The problem with this conceptual direction lies in its approximation, equivalence or confusion with the term 'immersion', also very widespread in transmedia context (as will be seen in the next subsection). Despite the initiatives to differentiate them (Douglas and Hargadon 2000; Brown and Cairns 2004), the results fall to parameters that are not very consensual and do not effectively present the design aspects I want to discuss here.

For this reason, I resort to the marketing field, more precisely to the work of Brodie et al. (2011), which defines engagement as a psychological state arising from the interactive and co-creative experiences of customers with a focal agent or object (such as a brand, for example) in service relationships that occur in a specific set of conditions dependent on a context. Thus, loyalty, commitment and other terminologies usually taken as a synonym for engagement are, for the authors, causes or consequences of the experience itself.

About these services, they consider mainly the new dynamic processes between the organization and the stakeholders, differently from the traditional perspective of good transactions. That is, each individual participating in these consumer relations is part of a collective construction process, in contrast to interactions only based on buying and selling. This approach reinforces the relevance for transmedia context since it meets with more horizontal hierarchical relations and prossumption behaviors.

This engagement definition based on interactions that result in some type of collaboration finds strong support in digital marketing, that refers to activities metrics and analysis that generate some material, whether given through interactions (clicks, accesses, views, etc.), as well as content from users' contributions (likes, shares, comments, etc.) (Okada 2012).

Considering the transmedia circumstances pointed out here, I assume the conceptual proposal of Brodie et al. (2011) but putting the storyworld as the focal object. So, the engagement is related to the behaviors of the actors that produce some kind of contribution to the narrative.

Pratten (2015), in this regard, offers a relevant classification, in which the existing engagement levels are scored based on the combination of the different forms of commitment and contribution in a transmedia project: attention, evaluation, affection, advocacy, and contribution. On attention condition, the actors consume the narrative content, but do not take any further action, nor are there any signs or promises of any involvement continuity. The evaluation state refers to the moment when it is being decided whether there will be any commitment, even evaluating what resources are necessary (time, money, effort, etc.). Affection considers some contribution to the narrative, such as commenting, evaluating a post, writing reviews or joining a community. The advocacy level refers to the moment when actors start to encourage others to get involved with the content through forwarding information, sharing content, completing satisfaction surveys and others. And the contribution goes from participation in forums, events, and other activities to the production of new storyworld extensions.

As can be seen, the stages of attention and evaluation do not make any contribution to the narrative and, therefore, for the criterion adopted here, they are not recognized as engaging behaviors. However, at each of these levels, even the initial ones, it is possible to notice different types of mechanisms, strategies and design arrangements that can be explored in order to contribute to engagement, from windows, highlights, advertisements and other informational and aesthetic elements of persuasion, even buttons, polls, forms that allow the creation and sharing of content.

5.3 Immersion

Another experiential aspect that permeates the field of arts, communication, interactive technologies, and recurrently transmediality is immersion (Massarolo and Mesquita 2014). According to Murray (2017), the term makes a metaphorical allusion to an aquatic dive that subjects the individual to a series of particular stimuli and sensations, as well the user in a fictional space in the media context.

Despite that, the concept also presents a conceptual imprecision, not only because of the confusion with the term engagement, as mentioned earlier but more about what would characterize cognitively this 'dive'.

Jenkins (2009, 2010), the author who defends immersion as one of the essential for transmedia projects, believes that it would be conditioned on the individual's ability to ignore reality, that is, something similar to the idea of "suspension of disbelief" (Laramée 2002).

Salen and Zimmerman (2004), however, believe this is a great fallacy, at least in the context of games. They argue the immersive process occurs in a double consciousness state, a psychic agreement which allows access to emotional stimuli of the fantasy world, without losing the real consciousness. In consonance with these arguments, Fragoso (2014) defends the "voluntary suspension of disbelief" concept, preserving the occurrence originally introduced by Coleridge (1817) in the literature field.

This argumentative line is also corroborated by Bolter and Grusin (1999) in digital media scenario with their significant theory called "remediation", which consists of the coexistence between "immediacy", the capacity for sensorial reproduction of an alternative reality, and "hypermediacy", the notion of that artificial construction. In other words, no matter how emotionally involved viewers, players or users are with the narrative of a show, a game or a website, they do not forget they are facing elements that do not belong to fictional space. The remote control, the joystick, and the mouse, apart from the delimitations offered by the screens formats, are elements that are not ignored during the experience. Even because they are fundamental for their accessibility and interaction.

Furthermore, according to Fine (1983), there is still a third mental condition to be considered, especially when it comes to immersion in narrative worlds. From RPGs universe perspective, he points out the performers assume a consciousness triple-state: as a character in the fictional world, a player in the game and a person in the real world.

These stages also seem to be significant among actors who are inside a multimedia storyworld, which may vary between real and fictional instances and can assume eventually the role of characters. Thus, I propose the following classification: (a) *Character in the storyworld*, when assumes the traits, personalities, languages and actions of a specific character in the story, whether in an ARG or a social network profile; (b) *Actor in the media context*, which is aware of the resources and operations necessary to bring the character to life; And (c) *person in the real world*, that is related to actions, postures and/or emotions aliened from the character, such as marketing strategies, personal satisfaction, among others.

However, regardless of the consciousness level, the primary idea that involves an immersive process is in the first-person relationship that the participant maintains with the narrative (Laurel 2013). A condition that is associated with the agency sense (Murray 2017), an aesthetic pleasure characterized by the ability to effectively perceive the virtuality effects from actions with its surroundings, which suggest certain freedom of choice and induce an interactor's command feeling.

A situation that is usually associated with the virtual reality and its multisensory stimuli (Bolter and Grusin 1999; Laurel 2013; Murray 2017), but also can applied to the mixed or hybrid reality (including augmented reality/virtuality), which do not necessarily imply a shift to another dimension but in approximations or intersections between the real and fictional worlds (Milgram and Colquhoun Junior 1999).

This issue may also be related to the extractability, pointed out by Jenkins (2009) as another principle of a transmedia project, precisely placed in dichotomy with his immersion concept. Is happens because the term refers to the absorption or capture of a storyworld element to reality, like a theme park gift shop purchase. The opposite of what is considered by him as a total cognitive and/or physical dive in the narrative universe. Still, when we analyze the blurred boundaries between fiction and nonfiction, this partial appropriation (physical or virtual) seems to me just a different stage of immersion, perhaps only less profound than a virtual reality experience.

Besides the analysis of immersion possibilities, it is interesting also to check the design strategies for this state. Murray (2017), for example, highlights the need for informational organization of the virtual spaces in digital narratives, such as taxonomic control, navigation consistency and limiting definitions.

But one of the most relevant cited by the author, mainly considering the complex systems of the multimedia storyworld, seems to the simulation concept. The first-person view, the spatial three-dimensionality and the reproduction of the objects' physicality are evident simulation samples present in digital games and other media with some virtual reality. However, it is possible to consider more sophisticated constructions, such as a character who communicates on a social network.

Another mechanism that can also be considered is the metaphor, defended by Salen and Zimmerman (2004) in the context of games when arguing the compatibility lack with real-world aspects does not necessarily compromise involvement and playfulness. As well as a digital space war game can give up the gravity theory in favor of gameplay, it is feasible for a theatrical spectacle uses non-figurative representations for a story on the Moon, without actually having to present any commitment to situations that involve weightlessness (shortness of breath, slower movements, etc.).

5.4 Mapping

Another crucial foundation of a transmedia narrative is "worldbuilding" (Jenkins 2009; 2010), which refers to the process of thinking about the different components or narrative systems as part of a single ecosystem. An idea based on the discourse about the encyclopedic capacity (Murray 2017) of digital narratives, which enables endless information storage and consequently emerges the need for mastering, organizing and mapping them.

This world notion can be also complemented by two other valuable properties also offered by Murray (2017) regarding digital environments: spatiality and procedurality. About the first, the author describes the human predisposition to 'spatialize' experiences. 'Visiting a website' is an expression that uses dimension metaphors that exemplify it. As well as maps, graphs, models, among other multimodal resources, which serve not only for the organization but also for the establishment of the place condition on interfaces.

The procedural aspect is associated with the rules, parameters, and instructions that allow the development of computer processes. In transmedia systems, this property may be interpreted as the criteria developed by the actors—producers and consumers—which define the elements that belong or not to the storyworld. Something analogous to the concept of "magic circle" (Salen and Zimmerman 2004), the game's imaginary frontier which establishes its own time and space with physical (board, books, cards, etc.) or intellectuals (instruction manuals or rules previously agreed) components.

About franchises, the elements considered belonging to this circle are the canons, which correspond to the rules, events and other materials accepted as belonging to the storyworld (Toledo 2012; Rosendo 2015). The term, as the religious expression, alludes to the texts assumed and worshiped by believers as the official to the story (Toledo 2012). The word 'bible' was also incorporated into the glossary of the media industry to define the documents that organize, specify and make explicit the canons, like on television to ensure narrative consistency between episodes (Dena 2009).

However, canons and their bibles suggest that the worldbuilding takes place in an imposing or regulatory manner by those responsible for the production, authorship or intellectual property of a particular work. A condition that seems to confront another transmedia criterion punctuated by Jenkins (2009, 2010), the multiplicity, which deals with alternative versions emergence of characters, events and other story components in a storyworld with deliberately inconsistent narrative properties.

On the other hand, Toledo (2012) and Rosendo (2015) converge to the understanding that canonicality is the result of a negotiation process between the actors involved. Therefore, extensions created by fans, which were not necessarily previously conceived by the original authors of the work, can eventually be made official based on a partial or integral consensus between producers and consumers in a given storyworld. Furthermore, the dynamics related to criticizing, discussing inconsistencies, defending apocryphal texts, producing alternatives, among other activities associated with what is canonized, cannot be ignored as part of the whole experience involved (Toledo 2012).

Faced with this complex scenario, the design participation does not seem to be related to the content of the canon, but in the relations or interactions existing between the actors and the canonical systems. In this regard, Rosendo (2015) offers two significant concepts: the territories (space-time correlation, characters, and events) and the maps (organization and structuring of the territories). The canons, in this case, correspond to the materials that build the territoriality of the project, while the bibles to the maps themselves.

Although there is a design contribution in the territoriality (mainly about appearance), it is in the mapping process that seems to concentrate the main one. It contemplates all the mechanisms or spaces which allow the articulation of discussions or information (canonical or not) referring to the worldbuilding. In this sense, it is possible to glimpse other instruments besides bibles, such as wikis, blogs, forums and channels on social networks (Rosendo 2015).

Another complementary aspect highlighted by Rosendo (2015) is to understand the maps should not be treated as limiting territories. They must support new conquests and territorial movements, become an updatable and dynamic document, aligned with the organicity and complexity inherent to the world sense.

Besides technological and intellectual resources, it is possible the mapping depends on human agents, as in the case of the RPG master, who not only guarantees respect for narrative prerogatives during the journey but can also be open to concessions, discussions or propositions about narrative paths proposed by other players.

In the case of an ARG, this role corresponds to the puppetmasters, despite their substantial differences. From the observation of the players' behavior during the journey, they make interference and adjustments in the stories and the game mechanisms, not necessarily to facilitate the actions (McGoginal 2008; Olbrish 2011).

Regarding franchises, this function is usually the responsibility of the transmedia producer, responsible both for maintaining the continuity of the narrative between the platforms and for stimulating opportunities to bring the audience closer to their canon (Producers Guild of America 2016).

6 Final Considerations

The dimensions presented, especially the elements associated emphasizes the participation and potential of transmedia design and can be used as criteria in the analysis and creation process of multimedia storyworld interfaces.

However, it is worth mentioning in the same way this work highlights his importance, it also demonstrates the limits of the design. After all, a project of this nature involves other areas related to the construction of the narrative objects and not just the interactions involved. A website, a book or a film has components that do not usually compete with the designer's performance, mainly in relation to texts, in their most varied types, styles, and formats, but to journalists, copywriters, screenwriters, bloggers, and other social actors who deal with the process of conceiving and telling stories.

At the same time, the intersection between the construction and the formalization of the stories cannot be denied. That is, even if the work of the designer does not normally involve the design of a fictional script, the characters costumes, the signs 'typography, the scenarios' appearance, and the menu buttons layout definitely influence how the story is perceived and experienced, which contributes to the narrative development itself.

Furthermore, it is not just about narrative systems created by screenwriters and designed by a priori designers, but dynamic organisms in continuous expansion and constant maintenance by the actors involved. In this sense that perhaps lies one of the main roles of transmedia design, which is to provide opportunities and encourage the entry of new agents and content to these multimedia universes, while managing and optimizing the interactions developed from the emergence of new components.

References

Anderson C (2009) Free. Hachette Books, New York

Askwith I (2006) This is not (just) an advertisement: understanding alternate reality games. MIT Convergence Culture Consortium

Barney JB, Ketchen DJ, Wright M (2011) The future of resource-based theory: revitalization or decline? J Manag 37(5):1299–1315

Beddows E (2012) Consuming transmedia: how audiences engage with narrative across multiple story modes (Faculty of Life And Social Sciences). Swinburne University Of Technology

Bernardo N (2011) The producer's guide to Transmedia. Beactive Books, Lisboa

Bolter DJ, Grusin R (1999) Remediation. MIT Press, Cambridge

Brodie RJ, Hollebeek LD, Juric´B (2011) Customer engagement: conceptual domain, fundamental propositions, and implications for research. J Serv Res 14(3):25–271

Brown E, Cairns P (2004) A grounded investigation of game immersion. Chi ea'04. ACM, New York, pp 1297–1300

Bruns A (2006) Towards produsage: futures for user-led content production. Cultural attitudes towards communication and technology. Tartu, QUT, pp 275–284

Bryson JR, Daniels PW, Rusten G (2004) Design workshops of the World (Working Paper). Oslo. Retrieved from http://org.uib.no/design/a5304.pdf

Csikszentmihalyi M (2008) Flow: the psychology of optimal experience (harper perennial modern classics). Harper Perennial, New York

Dena C (2007) Patterns in cross-media interaction design: it's much more than a URL. In CMID'07: the first international conference on crossmedia interaction design, pp 4–10. Umeå

Dena C (2009) Transmedia practice: theorizing the practice of expressing a fictional World across distinct media and environments (digital cultures program). University of Sidney

Cambridge University Press (2020) Cambridge Dictionary. Retrieved from http://dictionary.cambridge.org/

Coleridge ST (1817) Biographia literaria. Retrieved from http://www.english.upenn.edu

Davis CH (2013) Audience value and transmedia products. In: Storsul T., Krumsvik A. (eds) Media innovations. Nordicom, Göterborg, pp 175–190

Dinehart S (2011) Defining interactive narrative design 2. Retrieved from https://web.archive.org/web/20110227230834/http://narrativedesign.org/2009/06/defining-interactive-narrative-design-2/

Ding W, Lin X, Zarro M (2017) Information architecture: the design and integration of information spaces, 2nd edn. Morgan and Claypool Publishers

Douglas Y, Hargadon A (2000) The pleasure principle: immersion, engagement, flow. Hypertext'00. ACM, San Antonio, pp 153–160

Dowd T, Fry M, Niederman M, Steiff J (2013) Storytelling across worlds: transmedia for creatives and producers. Focal Press, Burlington

Evans E (2011) Transmedia television: audiences, new media, and daily life. Routledge, Nova York

Fine GA (1983) Shared fantasy: role-playing games as social worlds. The University of Chicago Press, Chicago

Fox M, Kemp M (2009) Interactive architecture. Princeton Architectural Press, New York

Fragoso S (2014) Imersão em games narrativos. Galaxia 1(28):58–69

Gambarato RR (2013) Transmedia project design: theoretical and analytical considerations. Baltic Screen Med Rev 81–100

Gaver W (1991) Technology affordances. In: CHI. ACM, New York, pp 79–84

Gibson JJ (1979) The ecological approach to visual perception, 2nd edn. Houghton Mifflin, Boston

Giovagnoli M (2011) Transmedia storytelling: imagery, shapes and techniques. ETC Press, Pittsburgh

Hartson R (2003) Cognitive, physical, sensory, and functional affordances in interaction design. Behav Inf Technol 22(5):315–338

Hayes G (2008) The myth of web 2.0 non-participation. Retrieved from https://www.socialmediatoday.com/content/myth-web-20-non-participation

Hayes GP (2011) How to write a transmedia production bible: 2011. 20 p. Australia: Screen Australia. Retrieved from http://www.screenaustralia.gov.au/getmedia/2b6459ab-3d05-4607-8fc6-10e1a8fff13d/transmedia-prod-bible-template.pdf

Jenkins H (2001) Convergence? I diverge. Retrieved from https://www.technologyreview.com/s/401042/convergence-i-diverge

Jenkins H (2003) Transmedia storytelling: moving characters from books to films to video games can make them stronger and more compelling. Retrieved from http://www.technologyreview.com/news/401760/transmedia-storytelling

Jenkins H (2006) Convergence culture: where old and new media collide. New York University, Nova York

Jenkins H (2009) The revenge of the origami unicorn: seven principles of transmedia storytelling (well, two actually. Five more on Friday). Retrieved from http://henryjenkins.org/blog/2009/12/revengeoftheorigamiunicorn.html

Jenkins H (2010) Transmedia storytelling and entertainment: an annotated syllabus. Continuum 24(6):943–958

Jenkins H (2011) Transmedia 202: further reflections. Retrieved from http://henryjenkins.org/blog/2011/08/definingtransmediafurtherre.html

Kalbach J (2007) Designing web navigation, 1st edn. O'Reilly Media, Sebastopol

Kinder M (1991) Playing with power in movies, television, and video games: from Muppet babies to teenage mutant ninja turtles. University of California Press, Califórnia

Laurel B (2013) Computers as theater. Addison-Wesley Publishing Co, Massachusetts

Landow GP (1997) Hypertext 2.0: the convergence of contemporary critical theory and technology (Parallax: revisions of culture and society), 2nd edn. The Johns Hopkins University Press, Baltimore

Laramée FD (2002) Game design perspectives. Charles River Media, Rockland

Lawless KA., Schrader P (2008) Where Do we go now? Understanding research on navigation in complex digital environments. In: Coiro J et al. (ed) Handbook of research on new literacies. Lawrence Erlbaum Associates, Nova York, pp 267–296

Long GA (2007) Transmedia storytelling: business, aesthetics and production at the Jim Henson Company (Master of Science in Comparative Media Studies). Massachusetts Institute of Technology

Lopes EC (2012) Uma (re)visão do conceito de experiência do usuário: a experiência como narrativa (Curso de Especialização em Comunicação Digital). Universidade de São Paulo

Marcotte E (2010) Responsive web design. Retrieved from https://alistapart.com/article/responsive-web-design

Massarolo J, Mesquita D (2014) Imersão em realidades ficcionais. Revista Contracampo 29(1):46–64

McGonigal J (2008) The puppet master problem: design for real-World, mission-based gaming. Retrieved from http://www.electronicbookreview.com/thread/firstperson/curtained

Milgram P, Colquhoun Junior H (1999) A taxonomy of real and virtual World display integration. In: Ohta Y, Tamura H (eds) Mixed reality: merging real and virtual worlds. Springer, Berlim, pp 5–27

Murray J (2017) Hamlet on the holodeck. The MIT Press, Cambridge

Norman DA (1999) Affordance, conventions, and design. Interact 6(3):38–43

Norman DA (2010) The transmedia design challenge: technology that is pleasurable and satisfying. Interact—Tangible Interact = Form + Comput 17(1):12–15

Nielsen J (2011) Transmedia design for the 3 screens (make that 5). Retrieved from http://www.nngroup.com/articles/transmedia-design-for-3-screens/

O'Brien HL, Toms EG (2008) What is user engagement? A conceptual framework for defining user engagement with technology. J Assoc Inf Sci Technol 59(6):938–955

Olbrish K (2011) The ABC's of ARGs: alternate reality games for learning. Retrieved from http://elearnmag.acm.org/archive.cfm?aid=2019544

Osterwalder A, Pigneur Y (2011) Business model generation, 1st edn. Alta Books

Okada SL (2012) Web analytics: modelos de métricas de engajamento em mídias emergentes. Revista Brasileira de Marketing 10(3):107–126

Peters C, Castellano G, de Freitas S (2009) An exploration of user engagement in HCI. Affine'09. ACM, Boston, pp 1–3

Pratten R (2015) Getting started with transmedia storytelling: a practical guide for beginners, 2nd edn. Createspace Independent Publishing Platform, Seattle

Producers Guilds of America (2016) Code of credits—new media. Retrieved from http://www.producersguild.org/?page=cocnmtransmedia

Resmini A, Rosati L (2011) Pervasive information architecture: designing cross-channel user experiences book review. IEEE Trans Prof Commun 54(4):408–409

Rouse M (2016) Platform. Retrieved from http://searchservervirtualization.techtarget.com/definit

Rosendo N (2015) The map is not the territory: bible and canon in the transmedial world of Halo. Image—J Interdiscip Image Sci 1(22):54–64

Rosenfeld L, Morville P, Arango J (2015) Information architecture, 4th edn. O'Reilly Media, Sebastopol

Ruppel M (2009) Narrative convergence, cross-sited productions and the archival dilemma. Convergence 15(3):281–298

Sabourin E (2002) Desenvolvimento territorial e abordagem territorial—conceitos, estratégias e atores. In: Sabourin E, Teixeira OA (eds) Planejamento e desenvolvimento dos territórios rurais—conceitos, controvérsias, experiências. Embrapa Informação Tecnológica, Brasília, pp 21–37

Salen K, Zimmerman (2004) Rules of play. MIT Press

Schade A (2014) Responsive web design (RWD) and user experience. Retrieved from https://www.nngroup.com/articles/responsive-web-design-definition/

Scolari C (2009) Transmedia storytelling: implicit consumers, narrative worlds, and branding in contemporary media production. Int J Commun 586–606

Scolari CA (2013) Narrativas transmedia. Centro Libros PAPF, Barcelona

Sens AL (2017) Design transmídia: um sistema para análise e criação das interfaces de mundos narrativos multimidiáticos (Doutorado em Design, Universidade Federal de Santa Catarina). Retrieved from https://repositorio.ufsc.br/handle/123456789/187564

Sens AL, Palazzo LAM (2016) As hashtags como expressão da cultura transmidiática. In: Calegari C (ed) Cibersociedade: Fragmentos e reflexões. Deviant, Erechim, pp 113–122

Solomon MR (2016) O Comportamento do Consumidor: Comprando, Possuindo e Sendo, 11th edn. Bookman companhia editora LTDA

Stackelberg P (2011) Creating transmedia narratives: the structure and design of stories told across multiple media (School of Information Design and Technology). State University Of New York, Institute Of Technology

Tenderich B (2014) Transmedia branding. Eimo, Frankfurt

Tofler A (1980) *Choque do futuro,* 2nd edn. São Paulo

Toledo GM (2012) *Aspectos Canônicos da Narrativa Transmidiática em Lost* (Programa de Pós-Graduação em Imagem e Som). Universidade de São Carlos

Ytreberg E (2009) Extended liveness and eventfulness in multi-platform reality formats. New Media & Society 11(4):467–485

Zanetti D (2009) Repetição, serialização, narrativa popular e melodrama. Matrizes 2(2):181–194

Improving Sleep Awareness: Design and Development of an M-Health App

Mafalda Monteiro, Marina Moreira, Telma Arzileiro, and Pedro Amado

Abstract The current research on M-health shows a poor quality of sleep in Portugal. This paper presents the development of a high-fidelity visual prototype of a mobile application—Moon App—that aims to improve the user's sleep through self-assessment. Developing it was the result of our concern surrounding the lack of sleep being experienced in today's society. The app intends to offer both informative and practical content, and also to promote a self-analysis of the user sleep performance. By establishing a connection between the users' dreams or nightmares, and the overall quality of the sleep. Considering these goals, the features were defined with the objective of giving the user a distinct experience in the fields already mentioned. The methodology adopted consisted mainly of an User-Centered Design approach to software development and evaluation: an initial analysis of the state of the art of other mobile applications within the sleep domain; exploratory data-gathering interviews with end-users; the information collected was used for the development of the features, based on a persona and scenarios of use; and finally we've conducted usability tests on the prototype. The feedback of the dream log and the calendar features implemented was positive. The majority of users would use these features to register their dreams and use the log to self-access their sleep quality history.

Keywords Invision studio · Interaction design · Mental health · Usability evaluation

---

M. Monteiro · M. Moreira · T. Arzileiro · P. Amado (✉)
Faculty of Fine Arts, University of Porto, Porto, Portugal
e-mail: pamado@fba.up.pt

M. Monteiro
e-mail: mafalda.ines.monteiro@gmail.com

M. Moreira
e-mail: marinamoreira.mra@gmail.com

T. Arzileiro
e-mail: telma_019@hotmail.com

P. Amado
i2ADS–Research Institute of Art, Design and Society, Porto, Portugal

N. Martins et al. (eds.), *Perspectives on Design and Digital Communication*, Springer Series in Design and Innovation 8, https://doi.org/10.1007/978-3-030-49647-0_10

1 Introduction

Before conceptualizing *Moon* App, it was important to understand furthermore the raising phenomenon of M-Health applications and perceive what could be significant to develop on this vast topic.

In the matter of M-Health, Prof. John Orzechowski, clinical assistant professor at UIC, tells how "Mobile Health continues to reach heightened interest levels and activity across the globe". He says that,

> (…) its solutions hold the promise to provide new, innovative care access and delivery models that produce better outcomes, and that M-Health is being viewed increasingly by many as an important technology metaphor to achieving a patient-centric paradigm change. (Orzechowski 2014)

After realizing the importance of developing an app surrounding the quality of sleep, due to observing data providing further acknowledgment of the increasing of unhealthy sleeping routines, it was decided to work on the matter of the dream. It was a mutual goal to approach this topic with a less explored area on mobile applications since there were already many well accomplished on the sleeping field.

On the following sections we'll showcase data concerning the sleep habits of the current society provided by platforms such as DECO; Afterwards, focusing on the premise of the app, there will be shown studies surrounding the connections between dreaming and sleep routine; With the purpose of studying the current market, it will be shown our research on existing applications of the same field to compare their weaknesses and strengths; Closing our research, it will be presented the concept of our application and the features developed; Usability tests were conducted on May to evaluate the experience of possible users and then we provide the results and the improvements realized after analyzing the data collected.

2 M-Health as a Tool for Behavior Change

We understand that the connection between sleep quality and electronic devices presents an open space for discussion. The debate upon the relationship between mobile devices and sleep quality is a worldwide matter that focuses mostly on the problematic use of mobile devices, nevertheless, recent studies show us that a core subject to be explore is how to relate with them.

A research conducted by Shin et al., *Mobile Phone Interventions for Sleep Disorders and Sleep Quality: Systematic Review,* reveals that m-health applications can be beneficial to improve sleep disorders and sleep quality. Through a strict study selection criteria of research articles, published between 1983 and 2016 and a primary selection of 2674 articles from four electronic databases (PubMed/Medline, Scopus, Web of Science and EBSCOhost), the researchers focused only on mobile phone interventions to determine the effectiveness of mobile technology in sleep quality, quantity and sleep disorder. The result "supports the evidence that mobile technology-based interventions are an effective tool to improve symptoms of sleep disorders and quality of sleep than traditional intervention without a mobile phone" as well as the potential of mobile devices as a tool for behavior change.

Grigsby-Toussaint et al. evaluated the role of m-health applications has a tool for motivating behavior change. To examine the integration of behavior constructs in sleep applications, a selection of 330 unique applications were found in the Google Play Store and iTunes App Store, in September 2015. The descriptive analysis of sleep applications performed by the researchers reveals that although a few embodied features to support behavior change, at the time of the selection app process, "an opportunity exists to encourage sustainable sleep hygiene practices using mobile phones Grigsby-Toussaint et al. (2017)."

As far as our best knowledge, considering the lack of research that aims to investigate directly the effectiveness of m-health applications in sleep quality, the above researches represent major references to minimize our concerns regarding not only a non-problematic use of mobile devices before sleep, furthermore the potential benefits of m-health applications. Therefore, as a growing market m-health applications represents an opportunity to take advantage of mobile phones to meet users' needs.

3 Sleep/Sleeping Habits Today

A survey made by *Deco Proteste* (DECO 2016) verified certain concerning numbers about the common sleeping habits of the Portuguese: two-thirds responded that, on average, they didn't have a good night of sleep. These numbers have duplicated since the last survey made by the same source back in 2004, which reveals a tendency of worst sleeping habits by the Portuguese in 12 years. These habits seem to progressively affect the daily life and routines since 4 in 10 answered that the lack of sleep made them experience concerning somnolence that influenced their productivity and increased risks of accidents (Garbarino et al. 2016). These tendencies, verified globally, need to be treated as a major global problem since the lack of sleep is not only associated with short-term negative effects such as accidents and illnesses but is also associated with a decrease in the general well-being.[1] The quality of sleep and the nightmare frequency have a direct relationship to well-being (Blagrove et al. 2004).

In 2019, a survey published by the Portuguese newspaper *Público* revealed more recent statistics concerning these matters (Mendes 2019). In this article, the pulmonologists Susana Sousa and Silvia Correia explain that even with the increasing awareness of the connection of bad sleeping habits with diseases, most people don't

[1] In 2003, professor and dream researcher Allan Hobson explain that even when humans dream, the brain is active. Through experiments he defends that understanding how we create dream´s narratives helps to understand the nature of consciousness and that dreams offer insight into humans waking lives. His research focuses not only on the dream's story itself but also in correlation with dreamer´s daily life experience.

attribute to healthy sleep the same importance as to healthy eating habits, or regular exercise.

With the statistics already mentioned, it leaves no doubt that this is an issue that needs to be tackled in the current young generations, as this problem will aggravate in the future. There is a necessity of raising awareness for better sleeping habits and studies surrounding the sleeping matter.

4 Connection Between Dreams and Quality of Sleep

On the first research, at a North-American sleep research platform, Sleep Foundation, can be found dozens of articles discussing everything surrounding the sleeping matter. At the most researched topics on the website, it is found at first place the following article questioning, "Do dreams affect how well you sleep?", which provides further acknowledgement how this connection between sleeping and dreams raises questions and curiosity of many people. Although the article claims that disturbing dreams don't affect how much time a person spends in different stages of sleep or the number of times it is awakened, there is still a concern that as they mention, (…) "there's no question that nightmares have ramifications that last even after you wake up (…) those scary images can affect your mood and behavior the next day, causing the equivalent of a bad-dream hangover Sleep Foundation (2019)."

Following this statement, the article tells that a person may feel less well rested as an aftermath of how long it takes to fall back to sleep after experiencing a nightmare. They concluded by referring furthermore how dreaming impacts an individual's well-being, and how it content can change people's sleeping experience, arguing that, "Research shows that good sleepers often describe their dreams as being more pleasant and joyful, while people who suffer from insomnia tend to have fewer positive emotions associated with their dreams" (…)

As there are studies about those possible connections, there are plenty of other questions about this topic that remain scientifically unanswered. Perhaps more complex to study is the actual content of the dreams, do they matter? Do they mean anything? Questions like these are answered in an issue of New Scientist magazine, in the article, "Dreams decoded: 6 answers to the mysteries of the sleeping mind", written by Rowan Hooper, who states that dreams play a key role in boosting creative thought, memory, learning and even mental health (Hooper 2018a, b). Answering the question if dreams have any meaning, Hooper states:

> (…) what you dream about and the emotional tone of the dream probably reflects what your brain considers important. Research shows that if you play Tetris all day long, your brain will decide that Tetris is what you need to dream about. If you are anxious about something, your brain may well give you a dream with anxiety as the dominant emotion. (Hooper 2018a, b)

He further explains Mark Blagrove's view on the topic, about how analyzing your dreams could be therapeutic and insightful, nevertheless Hooper states that further experimentations would be needed to test whether dreams convey important personal information.

Considering the following information provided by these resources, it was a mutual goal to approach the quality of sleep matter with a less explored area on mobile applications. Dreams represent something significantly personal to everyone, and learning about the connections of each dreams with daily life is a responsibility of each individual. Developing an application had to have the concern of providing a platform adaptable to everyone's experiences.

5 Moon: A Concept Application

The Moon application gives the user exercises and instructions for a better sleep routine. It explores the possible connections between our dreams and the quality of our sleep. The goal is to context the theme throw an analysis in order to provide an insight able to contribute to the development of the app and future advances. (Hobson 2002). Here, the developer team, being only specialized in Design, haven't searched for a scientific approach, but have given priority to designing the user experience in the development of a self-analysis tool for the users' sleeping health. The app presents three main features: (a) the first presents exercises and instructional plans to the users, aiming to promote better sleeping habits; (b) the user is invited to record/track his dreams in a dream log in order to promote a deeper insight on his dreams; (c) the final overall dream log activity can be viewed or reviewed in a global calendar.

In a first approach to the theme, a search was conducted on the Google Play Store, to understand what the market had to offer in the M-Health/Sleeping area. After choosing three key applications,[2] the aim was to study the features already accomplished by those apps and see what it would offer to the user. A final app was chosen to serve as a study case. Interviews with *Shleep*[3] users were made to understand what strengths and elements could be improved in a future app. This also allowed for the development of the personas, scenarios and the development of original features in a User-Centered Design approach (Cooper et al. 2014). Then the steps to develop *Moon* were presented through those interviews, which resulted in the present prototype application. To evaluate the usability of the app, two separated sessions with potential *Moon* users were developed. This was essential to test these features and understand what the user needed.

---

[2]The choice criteria of these key applications was based on the availability to test, considering their potentiality in further analysis.

[3]Mobile application. Available online at https://play.google.com/store/apps/details?id=com.shleep.shleepb.

6 State of the Art in Sleep Monitoring Mobile Applications: An Analysis of Three Study Cases

In terms of the digital applications universe, mostly directed to the sleeping area, a considerable number of apps were found in which the aim was to improve and control the user's sleep. We've searched Google Play Store using the keyword "sleep" in January 2020. From the first twenty-five applications presented were selected eight as study cases, all have English as their reading or audio language. Their characteristics, positive and negative, were considered in the conception of *Moon*. Their names are *Pzizz*,[4] *Sleep*,[5] *Sleepo*,[6] *Sleep Away*,[7] *Sleep Monitor*,[8] *Sleep Time*,[9] *Sleep Town*[10] and *Tide*.[11] Almost all of this sample presents sound as one of their features, four of them use relaxing and calming sounds as the main feature and a way of improving the sleep quality (they are *Pzizz*, *Sleep*, *Sleepo* and *Tide*). Two of them also use meditation as an immersive space for relaxation. Another feature that has proven to be common is the alarm clock, five apps in this sample offer an option for the user to set the bedtime and wake up time. Three of them also monitor sleep habits and analyze patterns to calculate sleep cycles, in order to present the user the best time to go to bed and the time to wake up, feeling healthy (they are *Sleep Away, Sleep Monitor* and *Sleep Time*). One important characteristic verified in this analysis is the distance created between the user and the electronic device during sleep time. Although there is an interaction between the two, this action is never direct, in a way that the user doesn't need to continuously touch or look at his device to use the app. This brings us to another one of the applications selected, who presents features that challenge the user to fight his phone addiction (this app is *Sleep Tow*). The app aims to maintain a regular sleep schedule for the user and avoid the contact between him and the electronic device during sleep hours. Through the search conducted of the apps analyzed we identified another application that shows characteristics very close to what we intend to develop. The app's name is *Shleep*, the only coaching sleep app that we could find, also offers relaxing sounds and meditation exercises to help the user to establish a calm environment for sleeping. This app presents two characteristics that we find very useful in the sleeping matter, the learning concept through lessons about healthy sleep habits and the practical content like breathing exercises and tips to help the user fall asleep.

After an initial analysis of the online information and initial testing of the apps in the mobile environment, we've gathered certain characteristics of the applications

[4]Idem at https://play.google.com/store/apps/details?id=com.pzizz.android.

[5]Idem at https://play.google.com/store/apps/details?id=com.bendingspoons.sleep.

[6]Idem at https://play.google.com/store/apps/details?id=net.relaxio.sleepo.

[7]Idem at https://play.google.com/store/apps/details?id=com.samuelbanas.sleepaway.

[8]Idem at https://play.google.com/store/apps/details?id=com.sleepmonitor.aio.

[9]Idem at https://play.google.com/store/apps/details?id=ru.olegfilimonov.sleeptime.

[10]Idem at https://play.google.com/store/apps/details?id=seekrtech.sleep.

[11]Idem at https://play.google.com/store/apps/details?id=io.moreless.tide.

Table 1 Analysis of the applications studied

	Audio used as main feature	Avoid direct contact with the device (sleep hours)	Visuals suitable for night time (colors not too bright)	Practical content	Informative content (learning concept)	Show progress (track sleep hours)
Pzizz	+	+	+	–	–	–
Shleep	+	+	–	+	+	+
Sleep	+	+	+	–	–	–
Sleepo	+	+	–	–	–	–
Sleep away	–	+	+	–	–	–
Sleep monitor	–	+	+	–	–	+
Sleep time	–	+	+	–	–	–
Sleep town	–	+	+	–	–	+
Tide	+	+	+	+	–	–

studied and compared them in the table presented next. We used the symbol positive (+) to indicate those applications where the aspect presented on the top of the table exists and the symbol negative (−) in those where it doesn't (Table 1).

After the analysis and use of the three applications, *Shleep* was the app chosen as a case of study. We have selected and conducted 13 interviews with users of this app. All the information collected until this point was used to plan how *Moon* could answer the real user's needs, using the strengths of the applications studied and minimizing their weaknesses. The first feature presented is the center of the app—the sleeping plan. It consists of different plans of audio with informative and practical content (each plan presents a different theme). To avoid direct contact, distract, or excite the user in relaxation times, the device's screen is turned off once the user starts to listen to the audio. Every time the user finishes a plan he or she gets a badge. This gamification element presents a way to motivate and promote the constant use of the app (Lister et al. 2014). The badges come in the form of characters with distinct personalities. Another main feature is the dream log. Resembling a diary for dreams, users can also share it with friends. This feature allows the user to classify his dreams or nightmares. Then this information is presented in the calendar which allows for the user to compare in a temporal scale the periods in which more dreams or nightmares were registered (Fig. 1).

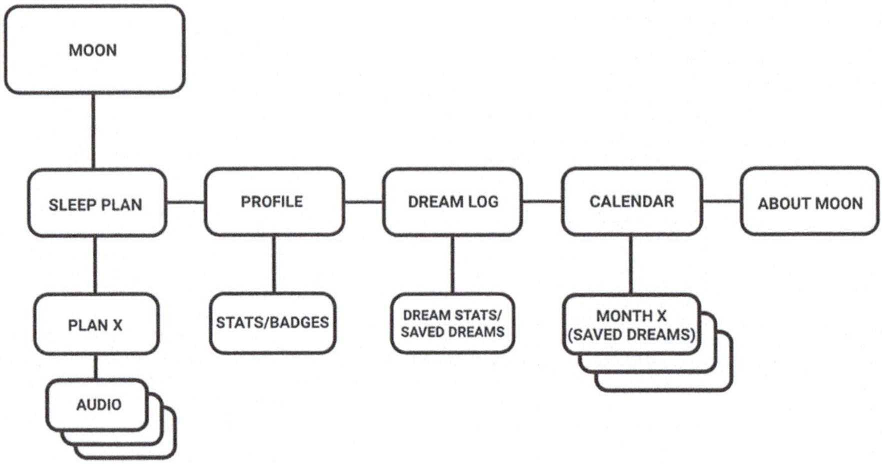

Fig. 1 Application structure, *Moon* sitemap

7 Development and Evaluation of Moon: A High Fidelity Interactive Prototype in Invision Studio

From the data gathered in the initial research and interviews, we knew that the persona's goals consist of sleeping better and at a regular schedule. The persona also aims to feel more energetic to complete the tasks that are asked of him during the day. Having trouble to fall asleep the persona feels that anxiety and stress may be influencing negatively his sleeping hours. The main occasion for the persona to use the app it's at the end of the day, specifically before turning into bed. Another possible use case scenario is in the morning, after waking up, this way the persona can register the dream(s). Having this persona's desires, needs and behaviors as a primary target user in mind, the app's system architecture and visual design were developed (Fig. 2).

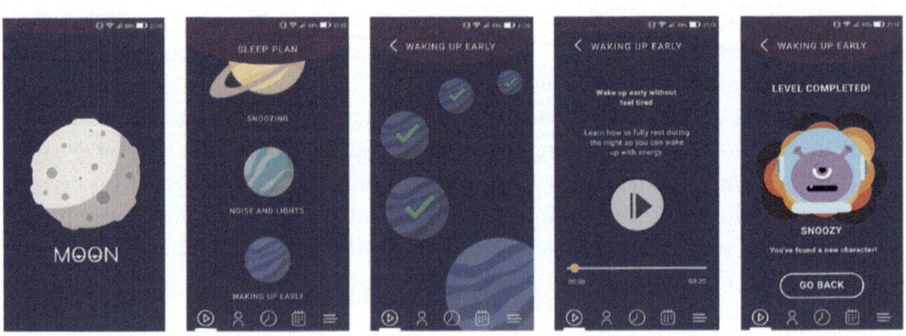

Fig. 2 High fidelity visual prototype of *Moon*

8 Main Features and Prototype

From the state of the art review and through the studies made, the main features of the app were implemented to then be tested with users. One of these features, already presented, is the sleeping plan that works along with the badges. Through the study of other applications, it was decided to encourage motivation and so the badges represent distinct characters so that the user would want to collect a specific one. The dream log is another important feature. It was developed to correlate the dreams and nightmares in a personal dreams' archive. The calendar was thought of so that the users could perceive visually their dreams/nightmares through different periods of their life's. These three features can be engaging to the user experience and can also allow a self-evaluation. Keeping in mind the study cases, it's intended for *Moon* to be capable of providing informative content but also entertainment to the user (Figs. 3, 4 and 5).[12]

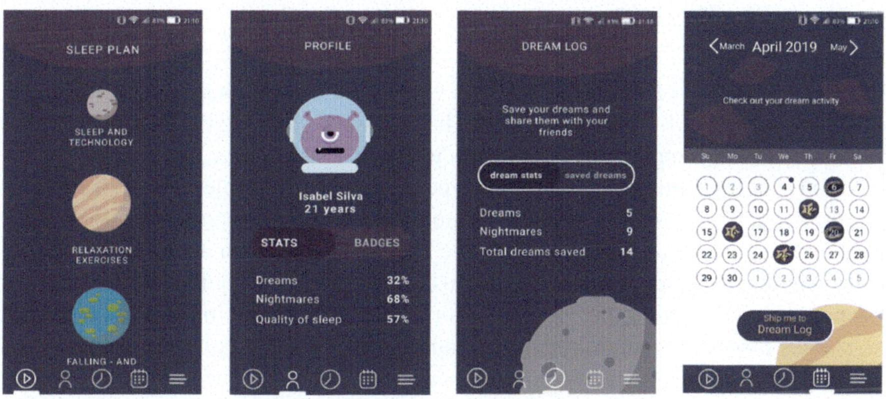

Fig. 3 High fidelity visual prototype of *Moon*: Audio Task

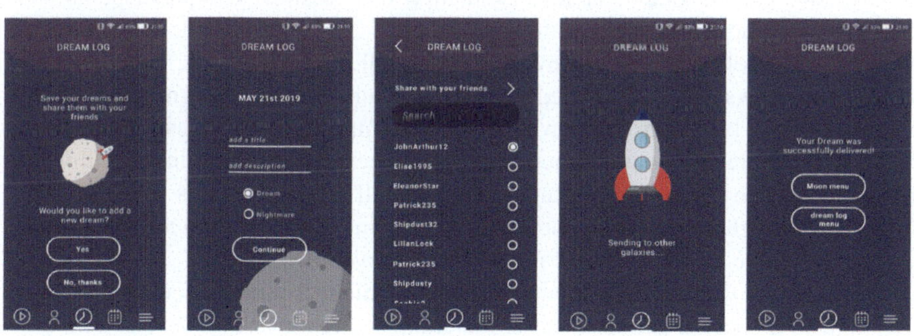

Fig. 4 High fidelity visual prototype of *Moon*: Dream Log

[12]It's important to note that the application aims to educate the users about the tools necessary to improve their quality of sleep, the app encourages the users to progressively detach from electronic devices, as it is known their influence on sleep. With that concern, the app presents features such

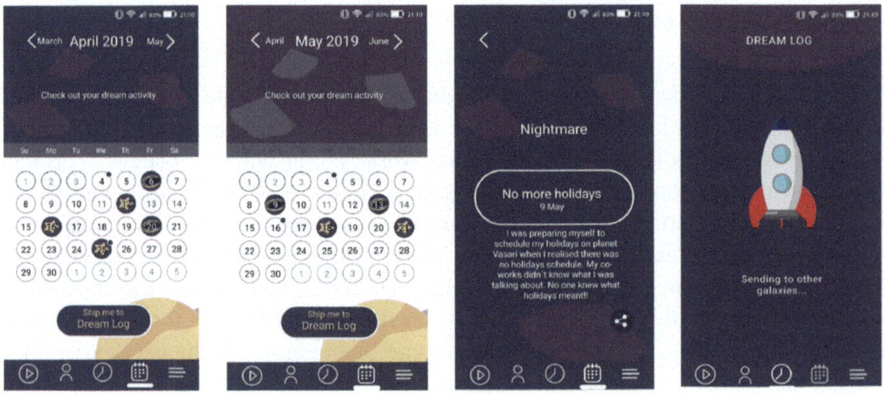

Fig. 5 High fidelity visual prototype of *Moon*: Calendar

9 Usability Evaluation

A primary analysis of the initial 13 interviews of the apps analyzed revealed that most of the people who were interviewed had irregular sleeping habits and the belief that if they could improve sleeping habits it would also improve their health.

Moon is a high-fidelity visual prototype designed and implemented in Invision Studio. After a primary analysis of the mobile prototype app, concerns were identified and required clarification during the usability tests, such as the possibility to rearrange the visual sequence of the audio clips to provide easy flowing progress. It was necessary, as well, to prove whether or not the user found interest in consulting the badges from the feature dream log, and also if verifying, consulting and adding dreams were eligible tasks through the dream log and the calendar.

The usability tests of the prototype Moon were conducted in two sessions, each with five participants following the guidelines proposed by Rubin and Chisnell (2008) in a classic "one on one" usability evaluation test session. The participants were students and student-workers, with ages ranging 20–44 years old. The tests took place, in a controlled academic environment for all the participants.

The interviews were conducted using a structured script, designed in advance. It started with a brief introduction to the subject matter, in which every participant consented to be recorded and filmed for the purposes explained. Using the "thinking aloud" technique suggested by Rubin and Chisnell the participants were invited to share their thoughts throughout the usability tests in order to supply a further insight of the experience and to correlate it with the observed behavior.

The usability tests were conducted upon three distinct scenarios, each one corresponding to a specific group of tasks matching the features in analysis. The tasks

as black screen while listening to audio and lessons about using a phone mobile at night, it was important as designers to create an educative app that could also provide an enjoyable collective learning experience.

goals and respective scenarios were described to the participants equally and beforehand. Each session was held individually and lasted, approximately, fifteen minutes each, followed by a debriefing session interview and SUS Questionnaire (Brooke 1996).

10 Results and Discussion

The first batch of usability tests provided a significant upgrade to the prototype. While allowing the developers to compare one session to another, it became clear that not only were the improvements necessary, but they also allowed verifying that the concerns related to the first session were suppressed.

Analyzing the data collected from the global usability tests it is possible to confirm that the progress of the three features impacts the way participants engaged with the app.

Through the badges, it was expected to encourage the participant's curiosity by describing badges or characters. The users were asked to explore this feature and, at the first session, the average time spent on this task was 1: 08 min while at the second session there was an increased average time of 1: 40 min. This happened because the guidance on the second session was null, this factor gave us a hint about the accessibility of the badges collected, as Participant X hinted: "I really like the illustrations, I am going to explore everything".

A further improvement would be a button who leads the user (after finishing a plan) directly to the badges.

During the first test, the calendar presented constraints regarding the navigation of one month to another with a swiping action as all of the 5 participants referred. This interaction was changed to a simple tap interaction and tested. In the second usability test, none of the participants referred to this as an issue. The calendar proved to be a way of self-evaluation of sleeping habits useful to provide data related to the participant own life, as Participant Y mentioned out loud: "(…) to have a notion of how you are mentally and create a connection with other things in life".

So far, the results of the usability tests revealed that the prototype is on the right path, aware that there is yet much work to do and feeling positive about directions for further development.

11 Conclusion

The *Moon* app's first steps were accomplished by the study cases of apps highly presented on the market. Observing those features determined what would be best to implement on an app concerning sleeping habits, it was a goal to use the strengths of the apps studied and minimizing their weaknesses.

Following those premises, we created *Moon* with its focus on improving the quality of sleep of the users and providing an opportunity for the user to study the possible connections of their dreams and sleeping habits.

The two sessions of usability evaluation were significant to evaluate the user overall experience and validate the relevance of the features developed for the end-users. The feedback provided in the usability sessions was positive on key features like the dream log and calendar. Users have also shown curiosity and the motivation to engage in a self-analysis of their own dreams while saving and sharing them with close ones. The tests revealed some weaknesses on the navigability of the app that soon was improved upon to favor the overall users' experience.

We believe that it will be necessary for future studies to establish a long-term positive effect on the continuous use of such an app. Further usability tests will also be necessary since the short time provided wasn't enough to shape a strong view of the features mentioned above. And, if the concept proves valid and relevant in the present national/local context, this mobile app should be developed as a fully functional mobile application either in native code (such as Java or Swift for Android or iOS) or in device-independent hybrid Web technologies (HTML, CSS & JavaScript packaged with development frameworks such as Cordova or PhoneGap).

Although this mobile application concept has been developed to improve the users' well-being through dream analysis, we believe that this architecture of self-awareness through logs, insights through calendar visualization, and motivation for the positive reinforcement through gamification elements such as badges can be applied to other areas such as learning or physical exercise. Nevertheless, the development of the *Moon* app aims to, in the future, work more profoundly on the sleep-dream connection, to study a part so abstract of the human essence.

References

Blagrove M, Farmer L, Williams E (2004) The relationship of nightmare frequency and nightmare distress to well-being. J Sleep Res 13(2):129–136. https://doi.org/10.1111/j.1365-2869.2004.00394.x

Brooke J (1996) SUS-A quick and dirty usability scale. Usability Eval Ind 189(194):4–7

Cooper A, Reimann R, Cronin D, Noessel C (2014) About face: the essentials of interaction design, 4th edn. Wiley, Indianapolis

DECO (2016). Mais de 60% dos portugueses com problemas de sono. Disponível em: https://www.deco.proteste.pt/casa-energia/dormir/noticias/mais-de-60-dos-portugueses-com-problemas-de-sono

Hooper R (2018) Dreams decoded: 6 answers to the mysteries of the sleeping mind. Available online at: https://www.newscientist.com/article/2164099-dreams-decoded-6-answers-to-the-mysteries-of-the-sleeping-mind/#ixzz6CkCUEQly

Hooper R (2018). Why dreaming is vital: unlocking the power of REM sleep. Available online at: https://www.newscientist.com/article/mg23731700-200-why-dreaming-is-vital-unlocking-the-power-of-rem-sleep/?intcmp=PAC|NSNS|2018-inlinelink_dreamsdecoded&utm_medium=PAC&utm_source=NSNS&utm_campaign=inlinelink_dreamsdecoded

Garbarino S, Guglielmi O, Sanna A, Mancardi GL, Magnavita N (2016) Risk of occupational accidents in workers with obstructive sleep Apnea: systematic review and meta-analysis. Sleep 39(6):1211–1218. https://doi.org/10.5665/sleep.5834

Grigsby-Toussaint D, Kim J, Shin JC (2017) Mobile phone interventions for sleep disorders and sleep quality: systematic review. Available online at https://mhealth.jmir.org/2017/9/e131/

Hobson JA (2002) Dreaming: an introduction to the science of sleep. Oxford University Press, Oxford

Lister C, West JH, Cannon B, Sax T, Brodegard D (2014) Just a fad? Gamification in health and fitness apps. JMIR Serious Games 2(2):e9. https://doi.org/10.2196/games.3413

Mendes F (2019) Quantas horas dorme? Menos de seis horas é a resposta de 46% dos inquiridos num estudo sobre o sono. Público. Availabe online at: https://www.publico.pt/2019/03/01/sociedade/noticia/portugues-25-anos-provavel-durma-mal-1863854

Orzechowski J (2014) Why is mHealth Important? In: MS in health informatics & BS in health information management blog. Consulted in 22nd June, 2019. Available online at: https://healthinformatics.uic.edu/blog/why-is-mhealth-important

Rubin J, Chisnell D (2008) Handbook of usability testing: how to plan, design, and conduct effective tests. Wiley, Indianapolis

Sleep Foundation (2019) Do Dreams affect how well you sleep? Available online at: https://www.sleepfoundation.org/articles/do-dreams-affect-how-well-you-sleep

Digital Design and Its Socio-Political Conditions: Visual Diversity in Urbanscapes

Washington Morales

Abstract The aim of this paper is to point out the theoretical importance of calling into question the socio-political sources of digital design. Precisely, by means of that idea of "sources of fiction" partly imported from the philosophy of literature and art, I postulate a distinction between digital design and visual world akin to that distinction between world fiction and natural and social world. If we comprehend the digital design in that way, many socio political aspects of our everyday visual world are as important as the specific technical, practical and theoretical characteristics of digital design. In order to achieve that aim, I introduce and analyze the special aestheticization of the urbanscape of Montevideo City (Uruguay). The general thesis of this paper is that a really democratic digital design is also that design whose more basic visual materials are socially heterogeneous, because the democracy is not only a set of agreements among the members of the whole social body, but also the public acknowledgement of disagreements.

Keywords Visual design · Democracy · Urbanscape · Aestheticization

1 Preliminary Notes

This paper tends to be an approach to the theoretical and practical relationships between aesthetics and democracy, and particularly between design and democracy. I argue that one ancient discussion on fiction and truth is a very useful resource to think about the socio-political conditions of a democratic visual design. From Plato to Karl Marx and beyond, this following question is still nowadays a battlefield of endless controversies: is the literary value of a work determined by its (propositional) truth content? Usually, the so-called aesthetic formalism argues that every good artwork has nothing to do with the linguistic, pragmatic, and epistemic properties of scientific

W. Morales (✉)
Universidad de La República, Facultad de Arquitectura, Montevideo, Uruguay
e-mail: wamm1756@gmail.com

N. Martins et al. (eds.), *Perspectives on Design and Digital Communication*, Springer Series in Design and Innovation 8, https://doi.org/10.1007/978-3-030-49647-0_11

and philosophical knowledge. Every artwork is a *heterocosm*. In that sense, a visual aesthetic piece does not inform anything about the social and natural world nor needs any extra-artistic information in order to be comprehended. It follows from that that the literature has not any cognitive benefice for us. It also follows from that that every reference to world found into an artwork is just a mere excuse to access into another world. Let just imagine now a formalist conception of visual design in those terms. Because, by definition, a visual communicative piece does need to use the entire human referential apparatus, the sole idea of a formalist visual design disappears. On the contrary, many forms of romantic and Marxist aesthetics argue that art is a refined kind of social or metaphysical knowledge, i.e., art, they say, is a specular image of the world. According to "contentist" doctrines, the specific nature of art is determined by a cognitive benefice; for its part, knowing extra-artistic information is a *sine qua non* condition to comprehend an artwork. Therefore, it follows that a good visual artistic piece is that whose cognitive benefices are high, that is, when we interpret an artwork as a reflection of its time—*the mirror and the lamp*. However, in some cases that doctrine reduces the value of art to ideology or to a metaphysical account. Hence, if a visual communicative piece is understood through these terms, interpreting its context becomes an important task.

Keeping in mind the formalist side, a fictional or representational artwork has nothing to do with the outside world. For its part, keeping in mind the contentist side, every specific property of a design piece would be dissolved into context factors, therefore its answer to our initial question is emphatically *yes!* Here I try to extend the so-called *opacity of the narrative* (Lamarque 2014) to the realm of visual art and design in order to deny two traditional beliefs about aesthetically produced images. These beliefs are the following ones: (1) there is not any relevant relationship between an image and its context and (2) an image is only its social content. Nevertheless, I am very interesting in one political consequence of denying these two beliefs. The visual communicative design is not exactly a mirror of its context, but its sources, ways of organization, its way of seeing, etc., are not the design itself. Because it is a fact that design nearly peeks to its visual surroundings, the research on its sources and on its specific visual transfigurations of such surroundings is the highest importance.

For a few years now, Montevideo City (Uruguay) has begun a global process of anesthetization of its public spaces. The walls of the downtown have become a public field of disputes, because, on one hand, the city council of Montevideo called for proposals to paint the metallic curtains set up on the main avenue of Montevideo and, on the other hand, these walls are usually employed by improvised graffiti artists to express social and political tensions. Since that public battlefield of dispute, I point out the importance of thinking about the visual public sources of design. A really democratic design needs to be attentive to beautiful accepted expressions, but also to distorted ways of visual expression. In the first three sections of this paper, I argue that the process of Montevidean muralization can be interpreted as a process of silencing dissenting voices. In the last two sections, I justify the application of the distinction between knowledge/world-fiction to the distinction between visual world-visual design.

The main idea of this paper is that if it is necessary for a democracy to visibilize the different voices in tension in and among different forms of life, then it is a responsibility for design to recognize the peripheral and distorted visual voices expressed in public spaces. In that sense, I argue that this proposal will be useful to designers as a general critique of visual design.

2 Montevideo's Muralization

On 27 December 2013, the City Council of Montevideo publicly announced an integral urban "revitalisation" plan for its main avenue, 18 de Julio. The objective of this plan was to strengthen the "commercial, cultural, creative, and touristic" activities of 18 de Julio (Obras 2013). Together with a group of owners of stores located in 18 de Julio called "Grupo Centro",— the Montevidean Government announced a strategy to reach this goal. This strategy includes, new streetlights, a new design of urban advertising, universally accessible pavements, a new design of traffic fluxes and traffic volumes, installation of new security devices, new urban furniture, and so on. In particular, muralization was one element of this set of urban political measures.

Four years later, on 3 November 2017, the Montevidean Government called for artistic projects. The call was named "Galería de arte a cielo abierto" ("Open-pit art Gallery"), and it was oriented to paint the metallic curtains of some stores in 18 de Julio. The call's rules—and one of the institutional statements—are crucial to interpret the political sense of muralization. According to these rules, the murals should "contain references to Montevidean distinguished celebrities, celebrities associated to 18 de Julio Avenue, or specific city's themes. Furthermore, the murals should promote gender equality and respect to diversity" (Convocatoria 2017).

The two general reasons given for why the call to pictorial interventions had these conditions were, on the one hand, "the vision by which the art would be a tool of social transformation" (Se presentaron 2017 and, on the other, according to Marcelo Carrasco, president of Grupo Centro –, the conception by which "art [would contribute to] fight the vandalism suffered by this avenue." (Se presentaron 2017). Finally, in the following year, another part of the avenue not muralized yet was muralized too in the context of a youth-based programme named "Movida Joven", which called for new muralizations. The purpose of this second call was to "promote artistic expressions in non-conventional places and to appropriate the public places by the community through an art which is accessible to everybody" (Movida muralista 2018).

3 Muralization and Graffiti

In order to interpret these two calls to muralization, it is necessary to keep in mind two elements: on the one hand, their objectives and governmental justification and, on the other, the avenue's geographic and political characteristics.

Concerning the first element, the muralizations are tools for: (1) the general urban revitalisation of Montevideo's downtown, (2) a communitarian self-recognition of cultural identity, as well as, a sense of belonging to a form of life), (3) the encouragement of the public awareness of social issues (4) the communitarian appropriation of a public area, (5) the democratization of visual arts and, finally, (6) the fight against the supposed visual vandalization.

Concerning the second element, we should not ignore the avenue's relevant political characteristics to Montevideo's social life. According to Carmona (2010), "Conceived as a structuring site, [18 de Julio] supports a public places' system, actually integrated by the squares Independencia, Fabini, de Cagancha, Explanada Municipal, de los Treinta y Tres, [and] Explanada de la Universidad" (p. 58). Moreover, also according to Carmona (2010), the "hierarchical avenue's conception [...], is reinforced by the presence of symbols of power and urban milestones which proclaim themselves [holding] intact their festivity and expression of citizenship." (p. 59).

To sum up, this avenue is a central city landmark. Firstly, because it is the backbone of the Montevidean heritage industry, since it is the topological vehicle where the "classical tourism" and the "directed authenticity" (Čepaitienė 2013, p. 54) are developed and, secondly, 18 de Julio is a central place to citizenship's public expression. For example, the political and sport festivities happen there, especially, expressions of social public dissents which can be conjunctural—protests against different governmental measures—or systematic and regular, e.g., the March of Silence in which the citizens demand information about those who 'disappeared' at the hands of the last dictatorship regime.

This is the double nature of 18 de Julio: it may be the most important tourist spot of Montevideo and, at the same time, it is the most visible spot to have public protests or, in general terms, to citizenship's political expression. Keeping in mind this double nature, it is necessary to ask which the links between these constitutive elements are. On the one hand, instances of vandalization are evident obstacles to enjoy the avenue, if we consider some aesthetic global patterns of tourism. On the other hand, a possible means of political dissent is the use of non-institutional graffiti in public spaces. Both aspects of graffiti are incompatible. Nevertheless, I do not focus on the incompatibility itself, but in the governmental solution to it. Can we conceive every graffito as a form of vandalization? I if we answer affirmatively, then every muralization is acceptable as strategy of urban revitalization. But, if we accept the possible political value of graffiti, hence it is not a *factum* that every muralization is politically fair.

4 Graffiti, Aestheticization, and Politics

Although they can be considered the softer forms of politic expression, graffiti are recognized as forms of politic dissent. As Dobratz points out (2013, p. 377), they are non-institutionalized political expressions, by people who usually live in the margins of normal political discourse (Hanauer 2004, pp. 29–30; Penn 2018, p. 323). But what are graffiti? According to Klingman and Shalev (2001), graffiti "refers to virtually anything that is drawn, painted, etched, scratched, or scribbled on any surface visible to the public" (p. 405). However, this definition does not grasp important aspects of graffiti; their non-institutional nature, their distorting visual nature, and their unclassifiable typographic nature—for exemple, the "wildstyle", that is, textures and colours saturated and distorted (Gottlieb 2008, p. 81).

Nevertheless, in their set of defining properties, graffiti are rebellious not exactly by virtue of their visual distortions or their critical semantics, but by virtue of their contexts, i.e., their illocutionary purpose (Searl 1972) or their perlocutive force (Austin 1962), that is, their pragmatics conditions are their defining ones. Contrary to the thesis held by Kan (2001, p. 19), what gives graffiti their real sense is a set of motivations and a pretended audience, because they presuppose dissatisfaction to someone or something. This dissatisfaction is materialized in a painted surface where pictorial interventions are not allowed. The mere act of depicting a prohibited wall turns the depictions into graffiti.

The graffiti exhibited in galleries or museums lose their performative nature because the "circumstances in which [...] graffiti [are] seen are major features in their meaning [i.e.] integration of the work [...] the history of the location [...] the social context and the political context" (Lewisohn 2008, pp. 134–137). As Dobratz (2013) pointed out, "the transforming legal status of graffiti from always illegal to something legal may have implications for its political utility because increasing legitimacy potentially undermines its effectiveness" (p. 379). Therefore, by virtue of their temporal and spatial context, graffiti can perform three main functions: (1) the expression of messages otherwise marginalized, (2) the expression of controversial thoughts, (3) the possibility to express a message in a public area (Randviir 2011, pp. 97–98; Zaimakis 2016, p. 72; Hanauer 2004, pp. 29–30). The mere choice of a symbolically relevant wall turns the non-institutionalized graffiti a tool of "expression of taboos [...] that [...] often becomes the most powerful and the easiest means of self-identification, territorialization and simultaneous differentiation from the 'normal', 'ordinary', society" (Randviir 2011, p. 102).

However, the politically incorrect nature of graffiti has been a target of civil and governmental regulation. The government of civic behaviour is not only juridical. The different organizations of an urban area can be recognized as material rules of behaviour (Schindler 2015), as the urban furniture and architecture also have a role in social behaviour by controlling movement (for example, the access to certain areas or the dynamics of social movement). Keeping in mind Keats' metaphor of literature as a mirror and a lamp (Abrams 1962), we can say that urban landscapes are the general image of social organizations. In this way, according to Alderman and Moreau (2011), it is likely that the "control of landscapes through the creation of strict, and sometimes punitive, policies that work to marginalize certain citizens and landscapes activities [are] widespread." (p. 106).

Regarding this, silencing can be, and has been, a tendency to rule urban landscape. Silencing social or individual expressions has been an efficient way to subtly rule a form of life or a dissident opinion (Ferguson 2003, p. 50). However, it is more curious that there are certain almost paradoxical forms of silencing practiced by civil organizations. Graffiti Hurts, an American anti-graffiti civil organization, paradoxically has given awards for the best walls' depiction (Alderman and Moreau 2011, p. 109). Therefore, we can say that institutionalized muralization is a tool of silencing dissenting voices, not only by the visual characteristics of those voices, but also by the contexts where they appear. As Alderman and Moreau pointed out 2011), "Graffiti Hurts offers an alternative strategy in its campaign against graffiti: community murals with historical themes, agricultural themes, ethnic pride, frontier History [...] through its notion of community responsibility, positive image" eliminates the graffiti which distort visual dominant imagination (p. 119).

5 Fiction and Design

Many philosophical doctrines usually hold that motto of *art for art's sake.* In Peter Lamarque's words, formalism in literature argues that "It is not, and could not be, *truth,* they say, that gives literature its value but rather inventiveness, imagination, clever plots or engaging characters. Fiction, surely, is the very opposite of truth!" (Lamarque 2014,123). And also, according to him, the *anti-truth* side argues that "Truth is the province of science or history, poetry resides in creativity and make-believe. Literature lifts us beyond the mundane world of fact and verification." (idem). Even when we do not read literature as literature, many times we are impelled to image fictional scenarios appealing to our knowledge of customs, places, songs, science, etc., whereby even in those more formalist aesthetic positions, understanding a literary artwork is possible only if we start up of our knowledge of the world. It is the case that epistemic values as truth are not clear conditions to literary evaluation, but it is also clear that if we do not keep in mind all our knowledge at the service of our imagination, then our aesthetic experience gets worse. Everyday life is the more common stuff which literatures appeal to in order to dispose our imagination to construct characters, scenes, scenarios, etc. At the same time, the ways in which literature constructs the fictive worlds give a lot of *perspectival* information about our everyday life. Precisely, although distinguishing between the fictional stuffs of literature form their thematic layers, we can assert, with Peter Lamarque, that the more fictional aspects of literature as well as the more thematic speculative elements of it are opaque; moreover, we can assert that such a opaqueness informs us about the many ways to see our surroundings and even how, under the subjectivity of the writer, our surroundings are. Once again, we can deny the thesis according to which evaluating literature depends on the truth content of a work, but we can not deny that comprehending any literary text requires a profuse image or images of the world which then is transformed, expanded or even emphasized precisely by virtue of reading. We can call that transformation of seeing a *cognitive benefice*.

However, it is not clear why this should matter to visual design, because one can say that even though we accept that the predominant characteristic of design is imaging, however it is not clear that such imaginary activity implies some form of linguistic imagination. Visual design, like visual arts, one can say, needs other cognitive tools rather than a codification of linguistic signs. I agree with that, but I do not believe that these different approaches to opacity—a linguistic one and a visual one—cancel the similarities among these different aesthetic procedures to produce a world image. Visual design also requires a rich source of everyday visual realities and, by using visual information of our everyday world, visual design transforms our perceptions of our everyday world. Visual design is as opaque as literature in that sense of showing a perspectival set of perceptions and beliefs. The visual components of design are not auto-sufficient; on the contrary, to interpret any visual piece, we need to keep in mind experiences, images, and knowledge of our everyday life that are transformed in visual pieces. May be the process involved in the codification of images is quite different from that of processing a literary language, but these eventual different procedures are not relevant to my thesis. When we are approaching to an image by Matilde Correa (Fig. 1) which was produced for a public campaign against a reform of the Uruguayan punitive system we also see the distorted typographies of Montevidean walls and also the austere but perturbing range of colours of our facades and finally an intended confusing composition common to our Montevidean urbanscape too.

In that sense, the visual design absorbs in very special ways not only other visual pieces already produced, but also many visual perspectives of our living environments. Visual design itself works a perspectival way to construct visual narratives by which we can emphasize, expand or, in general terms, transform our more basic visions of our everyday life. Nevertheless, it still is not clear why a democratic design requires a wide gaze on the urbanscapes heterogeneous urbanscapes at its disposition. I try to answer that question in the next section.

6 Design and Democracy

Visual design as well as the literature is not only constituted by an abstract thematic level, but also by what is called "subject-level" (Lamarque 2014, 128). The thematic level usually consists of abstract "… generalizations, sometimes explicitly given, sometimes derived by readers, on the work's subject." (idem). Meanwhile, the subject level is "often fictional" (idem) and can be content "… filled in, imaginatively or inferentially, by a reader." (idem). Because the thematic level is not independent from the fictional level—not even in these occasions where some character seems to assert certain judgment—, any sole controversy about general thematic implied in a literary work precludes the specific literary stuff from the discussion. In the

Fig. 1 Matilde Correa's piece against the reform of the Uruguayan punitive system. Public domain image

same way, interpreting Matilde Correa's visual piece can stimulate a general dispute over the right way to resolve the Uruguayan public safety problems, but to look at only to general thematic positions in that dispute implies to forget the specific perspectives that the image enlighten. It follows from that that a democratic visual design is not that whose thematic abstract level promotes democratic values, but that design constituted by diverse perspectival ways of seeing. The expression of any democratic slogan would constitute a condition for a democratic piece only under the assumption according to which a visual piece can be reduced without loss into an abstract propositional content. Nevertheless, by virtue of the perspectival manner in which any visual content is exhibited, there is no piece where the contents were more important than then way in which the contents are presented. The cognitive benefice of design as well as the cognitive benefice of literature are not transparent or unambiguous, but, on the contrary, their specific nature is the opacity, i.e., the particular and subjective ways in which we can recognize, extend, transform or maintain our gaze over the world. If the ways of seeing are not less important than the general contents themselves, then we can conclude that a democratic piece is that where the proper ways of seeing were democratic. But what do we mean by "democratic"? I am following the immanent critique of forms of life by Jaeggi (2018) to answer that question.

Until recent years, the major part of the philosophy of politics' controversies were determined by an ethical abstinence side and a political agonality side (Jaeggi 2018), that is, by different liberal positions—according to which respecting a form of life does not imply to call into question that form of life—and by those familiar approaches to Chantal Mouffe agonistic theory of democracy—according to which democracy is a process of tensions among different individual and social agents that find their agreements by mere negotiation, but not by means of an apparent unattainable ideal of rational agreement. Rahel Jaeggi argues that recognizing different social tensions is a condition to a real democracy as well as the implementation of a critique of forms of life. She intends to recover a normative dimension to social philosophy and, at the same time, does not forget the ways in which a community narrates itself in order to develop their practices and products. Therefore, silencing ways of expression by means of muralization can be interpreted as a regressive form of resolving social problems, because precisely it does not visibilize some disruptive voices in the public field. That aestheticization movement in Montevideo does not allow the recognition of spontaneous and disruptive ways of seeing; however, that null recognition has nothing to do with silencing explicit messages wrote in the Montevidean facades, but it is a reduction of perspectival ways of presenting visual contents. In that sense, a democratic gaze—eventual embodied in a visual piece of design—implies the expression of a heterogeneous set of abstract contents as well as a heterogeneous set of modes of presenting those contents.

7 Final Remarks

No visual piece of design is an island in our everyday visual experience. On the contrary, every visual piece is a particular form of communicating something about our everyday life. Keeping that in mind, it seems a responsibility for our actual designers to critically intervene in our everyday forms of seeing. It can seem obvious that if something becomes a visual piece of design, it will have a clear link to our societies; but it is not clear at all, from that insight, that there are many levels as means which design can be democratic. Even the thematic level of design is perspectival, so that a democratic design is that engaged with many forms of visual expression. The visual monopolization of contents and official forms of visual imagination seems to be a designer's problem, because visual design plays a fundamental role in the daily circulation of forms of seeing. That monopolization is not an exclusive problem of graffiti artists, but also a problem for visual designers. The standardization of our gaze, the aestheticization of our visual landscapes, the monopolization of our ways of seeing, the social tensions expressed in urban walls, the controversies among different agents of the civil society are, all of them, very important themes for visual designers. The ways in which designers express a propositional content are as important as the propositional content itself in its more generic and abstract form, so a democratic design will be that does not ignore the diversity gazes in tension expressed in her and his material surroundings.

Acknowledgements I am especially grateful to Victoria Lavorerio who patiently read the first sketch of this paper. I am in debt to Victoria for her English proofreading and also for her comments, questions, and suggestions. This paper would have been clearly less rigorous and interesting without her invaluable help.

References

Abrams MH (1962) El espejo y la lámpara (The Mirror and Lamp]). Editorial Nova, Buenos Aires, Argentina

Alderman DH, Moreau T (2011) Graffiti hurts and the eradication of alternative landscape expression. Geogra Rev 101(1):106–124

Austin JL (1962) How to do things with words. The William James Lectures delivered at Harvard University in 1955. Oxford University Press, Oxford, United Kingdom

Carmona L (2010) Avenida 18 de Julio. [18 de Julio Avenue]. In: Bonilla F (ed) Guía Arquitectónica y Urbanística de Montevideo (Architectural and urbanistic guide of montevideo). Intendencia Municipal de Montevideo, Montevideo, Uruguay, pp. 56–79

Čepaitienė R (2013) The Patterns of urban landscape commodification. Archit Urban Plann 8(1):50–59

Convocatoria (2017) Convocatoria para "Galería de arte a cielo abierto". 18 de Julio a puro arte. (Call for "Open-pit Art Gallery". 18 de Julio full of Art). Retrieved from: http://www.montevideo.gub.uy/institucional/noticias/18-de-julio-a-puro-arte

Dobratz AY, Walder LK (2013) Graffiti as a form of contentious political participation. Sociol Compass 7(5):377–389

Ferguson K (2003) Silence: a politics. Contemp Polit Theory 2:49–65

Gottlieb L (2008) Graffiti art styles. a classification system and theoretical analysis. McFarland & Company, London, United Kingdom

Hanauer DI (2004) Silence, voice and erasure: psychological embodiment in graffiti at the site of Prime Minister Rabin's assassination. Arts Psychol 31:29–35

Jaeggi R (2018) Critique of forms of life. The Belknap Press, London, England

Kan H-K (2001) Adolescents and Graffiti. Art Educ 54(1):18–23

Klingman AY, Shalev R. (2001) Graffiti. Voices of Israeli youth following the assassination of the Prime Minister. Youth Soc 32(4):403–420

Lamarque P (2014) The opacity of the narrative. Rowman and Littlefield, London, England

Lewisohn C (2008) Street art. The Graffiti revolution. Tate Publishing, London, United Kingdom

Movida muralista (2018) Jóvenes artistas pintaron en 18 de Julio. (Muralist Movement. Young Artists Depicted in 18 de Julio). Retrieved from: http://www.montevideo.gub.uy/noticias/infancia-y-adolescencia/jovenes-artistas-pintaron-en-18-de-julio

Obras (2013) Intendencia anuncia revitalización de 18 de Julio (Works. Government announced the revitalization of 18 de Julio). Retrieved from: http://www.montevideo.gub.uy/institucional/noticias/intendencia-anuncia-revitalizacion-de-18-de-julio

Penn R (2018) The phenomenal forms of political graffiti in Rome and Buenos Aires: a comparison based upon detailed descriptive analysis. Visual Stud 33(4):313–325

Randviir A (2011) Transdisciplinary in objects: spatial signification from graffiti to hegemony. Sign Syst Stud 39(2/4):88–123

Schindler S (2015) Architectural exclusion: discrimination and segregation through physical design of the built environment. Yale Law J 124:1934–2024

Searl JR (1972) Expression and meaning. Studies in the theory of speech acts. Cambridge University Press, Cambridge, United Kingdom

Se presentaron propuestas ganadoras de (2017). Galería de arte a cielo abierto. El arte se apropia de 18 de Julio. (It presents the winner projects for "open-pit art gallery. The Art appropriates 18 de Julio). Retrieved from: http://www.montevideo.gub.uy/institucional/noticias/el-arte-se-apropia-de-18-de-julio

Zaimakis Y (2016) Youth Precariat worlds and protest Graffiti in the Dystopia of the Greek Economic crisis: a cross-disciplinary perspective. Punctum 2(2):66–84

Collaborative Learning in a Shared Digital Studio

Denitsa Petrova and Sabina Savadova

Abstract CollaboratED is a research initiative exploring the opportunities and challenges for collaborative work between online and on-campus students within the Digital Media Design Masters programme at the University of Edinburgh, where group projects are an important aspect of the learning process. CollaboratED asks students and academic staff about the benefits and challenges to group work, looking to find ways to successfully bring on-campus and online learners into a creative and shared studio environment. This paper discusses the outcomes from the longitudinal research, involving questionnaires, observations, and individual interviews with students and lecturers on the programme. The research findings suggest that the challenges that online students face are mostly focused on balancing work and studies, but also relate to working from different time zones and overcoming cultural differences within the team. Despite these challenges, the students recognise the benefits of group discussion and sharing resources with their peers, mostly, however, they value the sense of being part of a community. Despite positive responses towards group discussion and collaboration, in both on-campus and online cohorts, the largest percentage of students prefer to work alone where course assignments are concerned.

Keywords Collaborative learning · Online learning · Shared design studio · Cross-cohort teaching and learning

1 Introduction

The Masters programme in Design and Digital Media (DDM) was launched in the then Department of Architecture at the University of Edinburgh in 1999 and has since steadily grown to a cohort of around 80 students. The programme offers a

D. Petrova (✉) · S. Savadova
University of Edinburgh / Edinburgh College of Art, Edinburgh, UK
e-mail: denitsa.petrova@ed.ac.uk

S. Savadova
e-mail: sabina.k.savadova@ed.ac.uk

N. Martins et al. (eds.), *Perspectives on Design and Digital Communication*, Springer Series in Design and Innovation 8, https://doi.org/10.1007/978-3-030-49647-0_12

broad coverage of digital design techniques and technologies; the students are not necessarily specialists in these areas but may, for example, aspire to become leaders of creative teams where they will need a nuanced understanding of different design disciplines and how these can effectively work together. The programme is taught using a design studio approach derived from traditional teaching, with a focus on practical design projects and group work. In the last five years, the programme has been complemented by the introduction of an online counterpart, Digital Media Design (DMD). DMD features online variations of all the DDM courses, achieved by capture and reuse of all lecture, seminar and tutorial sessions, asynchronous discussion, and where possible use of collaborative tools such as Skype and Blackboard Collaborate in order to facilitate synchronous discussion. These courses share virtual learning materials and most other resources and facilities. Through this approach, on-campus teaching is also online teaching.

Group work is an essential element for the programme in both on-campus and online cohorts. Core courses such as Dynamic Web Design depend on group work of two or more members in order to respond to the complexities of course requirements and whilst working in groups, students are also expected to create an independently identifiable component of the project. The work is assessed on the basis of the group result; however, the students are expected to present the outcomes in a way that makes it possible to identify individual contributions to the joint outcome.

Similarly, as part of the Digital Media Studio Project course, students work as a large group of five to eight members, bringing together their creative skills in the context of an exploratory project brief. Through this the students have the opportunity to expand their practical experience of design technologies and the creative arts. A key aspect of the course is the expectation that the students have to work in complex collaborative situations similar to those in professional circumstances. The successful outcome of the group collaboration is graded, but also calibrated against individual performance evaluated by the peer members.

Although the M.Sc programme in Design and Digital Media has been running for eighteen years, no substantial research has been conducted with the purpose of evaluating the effectiveness of the shared learning experience in the context of creative studio culture within the programme. The need of such investigation arose even further when the online cohort grew substantially reaching over 50 online learners in its fifth year. Thus, the research team of CollaboratED is looking to determine the effectiveness of such shared learning approaches and reveal the factors which are most crucial in terms of student experience and learning outcomes.

The aims of the project are to investigate the attitudes towards collaborative work between on-campus and online students and between different online students on this shared programme. The initiative is looking to chart these attitudes against one of the aims of the programme: to encourage collaboration between both on-campus and online cohorts. The key goal of CollaboratED is to develop and test approaches to overcome any barriers to collaboration, in particular those of the cross-cohort. Finally, the goal is to integrate successful collaborative mechanisms within the programme and share best practices institution-wide.

2 Background

Collaborative learning is recognised as a successful approach in higher education with the term 'collaborative learning' referring to a method of teaching in which students work together in a group of two or more in order to achieve a common goal (Gokhale 1995; Johnson et al. 2000). Collaborative learning may also describe a situation where particular interactions amongst students are expected to occur, which in turn would trigger learning mechanisms. Furthermore, peers do not learn because they are in a group, but because they perform activities based on their interaction. Such activities may be explanation, discussion, disagreement or mutual regulation. Dillenbourg (1999) argues that the field of collaborative learning is precisely about these activities and mechanisms and they may occur more frequently in collaborative learning than in individual condition. Thus, collaborative learning could be seen as a situation in which particular forms of interaction among people are expected to occur, which would trigger learning mechanisms. Sharing the learning process provides students with opportunities to engage in discussion, but also to take responsibility for their own learning and become critical thinkers (Totten et al. 1991).

Since the start of the online learning variation of the programme, requirements for group work amongst the online students have become more complex. There are a number of factors for this, such as different locations and time zones, technological barriers and communication and cultural issues (Goold et al. 2008). In addition, trust is viewed as an essential factor when working in a group, particularly for online students. This is partially because with face-to-face, collaborating team members can also interact socially with more ease (Alexander 2002). A probing argument has been made by Staggers et al. (2008) stating that "most successful teamwork occurs after team building, but too often this team building is lacking in online environments" (p. 474).

It has been argued that successful distance education students preferred an independent learning environment, and successful on-campus students preferred working with others (Gee 1990). Self-direction and independence are important when studying at a distance where students have the option to shape their learning environment themselves. In contrast, students in equivalent on-campus cohort, are significantly more dependent learners than the distance group. The online students displaying collaborative qualities are reliant on their need for structure and their willingness to participate as good citizens (Diaz and Cartnal 1999). Therefore, although online students prefer to study independently, they are willing to participate in collaborative work if the structure of the work has been initiated by the teacher. Furthermore, the on-campus students are more eager to work in class providing they can obtain rewards for working with others and for meeting teacher expectations. In contrast, the online learners are more driven by intrinsic motives and less motivated by the reward structure of the class. This represents a challenge for the tutors and course organisers, which CollaboratED is seeking to resolve.

3 Methodology

In order to capture social process and obtain a more detailed picture (Neale 2018) we used Qualitative Longitudinal Research (QLR) methods to identify factors influencing collaborative group work among on-campus students as well as between on-campus and online students allowing us to "[…] move away from snapshot pictures of the social world to construct a moving picture that captures social processes" (Berthoud 2000, p. 15).

Qualitative Longitudinal Research is conducted through time and "[…] time is the driving force for research design and practice" (Neale 2018, p. 2). In QLR design two 'planes of time' are differentiated: while in the first plane we can look at time prospectively and retrospectively i.e. looking to the future or backwards to the past, in the second plane it is related to tempos and time frames (Neale 2018). While tempo indicates the number of observations, time frame is concerned with the overall time dedicated to conduct the study, and together they constitute the longitudinal time frame which can be conducted intensively, that is through more frequent and continuous visits to the field, and extensively, i.e. with less frequent and less regular visits. In this study we attempted to explore time retrospectively and prospectively through intensive waves. Unlike large scale QL studies, the longitudinal time frame for this study was relatively more intensive as the study was small scale and each method was used to inform the next (Smith 2003).

The data collection lasted for a year and a half which included three term times at the university. The research design involved mixed-methods and had two steps. In the first step we conducted short questionnaires through university's online portal for on-campus and online students. In the next step we used qualitative methods such as observations and interviews. We employed purposeful sampling method to identify cases in order to gain insights into group work among students on-campus or in an online setting (Ritchie and Lewis 2003; Creswell 2012). In total, we conducted four observations with online and on-campus students where we attended their weekly meetings and observed their work progress together. Following the observations, we conducted nine face-to-face and online interviews with students. The interviews were semi-structured with mainly open questions eliciting information about students' experiences in collaborative learning environment. Furthermore, we interviewed three university tutors whose classes included group work. In addition to these interviews, we conducted individual semi-structured interviews with the directors of on-campus and online programmes.

We compiled short questionnaires for students for our first round of data gathering. The questionnaires included various types of questions to gather demographic data of students. Additionally, it included several open-ended questions to elicit participants' ideas about group work. In the first year of the data collection we launched these questionnaires after students had finished their group work that allowed us to solicit opinions based on their recent experiences. Although student questionnaires were aimed and launched specifically at their cohort (online or on-campus), there were similar and different questions as well. In the second round, we adjusted the questions and launched the questionnaire before the students started working in groups. This was a deliberate step as we wanted to explore students' attitudes towards group work before and after them having experienced working in groups as part of their university experience. In the third round we launched the questionnaires at the end of the group work element.

Initially, we identified group projects that were comprised of online and on-campus students within the Digital Design Media programme. In the first year there was only one group project that was undertaken in a cross-cohort setting—by one online student and six on-campus students. The online student joined the group work in the first several instances through Skype call, but in the final stages of the project the online student managed to travel to Edinburgh and attend the meetings on campus. This offered us a chance to document the differences and similarities between the two types of meetings that this cross-cohort group had: online and on campus. Upon receiving consents of the students and tutors, we attended weekly group meetings in the university and observed them without interrupting in any way.

We took pictures of the students in the group work meetings. Furthermore, in line with Creswell (2012) besides the interviews, we developed descriptive and reflective fieldnotes after each observation. The descriptive fieldnotes recorded what happened during the observations, while the reflective fieldnotes were an interpretation of the observed events (Ibid.). More specifically, our fieldnotes reflected interactions amongst the students themselves, with their tutor and the researcher's personal thoughts.

For the interviews, we recruited a diverse number of students from the on-campus and online cohorts in order to perform a more detailed analysis (Macmillan et al. 2011). During the observations, we identified 11 students and invited them to take part in an interview. The interviews were semi-structured in nature, with open questions, related to group work activities and lasted between 30 and 40 min. The interviews were also audio recorded.

In addition to face-to-face interviews with students in the university, we also conducted interviews with online students who were located in different parts of the world. Out of nine interviews, three were conducted through *Collaborate*, a university-wide virtual classroom tool which has the capability to allow multiple users to interact simultaneously and has built-in recording options for both video and audio. This system is also university supported and encouraged in order to meet the current General Data Protection Regulations for recorded research material.

In addition to the interviews with the students, we also conducted five individual interviews with tutors and course organisers who work with both on-campus and online students from the programme. Such interviews were an important part of the research process, as through them we were able to find out more about the challenges of cross-cohort student collaboration through the perspective of those who teach the students. As with the student interviews, these interviews were also audio recorded and lasted around 30–40 minutes.

4 Data Analysis

We employed thematic analysis in the data analysis process in order to identify topics and themes that would lead us to potential resolutions to our research questions. The analysis process was concurrent with the data collection, where each method informed the following method (Creswell 2012). The analysis process involved two stages: data familiarisation and in-depth analysis stage that were adapted from the framework analysis approach (Neale 2017).

In the data familiarisation stage we listened to the audio recordings, read the fieldnotes, and grouped the pictures according to the group projects. Whilst going through this process, based on the initial research questions and emerging themes during the fieldwork, we developed notes and frameworks, where possible. This kind of general reading of the raw data initially helped us to make sense of the data as a whole.

In the in-depth analysis stage we conducted rigorous coding and categorisation of the data. 'The process of coding is one of reducing a text or image database to descriptions and themes of people, places, or events (Creswell 2012, p. 261). We used Computer Assisted Qualitative Data Analysis Software (CAQDAS) in order to code the data both systematically and effectively (Silverman and Marvasti 2008). Initially developed codes were descriptive in nature for example, 'lack of time to communicate', 'communication problems', 'social media use' and so on. However, as we continued coding in the following stages, descriptive codes were turned into more thematic codes and we sorted them into sub-groups in order to create an initial framework to analyse the data in further detail. Furthermore, we compared and contrasted the codes during this process. As a result of this process, thematic codes and code-groups were developed, with the intention of identifying initial themes to use for categorisation purposes.

Moving on to more in-depth thematic analysis codes and code-groups were refined further allowing the regrouping, refining and eventually re-categorsiing of data. Emergent themes were based on the research aims and objectives, focusing on finding advantages and disadvantages of collaborative learning in a shared studio environment. As a result of the more detailed and conceptual coding process, final themes were then identified and developed across all cases allowing for the identification of commonalities and differences to be highlighted. Final themes were instrumental in identifying the advantages and disadvantages of collaborative learning as they address various aspects of collaborative learning. For example, 'assuming responsibilities', 'sharing knowledge' and 'timing' were helpful in developing the analysis results.

The initial results of the data analysis process are reflected in the following section where we introduce our results discussing them within wider literature relevant to this research study.

5 Results and Discussion

The first round of questionnaires and interviews identified two key areas for future evaluation—assessment and grading; and social learning opportunities. The latter factor seems to be particularly relevant for this research, as collaborative and social learning mechanisms are crucial for the groups project courses . The theory of social learning (Bandura 1977) proposes that behaviour and complex learning can be explained in view of a continuous reciprocal interaction, by observing other people's behaviour and their environments. Thus, leaning as a cognitive process, takes place in a social environment and occurs on a vicarious basis. Social interaction between learners and role models is therefore required for social learning to occur. This system of learning is extended further through the proposed model of vicarious learning, where learning can occur not only through participation in dialogue, but also through observing others participating in it. Evidence of such learning can be seen in situations when silent students in a tutorial group learn from discussions between the tutor and others or when readers on an online discussion forum benefit from reading contributions of others (Stenning et al. 1999).

The most prominent information to come from this study has been around students' perceptions of grading assignments undertaken as group work. Initial evaluation has shown that more than 80% of the students prefer to work on assignments individually rather than as a group. However, when delving deeper into the data, it was apparent that the focus of this perception was on grades and the feeling that grades given to groups may not reflect the individual effort of the student, or indeed lack of effort by class colleagues. This came through as the primary concern for students and tutors when discussing assignments and working with others for the purpose of assignment: "… the problem is not just with group work, but also group marks," (On-campus student 2).

The data did highlight desires by the students that grading for group assignment should be given on an individual basis rather than as a group. This has provided us with further investigation opportunities to delve deeper into the hesitation students feel around group work in a graded scenario. Similar views were shared by some of the tutors on the programme: "The biggest thing… you cannot give group marks. Do not give group marks. Give marks to individuals and peer group assessment helps to do that. … They asses themselves and that gives them their individual mark," (Lecturer 1).

It must be noted that the hesitation shown by students was not about the actual opportunities afforded by collaboration or indeed the act of group work itself. A high proportion, over 75%, responded that they see the value in collaboration and the biggest motivators in this being the social learning opportunities such as sharing of resources and ideas, opportunities for feedback and support from peers and the opportunity for in-depth discussion around course topics.

Almost 90% of students placed value on discussion in groups when related to their studies, indicating not only that they felt that they added valuable contributions to the group but also that they received benefits from being part of that discussion group when it came to their studies and assignments.

It was also revealed that online students perceived on-campus students to be more dedicated to their studies. However, this was not seen as an opportunity, but as an additional worry that on-campus students would be directly inconvenienced by the asynchronous nature of online study:

> In some ways I think it would be better to work with another online student simply because of timing of things because obviously campus students are very much dedicated to the course that they are doing other modules etc.,… I am actually doing my course later at night and working at odd times which might be better with other online students to handle it in the same way (Online student 3).

Data also revealed that the value of creating social bonds with classmates earlier in the process is appreciated, where online students indicated that they find it easier to collaborate when the students know each other: "Better to start the collaborative work from the start of the course," (On-campus student 7). Further concerns were expressed based on the type of collaborative setting and the allocation of roles: "Collaborative work depends on the project we are given. I believe that if it is a big project then a collaborative work is needed. However, every member should be focused on a particular part of the project" (Campus student 6).

Student concerns about isolation seem natural, considering the nature of online study. The benefits of social collaboration and inclusion were also seen for online students in creating community and combatting isolation: "Being in contact with other online students helped feeling less isolated," (Online student 4).

The tutors on the programme shared that they viewed the allocation of the roles in the student groups as something that is done independently of the teaching process delivered by them. At the same time, the data revealed that a number of online students found it necessary to naturally take on the role of a project manager in order to keep the others on track of the project progress. Such online students felt strongly that if they hadn't stepped in and taken on a managerial role, then no one else would have: "So it is basically more about managing the projects rather than actually the interaction between us that we had to figure out first… (Online student 3). This emphasizes the need for a more structured approach towards group course projects, initiated and mediated by tutors on the Masters programme. This was highlighted further by another online student: "Please consider the difference between new graduates who may need collaborative experience and professionals who may be looking for more freedom and individuality, and find it hard to juggle their study, family and work" (Online student 3).

Further information on how roles within the student groups were allocated was provided by the assumption from on-campus learners that the time of their online peers is very limited and they have to work more efficiently when group discussions are concerned:

> I think if there is an online student. He cannot be online all the time. So we have to discuss quickly, we have to be more focused on the topic. (On-campus student 4)

It also appeared that the behavior of on-campus students changed when they had an online colleague. They shared that they would have to work quickly as the time an online student had available was limited. This view was mirrored from an online learner, who indicated that their study pattern was disturbed when the collaborative work started:

> …actually, on the first semester, everything was going smooth, everything was fine and when this collaborating thing happened that when I felt the stress of the course (Online student 3)

Such behaviour could be interpreted as natural in a professional working environment, where social conversations are less common, in contrast to the life style of an on-campus student where social connections with peers are an integral part of the university experience.

6 Conclusion

The biggest motivators for group work for both on-campus and online cohorts are focused on sharing resources and ideas, receiving feedback from peers and the inclusion of community. There is still hesitation around the concept of grading group work at group level with students preferring to either work alone on assignments or that their individual work is recognized and graded rather than that of the group. The value of social engagement and strategic brainstorming is highly recognised, therefore going forward, the focus should be on student interactions that trigger learning mechanisms.

It would appear that the most successful examples of collaborative projects delivered through a cross-cohort setting occurred when an online student took on a leading role and managed the workload of the rest of campus team. Further insights into influence on the campus group from an online colleague emerged in situations where the campus groups had to be more organised for meetings and keep the conversations focused solely on the project when their online colleagues were present through the computer screen. This proposes a base for further research into the dynamic of the social relationship between students in a cross-cohort setting and the effect of this dynamic onto group course project. This opportunity is already being explored in the Masters programme in Digital Media Design through one of the core courses, which requires group work. A number of students from the online cohort have been assigned to work with one of their peers from campus, thus the on-campus student is acting as the 'live' link between tutors and on-campus students. There is also scope for further incorporation of the social and community building aspects of online and on-campus collaboration, to assist the creation of a shared studio environment intended by the creation of this cross-cohort programme.

Acknowledgements We would like to gratefully acknowledge that CollaboratED was funded by the Principal's Teaching Award Scheme of the University of Edinburgh. Without this support we would have not been able to conduct this research, so essential for the students and tutors on the programme.

References

Alexander PM (2002) Teamwork, trust and information. In: Proceedings of the 2002. Annual research conference of the South African Institute of computer scientists and information technologists on Enablement through technology (SAICSIT '02). South African Institute for Computer Scientists and Information Technologists, Republic of South Africa, pp 65–74

Bandura A (1977) Social learning theory. Prentice-Hall, Oxford, England

Berthoud R (2000) Introduction: the dynamics of social change. In: Berthoud R, Gershuny J (eds) Seven years in the lives of British families. Policy Press, Bristol, pp 1–20

Creswell JW (2012) Qualitative inquiry and research design: choosing among five approaches, 3rd edn. Sage Publications, Thousand Oaks, CA

Diaz D, Cartnal R (1999) Students' learning styles in two classes: online distance learning and equivalent on-campus. College Teach 47(4):130–135. Retrieved February 28, 2020, from www.jstor.org/stable/27558962

D P (1999) What do you mean by collaborative learning? In: Dillenbourg P, Dillenbourg P (eds) Collaborative-learning: cognitive and computational approaches. Elsevier, Oxford, pp 1–19

Gee DG (1990) The impact of students' preferred learning style variables in a distance education course: a case study. Eastern New Mexico University (ERIC Document Reproduction Service No ED 358 836), Portales

Gokhale AA (1995) Collaborative learning enhances critical thinking. J Technol Educ 7:22–30

Goold A, Craig A, Coldwell J (2008) The Student experience of working in teams online. Proceedings ASCILITE Melbourne 2008, Melbourne, pp 343–352

Johnson DW, Johnson RT, Stanne ME (2000) Cooperative learning methods: a metanalysis. University of Minnesota, Cooperative Learning Center, Minneapolis

Macmillan R, Arvidson A, Edwards S, Soteri-Proctor A, Taylor R, Teasdale S (2011) First impressions: Introducing the 'Real Times' third sector case studies. TSRC, Birmingham

Neale, B. (2017). Generating data in qualitative longitudinal research: a review of field told and techniques. Timescapes Working Paper No. 8

Neale B (2018) What is qualitative longitudinal research?. Bloomsbury Academic, London

Ritchie J, Lewis J (eds) (2003) Qualitative research practice. Sage, London

Silverman D, Marvasti A (2008) Doing qualitative research: a comprehensive guide. Sage Publications. Thousand Oaks, California

Smith N (2003) Cross-sectional profiling and longitudinal analysis: research notes on analysis in the LQ study 'negotiating transitions in citizenship. Int J Soc Res Methodol 6(3):273–277

Staggers J, Garcia S, Nagelhout E (2008) Teamwork through team building: Face-to-face to online. Bus Commun Q 71:472–487

Stenning K, McKendree J, Lee J, Cox R, Dineen F, Mayes JT (1999). Vicarious learning from educational dialogue. CSCL

Totten S, Sills T, Digby A, Russ P (1991) Cooperative learning: a guide to research. Garland, New York

Hands Versus Fingers: Leveraging Digital Technology Towards Sustaining Traditional Crafts and Industrial Practices

Abhishek Chatterjee and Heitor Alvelos

Abstract This chapter presents four instances of dissipating traditional industrial practices in Portugal whose common perceivable denominator for technological obsolescence is 'digital takeover'. For traditional industries relying strictly on manual skills and people-centric systems, their involuntary objectivity with new technological paradigms compromises livelihoods, devalues identities and legacies, and nullifies specialised knowledge often evolving over centuries. The chapter showcases how a design mediation project 'Anti-Amnesia' is addressing the observable divide by:

- acknowledging that traditional industries, including affected communities, are not always a part of the evolutionary process from manual to digital;
- articulating strategies to capitalise upon the advantages presented by digital technology as a means for industrial heritage management, and vice versa;
- recovering and re-contextualising the associated socio-cultural and material narratives with a view to reactivate creative and commercial potential.

Correspondingly, the project strategically employs new technology, particularly digital media, for developing a deeper understanding of associated immaterial values, and for supporting knowledge recovery and capacity building within traditional practice. Its actions are supplemented by active pedagogy which it perceives as a suitable interface to moderate the discourse between traditional and modern praxis, and as embodying the potential to enhance complementaries between crafts, design, and new media practices.

Keywords Heritage crafts · Digital divide · Industrial ethnography · Design for recovery

A. Chatterjee (✉) · H. Alvelos
University of Porto / ID+, Porto, Portugal
e-mail: achatterjee@fba.up.pt

H. Alvelos
e-mail: halvelos@fba.up.pt

N. Martins et al. (eds.), *Perspectives on Design and Digital Communication*, Springer Series in Design and Innovation 8, https://doi.org/10.1007/978-3-030-49647-0_13

1 Reactivating Dissipating Manufacturing Cultures Through Design Research

The design research mediation project 'Anti-Amnesia' is based on growing evidence that traditional small-scale manufacturing cultures in the Northern and Central regions of Portugal are facing critical viability challenges (Gomes 2016; de Almeida and Chatterjee 2016; Albino 2017), in the wake of new global commercial and industrial realities. These industries typically operate on older manufacturing paradigms that rely inherently on competencies which are manual in nature and which often exist within human-centric subsystems. In these cases, the influence of cybernated processes is still relatively limited—if not non-existent—notably confined to financial transactions, occasional online landing pages, and infrequently, market research.

The move to a digital future has not been a straightforward process of evolution for the associated communities in lieu of their primary vocation being established on hand-operated application and skills garnered through innumerable years of dedication to their respective practices. Therefore, the ensuing practice and identity balance—for example, being known as a weaver or a shoemaker—does not allow for a smooth transition from manual to digital paradigms without compromising on factors pertaining to:

- the authenticity of material and processual aspects of practice;
- continued intergenerational transfer of specialised knowledge built upon generations of individual and community involvement;
- implicit local/regional cultural identities;
- definitive customs and practices;
- and critically, means of sustenance in case of absence of conditions to undertake the required re-calibration.

Under these circumstances, the project considers the examples of the following set of traditional industrial practices towards uncovering further technicalities related to the multifaceted nature of factors involved.

2 Artisanal Weaving

Almalaguês is an 11th Century textile craft found to be in practice specifically in two rural communities located on the outskirts of Coimbra in Central Portugal (Gomes 2016). The artistry behind this homespun craft is characterised by subtle warp and weft manipulations that allow the weave to be presented as a stratiform with jacquard-like reliefs of geometric motifs displaying over a regular two-ply base. The handloom on which the textile is woven is configured in a manner that lends robustness to the weave structure, to such an extent that the eventuating products, such as bed covers and floor rugs have been known to last several generations of use upon being passed down as family heirlooms. A typical household industry run entirely by women, the craft's deep significance to the historical and cultural landscape of the region, and to Portugal overall, is marred by its relative obscurity, abetted by limited market ingress and a historical deficit of inscription in public/academic spheres. The situation is exacerbated by a growing impassivity towards this rare practice from within the newer generations of the weaving communities who are aware of the decimation of their traditional markets over the past decades, mainly caused by the influx of foreign machine-made products. Such competition offers greater variety at an inferior cost—a proposition which the regular customer segments have given clear preference to over the local craft's superior quality and authenticity which comes in at a slightly higher cost (Fig. 1).

In consideration of the lack of expertise and resources to counter such seemingly insurmountable challenges of scale and profitability, the younger generation of weavers has turned to alternative vocations for sustenance. However, for the more seasoned practitioners who rely solely on their craft to earn a livelihood, a similar occupational switch has proven to be infeasible. The ruling untenability of the situation is thus effectively imperilling not only the established means of subsistence for the weavers but is jeopardising the continuity of the related active and tacit streams of unique knowledge that is embedded in the craft's human, material and cultural aspects.

Fig. 1 The Almalaguês techniques, looms, and patterns have been passed down by mothers to their daughters as family heirlooms in the two practice communities

3 Azulejos Tilework

A definitive element of Portuguese architecture for the better part of the past millennium, *Azulejos* tiles, unlike Almalaguês weaving, have typically had a sound representation in the country's cultural discourses. The surge in tourism over the past decade has led to a corresponding rise in the tiles' perceived value, and thus demand, influencing guided tours and souvenir markets. The Azulejos theme is witnessing a variegated reinterpretation of its iconography in physical and digital realms, particularly towards communicating the idea of 'authentic Portuguese', however, this frenzy of symbolism is distracting the public gaze from the craft's deeply manual processual origin. A vital aspect of Azulejos that is routinely overlooked concerns the sheer mastery of the original tilemakers who blended math and mysticism by hand to arrive at a distinctive visual lexicon that conveyed diverse historical and cultural contexts belonging to Portugal. Graphical approaches have accordingly varied from tessellated and recursive patterns to pixel-based configurations for large-scale artworks such as murals that commonly adorn churches and train stations. Variations also exist in dimensional relief features created by patterns and textures that reveal further nuances of the practice. However, such 'handmade' proposition is the very feature of the craft that has borne the brunt of large-scale industrialisation—and correspondingly, digitalisation—with the traditional flatbed technique first conceding to the mechanized rotary presses, and then recently to inkjet printing, whereupon the production quantities have grown substantially, but progress has come at the cost of authenticity (Fig. 2).

The imminent discontinuation of the original technique in the present times of boom in tourism is instigating unprecedented paradoxical circumstances for the craft, wherein vintage hand-painted pieces are in significant demand, while traditional kilns that produced the Azulejos have already succumbed to desuetude. The culmination of this conflict is evident on the bald facades of once festooned edifices that have become casualties of tile theft, although, it is also not uncommon to find original Azulejos dislodged and dumped from old buildings that are giving way to new construction.

4 Traditional Shoemaking

As a larger and considerably more organised sector in Portugal than the crafts previously described, the traditional footwear industry may not readily give an impression of being under as much technological duress. Sizeable entities within the industry have been known to periodically upgrade their facilities, in line with the latest technological advancements and global production trends, including a recent push towards digitised value chains. Figures suggest incremental year-on-year growth in terms of revenue (APICAPPS 2019); however, they do not reveal the relative impacts of such modernization. In a sequential discourse similar to that of Azulejos, manual practices in shoemaking have long been replaced by mechanised production, and hence

Fig. 2 Vintage hand painted Azulejos tiles recovered from a renovation site in Porto, Portugal

a direct relationship cannot be devised between digital advancements and the shift from handmade. The implications are, however, far more evident if the circumstances are viewed in light of the significant priority upheaval of the sector as a whole—from a balanced domestic/exports model to an all-out exports centric approach which has marginalised local brands and small-scale manufacturers that were dependent on long-established domestic retail networks (de Almeida 2012; de Almeida and Chatterjee 2016). Eminent examples in this regard are Sanjo's (de Almeida 2012) and Cortebel (de Almeida and Chatterjee 2016) whose respective accounts of decline demonstrate the non-alignment of the perceived notion of progress with needs of locally circumscribed industrial cultures (Fig. 3).

On ground research conducted with industry professionals further consolidates this assessment, suggesting that in recent years, the industry's preoccupation with processual upgrades, specifically in larger firms, has compromised a proportional amount of deliberation due for sustaining small-scale ventures and indigenous labels. Thereby, despite legitimately sharing Portugal's industrial and cultural heritage, these localized creative entities are being systematically consigned to oblivion.

Fig. 3 Automated processes may draw consumer attention away from the virtuosity of the human touch in shoemaking, and further disconnect users with producers

5 Letterpress Printing

Contrary to the contextual impediments described in the earlier cases, letterpress printing is curiously undergoing a revival in the digital era, albeit in semblance of a niche activity, and as such presents a potential paragon for antiquated industrial cultures seeking reanimation. This once prevalent printing technique revolutionised the industry in its time of introduction on the basis of propounding a mechanised alternative to handwritten forms that lead to a greater scope for dissemination, which is comparable in terms of broader efficacy to each of the subsequent paradigm-changing innovations in the field, including lithography, offset and digital printing. Letterpress is characterised by a workflow that puts a strong emphasis on material and processual knowledge and an understanding of graphic design aspects such as visual harmony. Simultaneously, it invites practitioners to maintain a culture of experimentation and improvisation within their work environment, which leads to custom tacit learning, and further on, translates to diacritic flair in printmaking. The practice's recent revival can accordingly be attributed to its novelty with respect to:

- a distinctive aesthetic quality that stands in contrast to the sterile uniformity of modern processes.
- the evocation of a sense of control over aspects pertaining to procedures, results and refinements, which under current 'digital' conventions is inconceivable.

Fig. 4 With the acute proliferation of 'digital', manual skills and processes are being viewed with renewed interest by creative professionals looking to reconnect with the past

- the possibility of hands-on involvement through a spectrum of competences, such as graphic design, typography, and printmaking, which requires both artistic and technical skills.
- its approach to design and making that is typically architectural, and thus understanding of the mutual affinities between the related visual, material and physical factors (Fig. 4).

In consideration of the practice's present-day unconventionality, the demand for relevant expertise and original machinery is augmenting with time. However, the concurrence of its revival with the era of digital printing has meant that certain facets of the original technique have had to be adapted in order for the craft to retain and reflect value. One such aspect is the 'impression' of the print, which is a key element of letterpress since it is essentially a mode of relief printing. While modern-day practitioners revel in the greater quality of impression as against flatness of offset or digital prints, and routinely accentuate it as a distinguishing feature of their work, in the past, the hallmark of a fine letterpress printmaker was to produce prints precisely without any perceivable impressions. A further, more direct influence of digital technology on the original art of letterpress is evident from the emergence of photopolymer printing plates that are developed from vector images, and are digitally pre-aligned for printing, thereby substituting the manual task of setting forms but conforming to the rest of the procedure. These instances may signal divergence from the original protocol; however, in the context of the continuation of traditional knowledge, they represent diversification which is imperative for the craft to adapt to newer universes of discourse.

For project Anti-Amnesia, these four study contexts represent different degrees of technological and/or cultural obsolescence. Practices such as letterpress typography and hand-painted tilemaking are long outmoded, but arguably due to rekindled interest in manuality, they find renewed relevance within niche markets and interest groups; the millenary hand weaving practice, Almalaguês, on the other hand, represents craft practices that are unique but on the brink of disappearance, and thus in requirement of urgent intervention; and lastly, shoemaking is implicative of traditional small scale industries that are presently stable, but are beginning to receive indications of untenability in the long run, such as a gradual onset of market loss to a variety of internal and external factors, and a growing disinterest from young people towards considering a career in shoemaking. The project discerns the criticality of sustaining these antiquated practices and recovering the underlying knowledge structures towards creating an information base that can contribute to the configuration of a scholarly infrastructure—one which can potentially legitimize the value of traditional making in public and academic spheres, and showcase the enduring relevance of small-scale creative human enterprise to cultural and commercial territories currently dominated by large-scale manufacturing.

6 Expanding Interknowledge Between Design, Crafts, and New Media Through Active Pedagogy

Through its ongoing engagement with the four traditional industrial contexts as described above, the project Anti-Amnesia has secured vantage points for observing and interpreting the emerging interrelationship between traditional and digital praxis. The research, in this regard, is striving to imbibe both etic and emic perspectives that are emanating from such perceivable nerve centres of conflict between convention and contemporaneity. The underlying dialectic is to acknowledge determinants of viability related to craft practices that lie beyond standard financial valuations.

The holistic contributions of the crafts sector have become a focal point of creative and analytical studies in recent decades. As global economies are moving towards a paradigm that puts onus on knowledge and specialized skills for creating value, the discourse on crafts is gaining greater momentum.

For mediations focusing on the preservation of crafts heritage, Thomas et al. (2011) advise exploring working connections between relatively "new economic models such as social enterprise", and "models of working and thinking from earlier eras that have continued resonance"; and put emphasis on identifying links between specialized skills, innovation, and digital technology that can help facilitate traditional practices to contribute more meaningfully to creative economies. They additionally point out that "the value of making skills, the ability to adapt and innovate, and the social benefits that accrue when people collaborate" are imperative towards mitigating economic uncertainty.

Shwarz and Yair (2010) consider traditional making in "creative knowledge economies" as not just for producing artefacts, but also see the associated makers leveraging their "specialist skills, knowledge, and ways of thinking" towards attaining cross-disciplinary impacts, and augmenting economy-wide capacities. In the Portuguese context, Lains and Pereira (2010) emphasize the continual importance of human capital, which is an essential element of traditional industrial practices, and commend investing in "knowledge-based and knowledge intensive sectors" as strategic and necessary. Digital technology, in this regard, can potentially provide the required conditions for traditional makers to extend their value propositions to further economic and cultural sectors in a time efficient and resource effective manner.

Jokilehto (1999) correspondingly looks at the value factor as crucial to both state-of the art initiatives involving crafts, and conservation efforts focusing on heritage. Creative approaches based on the rigorous and yet intuitive nature of craft practices can find applicability in both contexts, wherein differential use of media, tools, and knowledge, on one hand, is supplementing cutting-edge practices such as independent game development (Westecott 2012) and additive manufacturing (e.g., Betatype); and on the other hand, is providing the means and methods for restorative interventions such as Anti-Amnesia to recover and reinterpret crafts' embedded empirical wisdom.

The project respectively comprehends that while it may not be its position to counter shifting manufacturing paradigms, it can make meaningful contributions towards the ensuring the continuation of specialized knowledge through evolving new media strategies that are based on its research findings. Accordingly, Anti-Amnesia pays particular attention to:

- advancing the public and academic inscription of traditional practice, detailing associated industrial legacies and social narratives.
- conducting on-ground ethnographic documentation to recover and archive informal, contingent, and tacit streams of knowledge in addition to related instrumentalities (Fleck and Tierney 1992).
- involving practitioners in impact-driven pedagogic activities with students of design that target critical issues concerning traditional manufacturing, such as communication and product innovation.
- building a collaborative network between the said industries, along with institutional and business partners towards potentiating knowledge and know-how exchange and examining future avenues of application.

The deep proliferation of digital technology in daily life has meant that the continuity of traditional making may depend on the introduction of digital skills, materials and processes in an incremental manner that gives enough time for associated practitioners to recalibrate. In the case of letterpress, for example, the described instances of digital infusion illustrate how small modifications can augment the technique itself, and how practitioners are actively introducing digital externalities that adapt seamlessly to age-old processes despite not sharing any technical provenance. It must be noted here that a large section of modern-day printmakers may not necessarily have any prior familial connection with the practice. They may also be more open to bringing experimentation, external expertise, and view non-conventional perspectives to the craft, including digital technology, as potential sources of innovation. Such practices are also typically based in urban areas with greater access to multisectoral skills and technology, and multidisciplinary and/or multicultural expertise. Hence, the newer generation of makers showcase more flexibility towards their craft's material and processual aspects as against what may be possible for multigenerational and predominantly rural artisans, such as the Almalaguês weavers, who are deeper set in their practice context, and have had limited exposure to comparable exogenous influences or expertise.

The project, thereby, works in close contact with such multigenerational practitioners from the study contexts in order to consensually explore pathways for maintaining resonance in contemporary times.

Its corresponding line of intervention operates on the inference that an approach centred on reciprocity can play a decisive role in the dignified recovery and sustenance of traditional making, while applying craft knowledge and approaches in the production of new media and technology that is intrinsically better informed and more responsible.

Accordingly, the research explores various pedagogical affordances of design-led interventions in crafts and analyses the propriety of reflecting upon the resultant solutions/artefacts as semiotic resources that can give new meaning to antiquated practices. Active pedagogy is thereby employed by the project in the form of an interface to moderate the discourse between traditional and modern. In this regard, the project conducts a series of complementary pedagogy-based research actions which embody the potential to enhance complementaries between crafts, design, and new media practices. These actions encompass ethnographic documentation, source material archiving, conceptualization of new product and communication strategies, and dissemination of project outcomes, using digital tools.

Anti-Amnesia's approach is thus broadly based on three intervention categories:

1. recovery: Activities comprise the audio-visual documentation of 'evidence' of traditional knowledge derived from traditional industrial contexts that include recording personal testimonies materials, processes, and protagonists. The project maintains physical and digital source material libraries that have been created to collate and provide prompt access to the gathered/generated research information.
2. re-interpretation: Activities include workshops with students of design that explore different application scenarios for the recovered information/material knowledge/specimens. Related sessions have been organized for conceptualizing new product categories that can be made with Almalaguês textiles.
3. dissemination: The project sees consistent dissemination as crucial to communicate the enduring value of traditional making and makers to the general public, and in this regard, involves student participation towards broadcasting outcomes

over channels like web and radio, and creating strategic and contemporized marketing/promotional content for practice communities.

The curricular integration of design students within these activities has generated considerable interest from their part towards acquiring and experimenting with craft knowledge. The collaborating practice communities, in turn, have also shown great receptivity towards assimilating the students' etic perspectives within their traditional praxis, and have welcomed resolutions based on new media tools and interpretations, whose incognizance has typically been a crucial disadvantage for some of the practices involved. In the case of Almalaguês, for example, a tactical workshop related to packaging design was conducted with students of graphic design on the basis of indications regarding the inadequacy of the craft's elementary packaging practices towards conveying its legacy. The respective premise for the workshop was to conceptualize packaging materials that gave more detailed information and were visually more appealing, towards enhancing the perceived value of the related products, and conveying the underlying human narratives to prospective buyers.

Another example in this regard concerns the development of an interactive online platform by students of digital design, that incorporates both research and tactical outputs generated by the project. The platform also seeks to bring together traditional practitioners, students, and individuals interested in traditional making towards fostering opportunities for knowledge and expertise transfer and capacitating collaborative exploration of new research and application avenues, during and beyond the project period (Fig. 5).

This integrated approach operates on the inference that by leveraging technological advantages that are presently afforded by contemporary media, pedagogical actions can become a means of mediation between the old and the new and ensure an effective and dignified recovery/reinstatement of facets pertaining to traditional making. Thus, the concept of media is projected as:

- means to rescue materials, documents, testimonies, and historical facts that may otherwise be lost or forgotten;
- a global platform for acknowledging the processes and protagonists of traditional industrial practices as heritage in themselves;
- a medium to communicate the allegorical and historical values that are intrinsic to these contexts, towards arguing for their distinctive uniqueness in present times;
- conditions for the prototyping of exploratory design work based on the hybridization of materials and aesthetics from the several study contexts, towards obtaining new product and market prospects;
- a connecting thread between the protagonists of traditional industries, and universities, administrative bodies and startup culture, within a collaborative environment geared towards mutual support and innovation.

In this way, the project subscribes to Droumeva and Murphy's (2016) vision of mobilising media production as "scaffolding and enabling students to explore critical issues in culture and society in ways that supplement and transcend traditional instruction and assessment, opening possibilities to make a direct impact on the

Fig. 5 Under the project ambit, students engage directly with practitioners, in order to gain a first-hand experience of the associated crafts before advancing to further research or design-led creative solution making

social issues they are exploring"; and that such real-world experiences "create greater motivation and spur more imaginative creations", and the corresponding productions "take on meaning as legitimate material artefacts in the wider (mediated) world."

The collaborative learning-based intersections of practice-led knowledge organized by the research are accordingly providing a clear evidence of how complementarities between the disciplines are evolving, and subsequently, generating semiotic resources that have the potential to:

- help past praxis transition to a digital future without marginalising communities or compromising individuality;
- prepare traditional knowledge systems to inform and find agency in newer manufacturing paradigms;
- create key intellectual assets for traditional making to sustain in the imminent era of knowledge-based economies.

By encouraging the practitioners to define their own narratives, communication parameters, and means to self-actualise, project Anti-Amnesia positions digital technology as a regenerative agent within traditional manufacturing, in place of the idea of a disruptive change that invalidates precursory nonconformist creative human enterprise.

The research is being developed within the framework of the project "Anti-Amnesia: design research as an agent for narrative and material regeneration and reinvention of vanishing Portuguese manufacturing cultures and techniques", co-financed by Portugal 2020, alongside the European Regional Development Fund and the Foundation for Science and Technology, Portugal (ID+/Unexpected Media Lab: POCI-01-0145-FEDER-029022; 2018-2020).

References

Albino C (2017) À procura de práticas sábias—Design e Artesanato na significação dos territórios. Presentation, University of Aveiro

APICAPPS (2019) Facts and numbers 2019

de Almeida P (2012) Brand archives: the rescuing of locally specific brand imagery as a graphic design response to the globalization of visual identity (Ph.D.). Central Saint Martins College of Art and Design, University of the Arts London

de Almeida P, Chatterjee A (2016) Sapatilhas: cultural significance and industrial legacy. Poster session presented at Ciência 2016, Lisbon

Droumeva M, Murphy D (2016) A sound pedagogy: active learning through media production. Edulearn16 Proceedings, pp 3974–3982

Fleck J, Tierney M (1992) The management of expertise. University of Edinburgh, Programme on Information and Communication Technologies, Edinburgh

Gomes A (2016) Design, tradition and craft: the case of Almalaguês. University of Porto, Presentation

Jokilehto J (1999) A history of architectural conservation. Butterworth-Heinemann, London

Lains P, Pereira SA (2010) From an agrarian society to a knowledge economy: Portugal. Working Papers in Economic History, WP10–09. Universidad Carlos III, Madrid

Shwarz M, Yair K (2010) Making value: craft & the economic and social contribution of makers. Crafts Council

Thomas, N.J, Hackney, F. and Bunnell, K. (2011). Connecting craft and communities, In Connected Communities. Arts and Humanities Research Council

Westecott E (2012) Independent game development as craft, Loading… J Can Game Stud Assoc 7(11), pp 78–91

Play to Design with *Cards GO*: A Card-Based Game for Game Design and Creativity

Fabrício Fava, Pedro Cardoso, Ricardo Melo, José Raimundo, and Camila Mangueira

Abstract Design thinking refers to a creative approach to deal with complex problems in design contexts. Originally harnessed by designers, it is today within everyone's reach, to be learned and employed in their practices. To make it accessible and tangible to those who are not designers, a number of tools began to be developed and systematized. Among those, we highlight the group of card-based tools, which enable individuals to develop their creativity and to generate innovative design concepts. In order to explore these tools and to provide a scenario for creative ideas, we developed a card-based game—*Cards GO*—and conducted a workshop experiment to evaluate the applicability of the game to conceive other game concepts. We assessed the results of the workshop from three points of view: (1) that of the researchers, through direct observation; (2) that of the participants, by means of a questionnaire about their intrinsic motivation; (3) that of three experts in game design. Overall, *Cards GO* presented itself as a valuable tool for game design, creative thinking and collaboration. However, it was observed that the developed game concepts needed to be better detailed.

Keywords Cards-based tools · Creative process · Design · Games · Methodology

F. Fava (✉) · C. Mangueira
i2ADS / Faculty of Fine Arts of the University of Porto, Porto, Portugal
e-mail: ffava@fba.up.pt

C. Mangueira
e-mail: camilasoares@fba.up.pt

P. Cardoso
Faculty of Engineering and Faculty of Fine Arts of the University of Porto, Porto, Portugal
e-mail: pcardoso@fba.up.pt

R. Melo
Fraunhofer AICOS, Porto, Portugal
e-mail: ricardo.melo@fraunhofer.pt

J. Raimundo
INESC TEC / Faculty of Engineering of the University of Porto, Porto, Portugal
e-mail: joseraimundo3d@gmail.com

N. Martins et al. (eds.), *Perspectives on Design and Digital Communication*, Springer Series in Design and Innovation 8, https://doi.org/10.1007/978-3-030-49647-0_14

1 Introduction

Design thinking is believed to be a good means to meet various needs of creative development and to foster innovation in business and industry sectors, while being apt to stimulate collaboration (Chasanidou et al. 2015; Seidel and Fixson 2013). The term gained prominence in the early 2000s (Brown and Wyatt 2010), in a context where organizations were seeking innovation. The principle behind this human-centered, creative, iterative and practical approach (Brown 2009) was to spread the idea that the ways in which designers deal with complex problems could be learned and employed by anyone—even by those who never imagined themselves as designers. To externalize and to make this knowledge tangible, a number of design and research processes, methods, techniques and tools started being developed and systematised. Among those, we highlight the group of card-based design tools, which were designed to enable individuals develop their creativity and to generate innovative design concepts (Roy and Warren 2018).

In addition to design thinking, games have also been used as a means of teaching and promoting creativity in distinct ways (Blanco-Herrera et al. 2015). Creativity has been explored both in the context of video game playing (Jackson and Games 2015) and in that of game development process (Cook 2015). Scientific research has also demonstrated a number of positive effects regarding interaction with video games (Green and Kaufman 2015), such as cognitive, social, emotional, and motivational effects.

With this into consideration, we start this paper[1] by briefly discussing some card-based tools for creative design. Then, we introduce *Cards GO*, a card-based game we designed to promote creative ideas. After that, we present an experiment we conducted in order to evaluate the applicability of *Cards GO* to create other game concepts. Afterwards, we present its results, and develop an analysis and discussion on those.

2 Card-Based Tools for Creative Design

In an insightful review of card-based tools for creative and systematic design, Roy and Warren (2018) stated that card decks appeared "alongside the movement to develop systematic design methods". The authors argue that these tools have been used for promoting innovative and creative thinking since the 1950s, when Charles and Ray Eames created *The House of Cards*,[2] a set of 54 picture cards with six slots on each to enable the player interlock the cards and build structures of myriad shapes and sizes.

[1] This paper is an expanded version of (Fava et al. 2019).

[2] *The House of Cards* (1952–1961, 1999—present), Eames Office, Retrieved from https://www.eamesoffice.com/the-work/house-of-cards-2.

Later, in the 1970s, Brian Eno and Peter Schmidt produced *Oblique Strategies*,[3] a set of over 100 cards containing suggestions of courses of action or thinking to assist in creative situations (i.e. 'Be dirty', 'Do nothing for as long as possible', 'Listen in total darkness, or in a very large room, very quietly'). Afterwards, in the 1980s, a number of decks appeared. Roger von Oech, for instance, designed the *Creative Whack Pack*,[4] a deck of 64 illustrated cards that offers strategies for stimulating creativity (i.e. 'How can you reverse the way you look at your idea?', 'What would a six-year-old see if he were looking at your project?').

In the 1990s, with the emergence of participatory design, such card-based tools started being created to trigger collaboration. One example of this is *CARD* (Tudor et al. 1993), a participatory technique for analyzing and redesigning task flows in software systems. Using the metaphor of a card game, *CARD* was designed as a means for communication and collaboration among users, developers, and designers. From the 2000s onwards, such tools started to focus on user experience design and aimed to help designers create user-friendly solutions. In this regard, the most known and used example seems to be the *IDEO Method Cards*,[5] a deck of 51 cards divided into four categories (Learn, Look, Ask, and Try), each describing one design method and a brief story about how and when to use it.

Card-based design tools have been developed for distinct purposes. Based on a review of 72 tools, Roy and Warren (2018) classified them into six categories:

1. *Systematic design methods and procedures*, which present general methods, approaches and techniques to find, analyze and tackle design problems;
2. *Creative thinking and problem solving*, which can be used to help solve problems from distinct fields;
3. *Human-centered design*, which aim to help one focus on designing for users, considering their requirements and needs;
4. *Domain-specific methods*, which provide methods, information or checklists for specific domains, such as game design, graphic design, designing products or services for ecological sustainability or for children, etc.;
5. *Team building and collaborative working*, which provide guidance to facilitate collaborative working, participatory and co-design;
6. *Futures thinking*, that deals with awareness of change and scenario planning, and for creative problem solving within future constraints or scenarios.

Although intended to be used in a broad context, card-based tools are often used and tested by the research or company teams that developed them, which means that they are developed based on a specific creative culture. This explains why those tools often need training programs in order to be used productively. Moreover, they also demand a previous understanding of design methods and techniques, as well

[3] *Oblique Strategies* (1975—present), Eno Shop, Retrieved from https://www.enoshop.co.uk/product/oblique-strategies.html.

[4] *Creative Whack Pack* (1989—present), Creative Think, Retrieved from http://creativethink.com/products.html.

[5] *IDEO Method Cards* (2003—present), IDEO, Retrieved from https://www.ideo.com/post/method-cards.

as a certain level of systematization of the creative process itself. Trying to go in a different direction, designers Ricardo Melo and Pedro Cardoso created a card-based game called *Cards GO*.

3 *Cards GO*: From Character Design and Storytelling to Interaction Design

Cards GO was created in 2016 for a workshop at the *FuturePlaces Media Lab.*[6] At the time, it aimed to subvert the game and the cultural phenomenon of *Pokémon GO* (2016), transforming what is a passive activity of roaming while paying attention at a mobile phone's screen to capture virtual creatures into an active, reactive, creative and transformative activity, where the tangibility of the surrounding physical world feedbacks at the observer.

Cards GO combines unexpectedness, chance and randomness to create the conditions for creativity and imagination to have a chance to emerge. This is accomplished by asking participants to write a *noun*, a *verb*, an *adjective*, or whatever they want (*wild card*) in each of the 12 playing cards they will draw, resulting in 3 of each type (Fig. 1). These cards are then scrambled and piled up according to their type of card (noun, verb, adjective or wild cards), at the center of the playing table. Participants are then divided into teams (*stage 1—set up the content*). Each team randomly draws four cards. Turn-by-turn, each team plays a card of their choosing, adding it to the pool of previously played cards. After playing a card, that team may draw a new card from any pile (*stage 2—set up the stage, the context*). At any point, anyone from any team can yell "GO". When this happens, the teams have to create something that combines the ideas/concepts written on the cards that were played—at the time, characters and their backstories. The turn's duration is dictated by the total number of cards played, each card corresponds to a minute (*stage 3—go and create*). When the turn is over, teams need to present their creations (*stage 4—present the outcome*). Teams win points by making successful correspondences between the concepts present on the cards and their creation: 1 point per card. The team that yelled

Fig. 1 *Cards GO* examples of cards written by participants (i.e. destruir/destroy, pequeno/small, bonito/beautiful, trump tower)

[6]More information at http://futureplaces.org.

"GO", starting stage 3, needs to address all cards, doubling their points. Otherwise, that team's score will be cut in half (*stage 5—score*). After this stage, the game goes back to stage 2, or even stage 1 if the content needs to be altered (Fig. 2).

Later, in another workshop in 2018, *disruption cards* were introduced in the game. Their content is previously written, and they increase their score by 2 points per card. These present tasks (e.g. 'cannot use hands', 'sing during creation act') that players must perform during the creative processes, with the goal of getting them out of their comfort zone. During the beginning of stage 2, teams can blindly pick any number of these cards. However, they are obliged to fulfill the tasks of all the cards they pick, otherwise they'll see their score cut in half.

Beyond the creation of narratives and fiction, we understood this game's potential for addressing various design of concepts in interaction and play. In order to adapt this game to the context of interaction and game design, and when Fabrício Fava

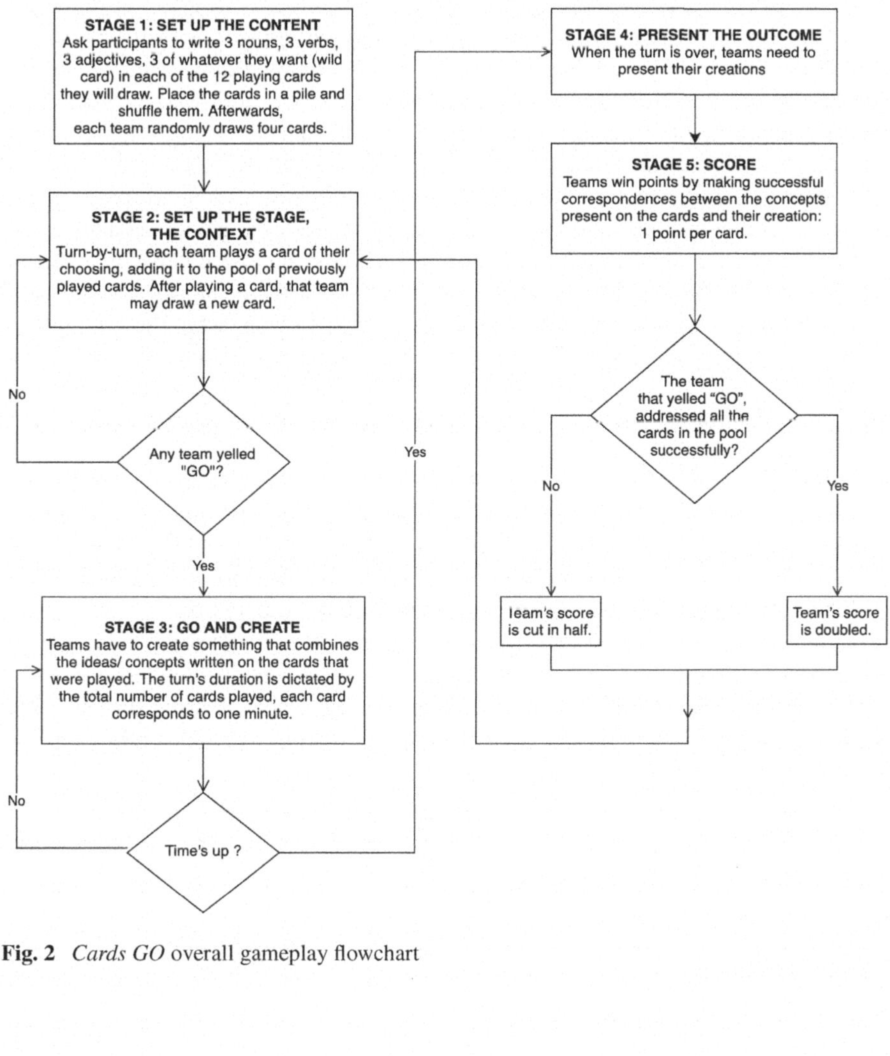

Fig. 2 *Cards GO* overall gameplay flowchart

joined in the design of this game, we created another set of cards: *user restrictions*. Their content is also previously written, presenting diverse user constraints (e.g. 'hands shake all the time', 'cannot see') to introduce such concerns into the creative process, with the objective to stimulate both user-centered design and empathy in players. These cards work in the exact same way as *disruption cards*.

4 A Game Design Workshop

In order to explore the possibilities of using *Cards GO* for the creation of game concepts, we conducted a 4-h game design workshop. A total of 9 participants (men = 4, women = 5), from distinct fields [design (n = 1), communication (n = 1), visual arts (n = 4), education sciences (n = 2) and games (n = 1)] enrolled in the workshop.

During its *first stage*, we presented a 45-min introduction to game design. The goal of this initial presentation was to provide the participants with the basics of game design and game mechanics. Then, we divided the participants into 3 groups of 3 participants, and presented *Cards GO*. This activity was followed by a warm up session that consisted of a tutorial on how to play the game.

During the *second stage* of the workshop, participants were invited to play a first round, aiming to create a game concept. As the game ended, we promoted a feedback discussion to expand the creative perspective of the games created. Each team had to present their ideas to the other participants, and these participants from other teams were able to give feedback on those concepts. Feedback consisted of writing down and speaking aloud, for the entire class to hear, what they thought it worked (strengths), what they thought it needed to be improved (weaknesses), and new ideas/suggestions for the presented concepts (e.g. alternative aspects, features or entire reformulations). After a 15-min break, the second round was played following the same dynamic of the first.

At the *third stage* of the workshop, all teams were invited to select one of the two game concepts they created, and to improve that idea considering the feedback given by their colleagues. This activity aimed to stimulate some critical thinking related to the creative process. After refining the concept, they had to document the idea by writing four aspects of the game: (1) goal (*What are players trying to do?*); (2) mechanics and rules (*What physical actions do players take?*); (3) components (*What are the materials of the game?*); and (4) space (*Where does the game happen?*).

The *fourth stage* was dedicated to participant assessment. During this moment participants were asked to assess Cards Go in four distinct subscales related to the Intrinsic Motivation Inventory (IMI)[7]:

1. *Interest/Enjoyment*: considers the self-report measure of intrinsic motivation.
2. *Perceived Competence*: is a positive predictor of both self-report and behavioral measures of intrinsic motivation.

[7]Center for Self-Determination Theory, Retrieved from https://selfdeterminationtheory.org/intrinsic-motivation-inventory.

3. *Pressure/Tension*: assesses the level of anxiety experienced during an activity.
4. *Value/Usefulness*: inspects if people internalize and become self-regulating with respect to activities that they experience as useful or valuable for themselves.

Assessing participants' subjective experience regarding those four subscales allow us to assess if *Cards GO* is capable of promoting an enjoyable experience, if the participants feel competent for the creation of games, their experienced level of pressure and tension during the creative process, and its potential for stimulating creative thinking.

After the workshop, there was the *fifth stage* of the experiment: the expert assessment. During this stage, we asked game design specialists to assess the conceived games regarding 4 aspects:

1. The level of *clarity* of the game's proposal;
2. The level of *creativity* of the game's proposal;
3. The level of *viability* of the game concept for future development;
4. The level of *consistency* of the game's mechanics towards the game's goal.

The expert assessment allowed us (1) to grasp how creative game concepts developed using *Cards GO* are from an expert point of view; (2) to confer if they are understandable for game designers; and (3) to acknowledge if they are viable for development.

5 Results and Discussion

5.1 Researcher Assessment

Cards GO presented itself as a productive tool for the design of games, as well as useful for the development of creative thinking. The gameplay experience promoted collaboration and engagement in players, most of which never had designed games before. Each team was able to create, discuss, select, refine, and document their own game (Fig. 3).

Regarding the content on the cards (verbs, adjectives, nouns and pictures), it was clear that the verbs usually determined the main objective or action of the game. This is related to the very notion of game mechanics, which determine the procedures and rules of the game (Schell 2008). However, verbs can be a limiting factor to the results, e.g. the goals of the games designed by the teams were very similar when the context presented by the game cards involved verbs, such as dancing.

The same is true for pictures. Visual elements that are already symbolically incorporated in the context of games usually promote similar forms of use, as was the case with the heart, which is usually applied in game design as a symbol of a character's life or health. When this element appeared in one of the game sessions (Fig. 4), the three teams used that same visual element for the same purpose. We do not consider this to be a negative approach to the exercise, but something to consider in the future.

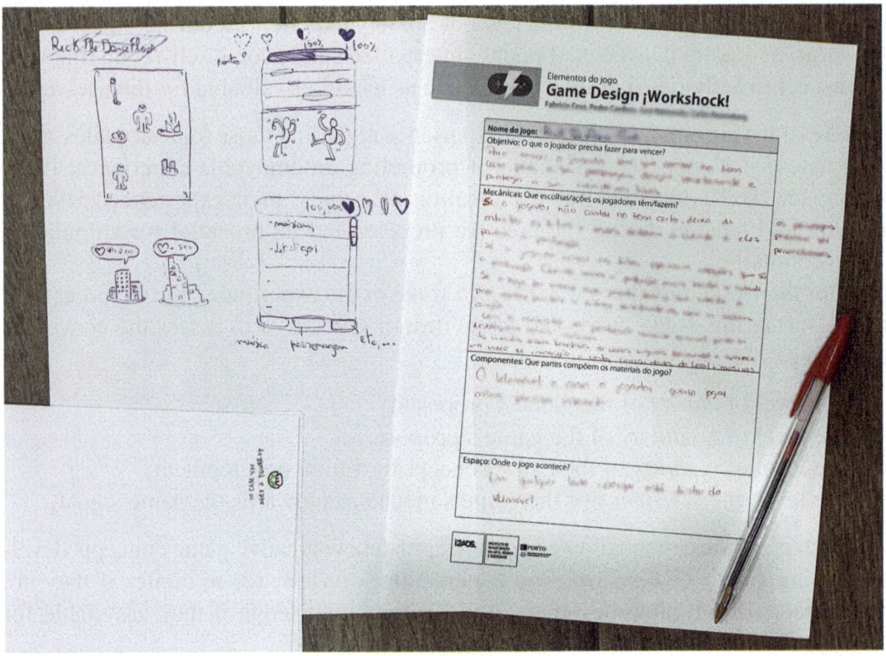

Fig. 3 Paper prototypes and documentation of one of the game concepts designed during the workshop

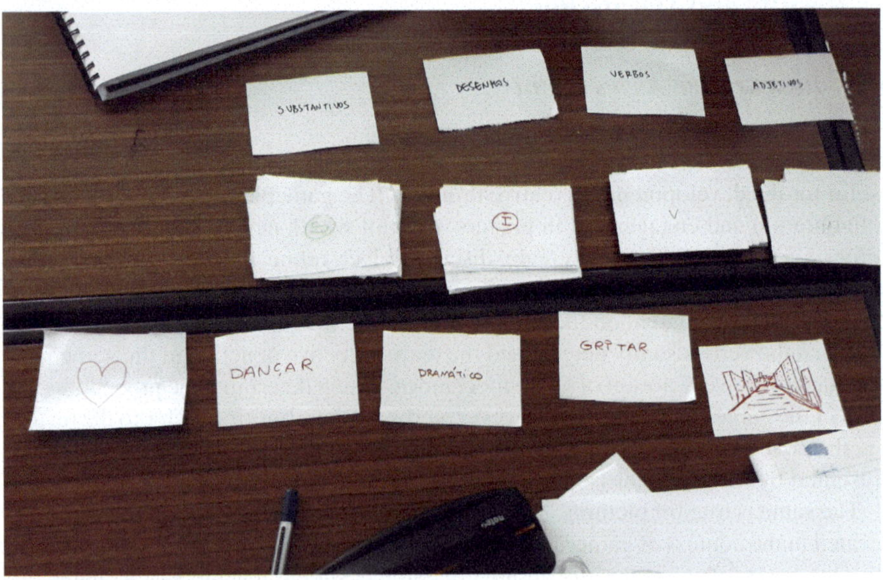

Fig. 4 Pool of cards (drawing of a heart, dançar/dancing, dramático/dramatic, gritar/shouting, and a drawing of an urban scenario) played in one of the game sections during the workshop experiment

Fig. 5 Post-its with participant feedback on a paper with game concept prototypes

Some participants presented some difficulty in providing feedback (Fig. 5). This may be related to a lack of experience with such collaborative creative process. In addition, we noticed that participants were not in the habit of taking notes of their ideas. They usually thought and evaluated their ideas well before writing their insights on paper, and ended up losing some along the way.

Participants also experienced some difficulty in describing the main mechanics of their games. The documentation of their own games seemed very restricted. In one of the game concepts, the mechanics and rules were described in a very broad and abstract way: "Challenges with great complexity and with levels. Differentiated score. They vote mutually"[8] (G3). This can be related to several factors: (1) the lack of knowledge about game design; (2) the fact that we usually fail to comment on aspects that are very familiar, because they are obvious to us (Norman 2004); (3) the time and intensity of the workshop. This last subject is something to consider in future experiments, since some participants were weary towards the end of the workshop.

[8]Original version in Portuguese: "Desafios com grande complexidade e com níveis. Pontuação diferenciada. Votam mutuamente".

5.2 Participant Assessment

Table 1 shows the average results of the intrinsic motivation inventory for each subscale considered in this study as well as the average result for each item assessed according to its respective subscale. As can be observed, two subscales (Interest/Enjoyment and Value/Usefulness) presented scores above 4, and the other two (Perceived Competence and Pressure/Tension) present scores below 4 in a scale of 1–7. The subscale that presented the highest average was Value/Usefulness (6.11) and the one that presented the lowest was Perceived Competence (3.39).

The results from the subscale Interest/Enjoyment (5.79) shows that the participants consider playing *Cards GO* as an interesting and enjoyable experience. Self-reported results showed that the activity was capable of engaging the participants, conferring a high level of fun and enjoyment (see items 2, 3 and 7, in Table 1). This is a positive result, as Interest/Enjoyment is the only subscale that assesses intrinsic motivation per se.

The Perceived Competence subscale presented a score of 3.39. Such result shows that playing *Cards GO* did not provide participants with the awareness of becoming more competent in the creation of games in comparison with their abilities prior to the workshop.

Pressure/Tension was another subscale that presented a score below 4 (3.78), but since it is theorized as a negative predictor of intrinsic motivation, and besides the fact that the value itself is rather neutral, lower values can be considered as positive results for this study. To experience a low level and pressure can also be considered a positive factor in an activity to exercise creative thinking, since relaxed and happy persons are not too focused and are able to expand the field of possibilities, becoming more creative and imaginative (Isen 1993).

The Value/Usefulness subscale presented the highest average value in the study (6.11), showing that the playing *Cards GO* was useful and/or valuable for the participants. Notwithstanding, the activity presented itself as relevant for stimulating creative thinking and for improving collaboration and creativity (see items 24 and 25 in Table 1).

5.3 Expert Assessment

Table 2 presents the results of the expert assessment for each observed item and their respective averages for each criterion. Overall, the developed games achieved higher averages regarding their viability (6.7, 6.7, and 4.7 respectively) and the lowest regarding creativity (4.7, 3.3 and 3.3 respectively).

Regarding Clarity, all games presented averages above 4 (5.3, 5.3 and 4.3 respectively), although game 3 maintained relatively at the centre of the scale (4.3). The deficiency in the description of the games as understood by the researchers (see Sect. 5.1) also was observed by the experts in their assessment: "the challenge and

Table 1 Average (AVG) for each item classified according to its respective subscale. The statements were randomly ordered in the administered questionnaire

Subscale	AVG (scale 1–7)	Item	AVG (scale 1–7)
Interest/enjoyment	5.79	1. I enjoyed doing this activity very much	6.1
		2. This activity did not hold my attention at all (R)	**6.2**
		3. This activity was fun to do	**6.2**
		4. While I was doing this activity, I was thinking about how much I enjoyed it	4.1
		5. I thought this was a boring activity (R)	6.1
		6. I thought this activity was quite enjoyable	5.6
		7. I would describe this activity as very interesting	**6.2**
Perceived competence	3.39	8. I was pretty skilled at creating game scenarios	4.2
		9. I think I am pretty good at game design	3.6
		10. I think I did pretty well at the workshop, compared to other students	3.2
		11. Creating game scenarios was an activity that I couldn't do very well (R)	2.8
		12. After working at the techniques for awhile, I felt pretty competent	2.9
		13. I am satisfied with my performance at creating game scenarios, compared to before the workshop	3.7
Pressure/tension	3.78	14. I was very relaxed in using the techniques (R)	3.2
		15. I did not feel nervous at all while using the techniques (R)	4.4
		16. I felt pressured while using the techniques	3.9
		17. I was anxious while using the techniques	3.9
		18. I felt very tense while using the techniques	3.4

(continued)

Table 1 (continued)

Subscale	AVG (scale 1–7)	Item	AVG (scale 1–7)
Value/usefulness	6.11	**19. I believe these techniques could be of some value to me**	**6.4**
		20. I think that these techniques are useful for creating game design solutions	5.8
		21. I think doing this activity could help me to be more creative	6.0
		22. I would be willing to do this again because it has some value to me	5.1
		23. I believe doing this activity could be somewhat beneficial to me	6.2
		24. I think this is an important activity for stimulating creative thinking	6.4
		25. I think this is important to do because it can improve collaboration and creativity	6.8

Note R, reversed score. Scale: 1 (total disagreement), 4 (partial agreement), 7 (total agreement)

focus of the game wasn't very clear, even with a certain goal in the game"[9] (S2); "Overall, detail in the way actions could be executed was missed"[10] (S3).

Creativity was the subject with the lowest average score. Only Game 1 presented a score superior to 4 (4.7); while Games 2 and 3 got an inferior score (3.3 each). This criterion was most subjective in the assessment, and even having available a space for writing comments, none of the three experts provided additional information. This fact does not allow us to present a more conclusive analysis.

Viability was the most well-assessed criterion. All the games obtained an average score above 4 (6.7, 6.7 and 4.7 respectively). This shows us that, besides having to deal with very random, uncertain and speculative, *Cards GO* allows the creation of game concepts capable of being developed.

Consistency is related to the relationship between game mechanics and goals created by the participants. Games 1 and 2 obtained a score superior to 4 (6.3 each); while, game 3 received an inferior average (3.3). Associated with game 3, this result

[9]Original version in Portuguese: "não ficou muito claro o desafio e foco, mesmo com um certo objetivo dentro do jogo".

[10]Original version in Portuguese: "De uma forma geral, faltou detalhamento como determinadas ações poderiam ser executadas".

Table 2 Game design specialists (S) individual scores and average (AVG) for each game concept according to its respective item

	Game 1				Game 2				Game 3			
Item	S1	S2	S3	AVG	S1	S2	S3	AVG	S1	S2	S3	AVG
Clarity: It is possible to understand how the game is played	7	3	6	**5.3**	7	3	6	**5.3**	4	6	3	**4.3**
Creativity: The game's concept proposal is creative	2	5	7	**4.7**	2	5	3	**3.3**	2	4	4	**3.3**
Viability: The game is possible to be developed	7	6	7	**6.7**	7	6	7	**6.7**	7	5	2	**4.7**
Consistency: The employed game mechanics are consistent with the game's goals	7	5	7	**6.3**	7	5	7	**6.3**	4	4	2	**3.3**

Scale: 1 (total disagreement), 4 (partial agreement), 7 (total agreement)

also points to the lack of clarity in the description of the game elements: "'The mechanics/actions' are not sufficiently developed in game 3"[11] (S3).

6 Conclusions and Future Work

We presented a brief panorama of the use of card-based tools in the context of design. Afterwards, we presented *Cards GO*, also a card-based game created by us and how it evolved from a creative instrument for character design and storytelling to a support tool for interaction and game design. Trying to understand new possibilities of use for Cards GO, we conducted a workshop focused on the design of game concepts. At the end of the workshop, participants answered a questionnaire focused on the assessment of their intrinsic motivation. Afterwards, the results of the workshop were submitted for assessment by three game design experts.

After the workshop, we observed that players of *Cards GO* were able to transform the combination of seemingly random concepts they wrote, drew or expressed somehow on the cards into creative solutions. Moreover, since the content of the cards (nouns, verbs, adjectives and wild cards) was not previously established, players worked with their own content, which may somehow be related with their current concerns about a given project or any other thing in their life.

Another perceived advantage of *Cards GO* is that it does not demand a previous understanding of design methods and provides a playful and collaborative way of creating stories, interaction and game concepts. This helps accommodate the game to players that are not designers, welcoming those with all sorts of professional backgrounds.

From the participant's point of view, the activity of game conception with *Cards GO* revealed itself as interesting, fun, and able to add value and usefulness. Self-reported answers presented the highest scores by relating their experience with the game with its ability to stimulate creative thinking and collaboration.

Notwithstanding, such opinion regarding creativity was not shared by the game design experts, although such lower scores may be related with the fact that these game concepts required to be better detailed to be properly communicated to third parties. On the other hand, all game concepts were assessed by the experts as viable for development and implementation.

The next steps of the research will focus on three aspects:

1. To conduct new workshops with larger groups, and with a control group to compare results with. Overall, despite having been classified as a positive experience, the number of participants and that of the produced game concepts is still low for us to draw more assertive conclusions.

[11]Original version in Portuguese: "'Mecânicas/ações' não são desenvolvidas o suficiente no jogo 3".

2. To explore more efficient strategies for documenting ideas. This aspect was noted by both the researchers and the game design experts, and is something to consider in future endeavours.
3. To explore the possibility for conducting the same workshop in distinct moments. Towards the end of the event, we observed that some participants were weary, and that may have negatively impacted the level of detail in their game concepts. One possibility is to divide the workshop in two distinct moments with a larger intermission in the middle—hours or even days apart.

References

Blanco-Herrera J, Groves C, Lewis A, Gentile D (2015) Teaching creativity: theoretical models and applications. In: Green G, Kaufman J (eds) Video games and creativity. Academic Press, San Diego, CA, pp 139–158

Brown T (2009) *Change by design*: how design thinking transforms organizations and inspires innovation. Harper Collins, New York

Brown T, Wyatt J (2010) Design thinking and social innovation. Stanford Soc Rev

Chasanidou D, Gasparini AA, Lee E (2015) Design thinking methods and tools for innovation. In: HCI international 2015 Los Angeles, vol 9186. CA, USA, August 2–7, 2015 proceedings, part I, pp 12–23. https://doi.org/10.1007/978-3-319-20886-2_2

Cook M (2015) Creating code creatively: automated discovery of game mechanics through code generation. In: Green G, Kaufman J (eds) Video games and creativity. Academic Press, San Diego, CA, pp 225–245

Fava F, Cardoso P, Melo R, Raimundo J, Soares CM (2019) *Cards GO*: A card-based game for game design and creativity. Paper presented at the DIGICOM: 3rd international conference on design & digital communication, Barcelos

Green G, Kaufman J (eds) (2015) Video games and creativity. Academic Press, San Diego, CA

Isen AM (1993) Positive affect and decision making. In: Lewis M, Haviland JM (eds) Handbook of emotions. Guilford, Nova York

Jackson L, Games A (2015) Video games and creativity. In: Green G, Kaufman J (eds) Video games and creativity. Academic Press, San Diego, CA, pp 3–38

Norman D (2004) *Emotional design*: Why we love (or hate) everyday things. Basic Books, New York

Pokémon Go (2016) https://www.pokemongo.com/en-us/. Last accessed 25 June 2019

Roy R, Warren J (2018) Card-based tools for creative and systematic design. In: Proceedings of the design research society DRS2018 conference (TBC), pp 1075–1087

Schell J (2008) *The art of game design*: a book of lenses. Morgan Kaufmann Publishers, Burlington, MA

Seidel VP, Fixson SK (2013) Adopting design thinking in novice multidisciplinary teams: the application and limits of design methods and reflexive practices. J Prod Innov Manage 30:19–33

Tudor L, Muller M, Dayton T (1993) A C.A.R.D. game for participatory task analysis and redesign. In: Conference: *Human-Computer Interaction*, INTERACT '93, 24–29 April, Amsterdam

Cinema, Education, and the Internet: Which Convergences?

João Pinto, Teresa Cardoso, and Ana Isabel Soares

Abstract This chapter addresses the relationship between cinema, education and the Internet. We focus namely on the contributions of cinema to learning in present society and on new paths for its integration in educational contexts, according to recent paradigms of teaching and lifelong learning. To study this relationship in the context of current digital lifestyles, we take into account phenomena of transmedia and media convergence made possible by the evolution of the Internet. Technological (r)evolution brought a profound transformation into users: from passive consumers of information produced, they have become also producers and distributors of content (their own, or otherwise), which continues to have a profound social and cultural impact on contemporary society. In view of these dynamics, cinema as an industry presents new opportunities and possibilities to intervene and finds a new type of audience, which, in addition to being spectators, can be producers of audiovisual content in their daily lives. We continue to explore the strong pedagogical potential of cinema, as the information conveyed and the audiovisual stimuli composing it are easily assimilated by viewers, while cinematographic content takes on increasing and transversal importance in the various digital media and platforms.

Keywords Cinema · Education · Internet · Transmedia · Convergence culture

J. Pinto (✉) · A. I. Soares
CIAC, Centro de Investigação em Artes e Comunicação, Universidade do Algarve, Faro, Portugal
e-mail: jppinto@lead.uab.pt

A. I. Soares
e-mail: asoares@ualg.pt

J. Pinto · T. Cardoso
LE@D, Laboratório de Educação a Distância e E-learning, Universidade Aberta, Lisbon, Portugal
e-mail: teresa.cardoso@uab.pt

N. Martins et al. (eds.), *Perspectives on Design and Digital Communication*, Springer Series in Design and Innovation 8, https://doi.org/10.1007/978-3-030-49647-0_15

1 Introduction

According to Castells (2011), a technological revolution has emerged in a network society in which people see themselves as active citizens, constructing a collective intelligence, and not merely passive consumers of a culture created by others. Social networks have become the new means of dissemination, with innovative possibilities for interactions (Pinto 2017), and the emergence of new communication devices in our day-to-day lives, which continually revolutionize the way audiovisual is experienced (Reia-Baptista 2006). This, in turn, found in cinema—since its emergence in the last decade of the 19th century—one of the most comprehensive modes of cultural expression in the contemporary industrial and technological society, and one that would profoundly shape the way of experiencing images.

In the context of what is meant by formal, informal or non-formal education, the relationship between cinema and education has been part of the history of cinema since the beginning of the cinematic age, because cinematographic works were more or less explicitly understood as means for propagating educational messages beyond the purpose of entertainment they had as the fair event they started out to be. However, and in an almost simultaneous paradox, according to Duarte (2002), even as the Seventh Art asserted itself as a fertile source of knowledge, it is not always understood in this way, mainly by educational entities and institutions. Now, in view of the dynamics that emerge around new media such as transmedia narratives and media convergence, and although cinema has always assumed an educational role in society, nowadays it finds new possibilities and ways to intervene in the educational landscape of society, and it has participatory audiences, which, in addition to being passive, inert consumers, can be producers of audiovisual content (Oliveira and Caetano 2017, p. 55).

In this text we are interested in considering cinema not only as a form of expression that belongs among the various arts (and which Canudo [1923, p. 3] considers as the "seventh art"), not only as an "entertainment product" (Toldo and Lopes 2017, p. 172), but, above all, as a "learning support agent" (Linhares and Ávila 2017, p. 99). In the technological context of the "network society" (Castells 2011), we will also undergo a reflection about cinema and education in the face of the dynamics created by the Internet—more specifically, we will take into account the phenomenon of social networks, "cyberculture" (Lévy 1999, p. 17), "transmedia" (Jenkins 2006), and media convergence (Navarro 2010, p. 14).

The considerations we will undertake here also intend to contribute to the consolidation of the theoretical framework of the research project on "Education, Cinema and Social Networks: a research study on the National Cinema Plan" developed under the aegis of the Arts and Communication Research Center of Algarve University in Portugal (CIAC) with support from the Portuguese Foundation for Science and Technology (FCT) and integrated in the Ph.D. plan in Digital Media Arts of the first author, under the scientific supervision of the second and third authors of this chapter.

Created in 2013 upon a joint government initiative of the "Presidency of the Council of Ministers, through the Secretary of State for Culture, and the Ministry of Education and Science, through the Secretary of State for Basic and Secondary Education" (cf. Dispatch 15377/2013 of September 26 issued by the Presidency of the Council of Ministers, which creates the Project Group for the National Cinema Plan [PNC]), the goals of the PNC are, among others, "to promote cinema literacy" and "to disseminate national cinematographic works" among the school public, guaranteeing essential instruments for viewing and interpreting these works with the students of the schools under the program (cf. text of the same governmental Dispatch). Through our research study, we intend to understand the ways in which this government initiative has resorted, in its implementation, to online digital social networks, to systematize good practices and to contribute for the definition of a set of recommendations to improve the use of the tools used. In the context of the new paradigms of open science, we believe, therefore, to contribute to the simultaneous scientific knowledge of the areas of Education, Cinema and Social Networks.

2 Cinema and Education: A Few Approaches

A few years after it appeared, cinema came to be understood as an artistic expression and its creators worked to consolidate this statement with each new work produced. In 1911, Ricciotto Canudo presented a series of lectures, later published under the title *Manifeste des Sept Arts* (Canudo 1923, p. 3), in which he defended cinema as the "seventh art (…) giving it an aesthetic character" and recognizing "Cinema as a language, capable of renewing, transforming and disseminating other Arts, in a Total Art project" (Brandão 2008, p. 7). According to Canudo referring to cinema,

> But this sort of total synthesis, this fabulous newborn child of the Machine and of feeling, begins to cease its wailings, enters its childhood. Soon adolescence will come to grab its intelligence and multiply its dreams. We demand that the development be precipitated, that the advent of its youth be accelerated. We need the Cinema to create the total art toward which all the others have always tended. (1911)

In the beginning, the exhibition of the films was a demonstration of a novelty; from the affirmation of cinema as an art, its almost natural evolution was toward the artistic sense, a course beyond the purpose of entertaining and turned, also, to an understanding of itself. The stories told in each film started to comprise narrative structures with plots, characters and other elements, incipient in some of the first experiences, and increasingly complex, which went beyond the aesthetic sense that a meta-artistic, or autotelic attention, necessarily involves.

The First World War (1914–1918), whose battlegrounds were located primarily in Europe, forced film production out of the Old Continent and into the United States: Hollywood then became the center of the film industry, and cinema would function largely as a product of pure entertainment and mass alienation, in a logic governed by the markets and financial return. For Toldo and Lopes (2017), this industrial ideology did not seem concerned "with aesthetic innovation" (p. 172), nor with the options of the authors, but privileged rather the commercial concerns of producers. For its part, the Nouvelle Vague, an artistic movement in French cinema, which surged mainly during the 1960s, defended "the authorship of the director in the cinematographic work and [brought] to the cinema, young themes, unethical heroes and breaks with language classic" (Toldo and Lopes 2017, p. 173). Such ideas would eventually influence the industrial cinema produced by Hollywood, inspiring new authors and directors, among others, with "new themes and new aesthetic propositions to films" (p. 190). However, these authors recall that the ambivalence of art cinema versus the industry-leisure/entertainment is an issue as old as cinema itself, something that is reflected in the way it is still seen by education agents.

As was stated above, the association between cinema and education goes back to the beginning of cinematographic history itself (cf., for example, Pinto et al. 2019, p. 5). Film producers and directors considered cinema, from its outset, as a powerful tool for the formation, education and reflection of the individual in human society. When analyzing the relationship between cinema and education, Linhares and Ávila (2017, p. 99) emphasize that it has always been "considered as a leisure instrument combined with the capitalist market in order to manipulate society" (p. 99), but which, on the other hand, was seen as a "learning support agent" (p. 99). The authors conclude that this dichotomy contributed to create some distance between cinema and education, as well as to the lack of appreciation of the potential of cinema in learning, since the works of the Seventh Art were more often associated with leisure and entertainment products—which, namely for the uncritical common sense, diminished the credibility of cinema.

Bearing into account the diversity of knowledge comprised in a film, one can conclude that its exhibition represents much beyond an audiovisual stimulus or an illustration of reality. The use of cinema in the field of education is therefore "a means of teaching and learning" (Pinto et al. 2019, p. 5), which helps shed light on social, cultural, historical, literary and political aspects. In a classroom context, the use of viewing cinematographic works is seen by Silva (2007) as a fundamental element to break barriers between the school's daily life and that of life outside of the classroom, as well as to reduce methodological fences separating thinking, feeling and learning, which expands the possibility of listening and reflecting the student. Trevizan and Crepaldi (2009) in Alves da Silva (2014, p. 363) mention that "the audiovisual language is very attractive and can produce different and enriching experiences in the classroom" (p. 363). Therefore, concludes this author, "films can be used as a 'gateway' to information that generates knowledge, which does not end in itself". In other words, through film analysis, a wide process of perception and reflection on the knowledge and practices inherent in the cinematographic language can be activated, enabling the process of learning that leads to the construction of knowledge. We tend to agree with Linhares and Ávila (2017), namely when they affirm that "the approaches of cinema and education are multiple and complex, extrapolating the simple association of film with content" (p. 89). It is in this sense that we then explore such approaches, complexifying the equation when observing them in the light of convergences brought about by the new digital world.

3 Cinema and Education: A Few Convergences Around the Digital

In a technological society such as the one we live in, highly mediatized, audiovisual content has gained particular prominence in social networks, and interest is increasing in "telling stories with images, sounds and movements" (Fantin 2007, p. 1). This leads us to consider one of the main characteristics of cinema, a narrative art par excellence. This reality of the confluence of two media—that of social networks and that of cinema—to which students are permanently exposed has equally implications for the way in which learning occurs, whether in formal/schooled contexts, or in informal or non-formal contexts. Education should therefore "consider new directions, strategies and methodologies, so that it can respond to the needs of individuals and institutions" (Pinto 2017, p. 8).

The digital technological revolution brought about a new social paradigm, described, as previously referred to, by Castells (2011) as a "network society," in which people interact daily with the most varied digital content as if it were inside a "media tsunami" (Trültzsch-Wijnen 2019, p. 61) causing "impacts on the lifestyle and behavior of individuals in society, as well as on the way they learn" (Pinto and Cardoso 2017, p. 79). This gives new meanings to the concepts of time and space, and profoundly transforms the processes of communication and perception of reality, into a "broad present" (Gumbrecht 2014, p. 87) expanded by and with the experiences of communicative simultaneity. While they change the entire dynamics of resource and exposure of individuals to the media, these transformations vest users with a series of skills and effective power: instead of being a mere consumer of content, each individual in this media society becomes equally potentially and often the actual producer of those same contents. Bruns (2006) coined the term "produsers" (p. 3) to refer to these new citizens in a networked world. The concept emerges from phenomena such as cyberculture and participatory culture, and has transversal implications for the various dimensions of the lives of individuals. In order to understand such transformations better, it is important to mention the contributions of Pierre Lévy (1999), who defines cyberculture as a "set of practices, attitudes, modes of thought and values that develop together with the growth of cyberspace" (p. 17), and Rheingold (2012), when he identifies the "emergence of a participatory culture [in which] the people who think they are able to create and also to consume are different citizens. And their participation makes society different and better" (p. 249).

A scenario thus designed grants the relationship between cinema and education a series of new meanings and challenges, given the "enormous potential for knowledge sharing" (Santos 2012, p. 83); therefore, the culture of participation is ratified, as it encourages connectivity, interactivity and cooperation through the Internet, with reflexes on the ways of learning.

Technological developments, namely in digital media based on the Internet, have radically transformed the "production, dissemination and consumption of audiovisual works, even cinematographic work" (Barone 2009, p. 45). Web spaces, with emphasis on online social networks, are nowadays perhaps the most used means for the construction and dissemination of artistic and cultural content, including audiovisual ones. In this way, the access to participation of individuals, producers, is increasingly democratized, freed from physical, technical and geographical constraints.

The new ways of distributing, consuming and interacting with content are directly related to the technological evolution of the Internet itself, from the Web 1.0 to the current Web 3.0, so, even if briefly, we will highlight the evolution of this medium. The first Internet pages were characterized by being static websites, through which content was made available without any possibility of interaction with users. It was the 1990s and the most users could do in addition to viewing the contents was to select links that, triggered by a click of the mouse button, opened onto other pages and, at best, allowed to download content. This stage of the Internet would be known as the Web 1.0—Internet's first generation, characterized by allowing "read-only" uses and nothing else (Gil 2014, p. 1). Even so, it can be said that there was already "a real Information Society" (idem), due to the fact that users had at their disposal a "large digital library, allowing access to a large amount of content" (Santarosa et al. 2014, p. 2), available anytime and anywhere. Search engines, like Google, are the best example of this type of services offered in this generation, as they allowed to easily and quickly search for information on the Internet.

The Web 2.0 appeared in the wake of the 21st century. The designation of this second generation referred to a type of Internet pages that encouraged users to give opinions, share content and even build online spaces that provided content created by themselves, such as blogs (a designation that derives from the reduction of the term *weblog*, a kind of diary [log] made available on the [web] network). Here, participants can interact (by posting comments on publications, for example), suggest, criticize, oppose ideas and add content. Rheingold called this wider interaction an "architecture of participation" (2012, p. 2); but it might as well be called the "Social Web," an expression that emphasizes user participation as a consumer, producer and distributor of content. In such a context of sharing, discussion and critical reflection, "conditions are created to be able to affirm that the transition from an Information Society to the Knowledge Society is promoted" (Gil 2014, p. 2). Paradigmatic examples of the Web 2.0 are the aforementioned blogs (which allowed users without previous knowledge of web programming to create online spaces from the most varied types of content) and digital social networks, which would enhance possibilities for interaction that had not been available before. From a "passive user" (Santos and Petersen 2014, p. 66) on the Web 1.0, we deem another, "less utilitarian and more interactive, participatory, collaborative" (p. 66) user.

With the large-scale expansion of the Internet, questions of information management began to arise (how to organize, in a simple and efficient way, the huge amounts of content archived on the Internet), but also of information availability (how to offer easy search and access, according to the specific needs of each user)—issues related to the concept of "Big Data" as described by Tomás (2013, p. 24). From the answers to these concerns came the Web 3.0—the third generation, also known as the semantic web. The concept of "semantic Web" (Berners-Lee et al. 2001) is recent and it characterizes the capacity computer systems have to interpret the content available on websites and to be able to understand the meaning of words differently. In other words, the contents are interpreted according to the contexts in which they appear, considering the characteristics of each user and their profile, and the attempt is to present each user exactly with what he/she wants, based on what the computer systems manage to gather from the user's behavior online. Therefore, there is a "personalization of web browsing, with programs that perceive specificities and preferences" (Santarosa et al. 2014, p. 2). This fact profoundly changes our experience of the Internet, as "the artificial intelligence mechanisms imbued with semantics are capable of introducing different dimensions, both in the personal and social spheres" (Tomás 2013, p. 152) and to "promote, increasingly, personalization in an open (social) context of learning" (p. 60).

The increasing use of mobile devices such as smartphones, on the other hand, has opened up for the experience of the mobile Internet, whose access is guaranteed without constraints of place, time or device. This has changed the nature of the network: now the user tends to spend more and more time connected, in a state of permanent availability, "in constant communication with those with whom he has relationships, with the social networks in which he participates, using the recently acquired connectivity to inform his peers or his friends about what is happening with him and in his surroundings (…). In other words, since then it has stimulated the exchange and creation of integrated content of common interest" (Santos and Petersen 2014, p. 66). Table 1, reproduced from Santarosa et al. (2014, p. 2), summarizes the characteristics of the three web generations described:

In the evolution of the Internet, according to this summary, there is a change in usage, which "shifts from a primarily instrumental emphasis to a broadly relational one" (Santos and Petersen 2014, p. 64). At first, the use was fundamentally instrumental; that is, the Internet was used mainly as an instrument for activities of information research, collection and dissemination, but above all as a means of content consumption. Currently, the focus of users is on collective participation and interactive collaboration, so much so that the characteristics of an instrumental web lose relevance in favor of those of a relational web, strengthened by social interactions and bonds, that is, aimed at enabling "new forms of sociability" (Rheingold 2012, p. 192).

Thus, and briefly describing the evolution, it can be said that the Web 1.0 allowed content to reach the consumer, surpassing time and location factors; that the Web 2.0

Table 1 Main traits of the web generations

Web 1.0	Web 2.0	Web 3.0
Great digital library	Participation, cooperation, collaboration	Customized browsing
Low interactivity	Greater interactivity	Interpretation of preferences
User as viewer	Virtual communities	Information organization and analysis

brought along interactive features and made richer communication possible, as well as a return about the spectator's involvement with narratives; and that more recently, with the Web 3.0 it is possible to adapt the narratives to the consumer's profile and, in conjunction with the potentialities derived from artificial intelligence, to carry out innovative and gradually more personalized transmedia narratives.

One of the consequences of this technological (r)evolution is the emergence of new means of communication: these, also based on the Internet, carry along new models for the creation of narratives and a new paradigm of dissemination, in which contents are conveyed and spread through different means, configuring new forms of relationship between producer and consumer. It is in this context that the concept of transmedia storytelling or transmedia storytelling emerges (Navarro 2010). It defines the construction of narratives in different media, through which "each one […] makes his own contribution to the interpretation of global history" (Jenkins 2006). In other words, "at the most basic level, transmedia stories are stories narrated through multiple media. Nowadays, the most significant stories tend to flow on various media platforms" (Jenkins et al. 2006, p. 46). Because, as Jenkins (2006) notes, there are "narratives so extensive that they cannot be contained in a single medium" (p. 95). Lacalle (2011) illustrates this by stating that "comic books" are similar to the transmedia stories of the past, since they combine means of communication such as paper, television, and cinema, interconnecting text and consumer, and, more recently, Internet-based media.

In fact, the Internet allows producers to obtain an immediate return on users' actions, as well as to know consumers' demands in detail. It allows, therefore, to adapt the narratives to their tastes, but also to create a greater involvement among the various agents who participate in the process. If, in the past, narratives were concerned with the general public, with general and anonymous characteristics, with the development of the Internet as a means of communication, nowadays more restricted audiences or groups of consumers, even at the level of the individual, with more specific characteristics are considered. If we transpose this evolution into cinema—and cinema works are also part of the countless integrated and shared current Internet contents—, it can be affirmed that the films that started to be consumed by the masses, for example, in large cinemas, can now be consumed by the spectators in the isolation of the contact between the individual and his/her smartphone, in a kind of "reduction" of the human body to the sitting position in front of a minuscule screen (cf. Gumbrecht 2014, p. 87).

Lacalle (op. cit.) argues that film producers have long discovered the innovative possibilities of transmedia narratives, referring that already in the 1980s they began to use them in order to profit from the large investments forced into Hollywood films. Therefore, the construction of transmedia narratives was seen as a way of reaching greater audiences, and, consequently, as a strategy to maximize profit. In fact, the Hollywood film industry "is conservative and uses transmedia practices in relatively trivial ways, more focused on marketing than narrative" (Navarro 2010, p. 14).

Currently, however, as Jenkins argues in an interview with Navarro (2010), the media environment allows consumers to receive content through web platforms such as YouTube, and "transmedia narratives transform the way we think about cinema"

(p. 15). According to the author, our technological scenario is characterized by the re-appropriation of content and by cooperative and collaborative media production: it includes not only producers, but also consumers. Given this reality, Jenkins also reflects on the way in which information travels through different media platforms, and he proposes the term "Culture of Convergence" to define the way content is produced, disseminated and consumed, allowing its movement through different media and involving aggregation between different media industries. This dynamic should not be understood as an essentially technological process, through the creation of the technological platforms that make it possible, but rather as a cultural process resulting from a need felt by a society in which individuals are interested in consuming content through different means and formats, beyond the constraints of time and space. The process of creating new platforms responds to a social demand related to the enormous flows of information produced by society in the most varied formats (verbal text, image, sound, etc.), which converge on the electronic devices of our daily lives (as mobile phones). In addition to receiving this massive information flow, each individual can appropriate content, transform it, and, once more share it with the added value of more information, feeding these and other new flows.

The Culture of Convergence can thus be described as "a cultural phenomenon that involves new relationships between producers" and "consumers" (Navarro 2010, p. 14). These are seen as active and creative agents that help to define how media content should be used and, in some cases, shape it. Media convergence tends to expand participatory culture and collective intelligence, since it allows greater access to the production and circulation of culture. It is, therefore, an ally in the educational process, and, in articulation with cinema, namely through transmedia narratives, it can contribute to change the learning processes and the relation toward learning contents, in the constitution of new learning environments (Silva et al. 2012, p. 408), and within a highly competitive society, in which the acquisition of skills is a determining factor for the personal and professional development of the citizen.

In this scenario, according to Branco and Costa (2013), the development of transmedia narratives, "when conceived on purpose, [can] be an effective tool for all age groups and in all learning environments because they create transformative learning experiences" (p. 1278). These authors note that, as in other areas, for example in the area of entertainment, in which the use of transmedia narratives motivates consumers to engage with history, education can use this strategy as a means to create an involvement with learning contents. Thus, it might not only bring students closer to the topics at stake, through a fictional world created by the use of different formats and means of communication, but also open a way to make the creative processes used by this industry more familiar.

Long (2009) suggests "transmedia education" as a way of referring to this use of transmedia narratives in education. For that researcher, it is a strategy that, when implemented in the classroom, offers students the opportunity to learn from one another through the use of different types of media, which provides them with space for research, collaborative work and sharing. These, in a way, are characteristics associated with the work of the professional world, and certainly with education in lifelong learning.

In short, transmedia narratives can "offer great potential in terms of innovation in teaching organization processes" (Branco and Costa 2013, p. 1276). We therefore believe that cinematographic works should be integrated into these work dynamics, due to the characteristics they present, both in their technical aspects and as a source of knowledge, thus taking advantage of the capacity for involvement and depth of cinematographic content.

4 Conclusions

Throughout this article, we addressed aspects of the relationship between cinema and education, an affinity that goes back to the origins of cinema, and considered potential and desirable convergences in the Internet age. We live in a technological and audiovisual society in which new lifestyles—namely the digital—are incorporated, at a time when education is not exclusive to the closed space of the classroom, but occurs anywhere and anytime, conquering other means and assuming new pedagogical dynamics.

We acknowledge the fact that cinema has accompanied the evolution of education and technology, and that it now faces new challenges. The possibilities of sharing and cooperation, made available by the tools associated with multimedia and the Internet, encourage new educational practices, because "in the network society, people learn more and more informally in their personal and professional activities [...] Informal learning is, more and more, the true engine of human capital development" (Viana 2009, p. 21). Finally, we can conclude that cinema is a tool with a strong potential for education, since it is easy to understand information through audiovisual stimuli, and that transmedia narratives and media convergence, in particular, contribute to the strengthening of this relationship, given the phenomena of participatory culture and collective intelligence, so characteristic of a media society in which one lives in a network.

References

Alves da Silva J (2014) Cinema e educação: o uso de filmes na escola/Movies and education: the use of films in school. Revista Intersaberes:361–373. Retrieved from www.uninter.com/intersaberes/index.php/revista/article/viewFile/642/421

Barone JG (2009) Cenários tecnológicos e institucionais do cinema brasileiro na década de 90. Sulina, Porto Alegre, Brasil

Berners-Lee T, Hendler J, Lassila O (2001) The semantic web. Scientific American. Retrieved from http://www-sop.inria.fr/acacia/cours/essi2006/Scientific%20American_%20Feature%20Article_%20The%20Semantic%20Web_%20May%202001.pdf

Branco E, Costa F (2013) Narrativas Transmédia: Criação de novos cenários de aprendizagem. In: Gomes MJ, Osório A, Ramos A, Silva B, Valente J (eds) Actas da VIII Conferência Internacional de Tecnologias de Informação e Comunicação na Educação, Challenges 2013. Aprender a qualquer hora e em qualquer lugar. Centro de Competência da Universidade do Minho, Braga, pp

1275–1284. Retrieved from https://www.nonio.uminho.pt/challenges/download/atas-challenges-2013/

Brandão HSM (2008) A fábrica de imagens: o cinema como arte plástica e rítmica. Universidade de Lisboa. Retrieved from http://repositorio.ul.pt/bitstream/10451/341/1/19611_ulfl068913_tm.pdf

Bruns A (2006) Towards Produsage: futures for user-led content production. Queensland University of Technology, Australia, 2006. Retrieved from http://eprints.qut.edu.au/4863/1/4863_1.pdf. Acesso em 01 out. 2016

Canudo R (1923) La Gazette des Sept Arts. 2. Paris. Transcript on http://www.filosofia.org/hem/192/9230125.htm. Republished in La Gazette des Sept Arts. 10. Paris. Retrieved from http://www.cineressources.net/consultationPdf/web/o002/2687.pdf

Canudo R (1911) La naissance d'un sixième art. Essai sur le cinématographe in: ders., Les entretiens idéalistes, X, 6, Nr. LXI, pp 169–179

Castells M (2011) A Sociedade em Rede. A Era da Informação: Economia, Sociedade e Cultura (4.a ed.). Fundação Calouste Gulbenkian, Lisboa

Despacho nº 15377/2013 de 26 de novembro de 2013. Diário da República, 2.ª série, n.º 229. Presidência do Conselho de Ministros e Ministérios das Finanças e da Educação e Ciência. Retrieved from https://dre.pt/application/dir/pdf2sdip/2013/11/229000000/3453934540.pdf

Duarte R (2002) Cinema & educação: refletindo sobre cinema e educação. Revista Brasileira de Educação 23:126. https://doi.org/10.1590/S1413-24782003000200014

Fantin M (2007) Média-Educação e Cinema na Escola. Teias, 14–15. Retrieved from https://www.e-publicacoes.uerj.br/index.php/revistateias/article/view/24008/16978

Gil H (2014) A passagem da WEB 1.0 para a WEb 2.0 e… WEB 3.0: potenciais consequências para uma «humanização» em contexto educativo. Educatic—boletim informativo, 1–2. Retrieved from https://repositorio.ipcb.pt/handle/10400.11/2404

Gumbrecht HU (2014) Nosso Amplo Presente: O tempo e a cultura contemporânea. Trad.: Soares, A. S. UNESP, São Paulo 2015. ISBN 978-85-393-0600-8

Jenkins H, Purushotma R, Clinton K, Weigel M, Robison A (2006) Confronting the challenges of participatory culture: media education for the 21st century. The MacArthur Foundation, Chicago. Retrieved from https://www.macfound.org/media/article_pdfs/JENKINS_WHITE_PAPER.PDF

Jenkins H (2006) Convergence culture: where old and new media collide. New York University Press, New York

Lacalle C (2011) As novas narrativas da ficção televisiva e a Internet. MATRIZes 3(2):79–102. Retrieved from https://doi.org/10.11606/issn.1982-8160.v3i2p79-102

Lévy P (1999) Cibercultura. Editora 34, São Paulo, Brasil

Linhares N, Ávila É (2017) Cinema e educação para além do conteúdo. Revista Tempos e Espaços em Educação 10(21):89. Retrieved from https://doi.org/10.20952/revtee.v10i21.6335

Long G (2009) Transmídia: a narrativa da atualidade. In Revista PontoCom. Retrieved from http://revistapontocom.org.br/edicoes-anteriores-entrevistas/transmidia-a-narrativa-da-atualidade

Navarro V (2010) Os sentidos da convergência: entrevista com Henry Jenkins. Revista Contracampo—Brazilian Journal of Communication, nº 21. Universidade Federal Fluminense, Niterói. https://doi.org/10.22409/contracampo.v0i21.77

Oliveira S, Caetano R (2017) Literacia para os média e cidadania global: caixa de ferramentas. Lisboa

Pinto J, Cardoso T, Soares AI (2019) Educação, Cinema e Redes Sociais: um olhar a partir do Plano Nacional de Cinema. Translocal—Culturas Contemporâneas Locais e Urbanas, nº 4, ISSN 2184–1519. Universidade da Madeira. Retrieved from http://translocal.cm-funchal.pt/wp-content/uploads/2019/01/EducacaoCinemaERedes-Sociais_PNC.pdf

Pinto J (2017) Formação aberta e online, redes sociais e inclusão digital: o projeto Reviver na Rede. Universidade Aberta. Retrieved from http://hdl.handle.net/10400.2/6930

Pinto J, Cardoso T (2017) Redes Sociais e Educação Aberta: Que relação? Em Redes e Mídias Sociais (2a edição, pp. 75–92). Appris Editora, Curitiba, Brasil

Reia-Baptista V (2006) Regulation, awareness, empowerment: young people and harmful media content in the digital age. NORDICOM, Göteborg University. Retrieved from https://sapientia.ualg.pt/handle/10400.1/9125

Rheingold H (2012) Net smart—how to thrive online. The MIT Press

Santarosa LM, Debora C, Schneider FC (2014) Tecnologias na Web 2.0: o empoderamento na educação aberta. In Colóquio Luso-Brasileiro de Educação a Distância e Elearning. 3, Lisboa, 2013. Colóquio Luso-Brasileiro...: atas. Universidade Aberta, Lisboa. LEAD, pp 1–18. ISBN 978-972-674-738-3. Retrieved from http://repositorioaberto.uab.pt/handle/10400.2/3071

Santos AI (2012) Educação Aberta: histórico, práticas e o contexto dos Recursos Educacionais Abertos. Retrieved from http://aberta.org.br/livrorea/artigos/wp-content/uploads/2012/05/REA-santos.pdf

dos Santos F, Petersen C (2014) Redes sociais, redes de sociabilidade. Revista Brasileira de Ciências Sociais, 63–78. Retrieved from http://dx.doi.org/10.1590/S0102-69092014000200005

Silva RP (2007) Cinema e Educação. editora Cortez, São Paulo, Brasil

Silva S, Lima D, Versuti A (2012) Cultura da Convergência e Educação a Distância: Mapeando as Contribuições das Narrativas Transmídias. 3° Simpósio Educação e Comunicação. Universidade Tiradentes, Aracaju. Retrieved from http://geces.com.br/simposio/anais/anais-2012/Anais-398-410.pdf

Trültzsch-Wijnen CW (2019) Educação para os média como uma disciplina transversal. In: Brites MJ, Amaral I, da Silva MT (eds) Literacias cívicas e críticas: refletir e praticar, pp 61–68. Retrieved from www.lasics.uminho.pt/ojs/index.php/cecs_ebooks/article/view/3184/3078

Toldo GS, Lopes FD (2017) Cinema como arte ou entretenimento: uma visão de seus realizadores e a estrutura organizacional de suas produtoras. REAd. Revista Eletrônica de Administração 23(2):167–190. Retrieved from https://doi.org/10.1590/1413.2311.176.60848

Tomás C (2013) Web semântica e personalização: repercussões da interação semântica com recursos educacionais abertos na identidade virtual do estudante e nos ambientes de aprendizagem online. Universidade Aberta, Lisboa. Retrieved from http://repositorioaberto.uab.pt/handle/10400.2/3309

Viana J (2009) O papel dos ambientes on-line no desenvolvimento da aprendizagem informal. Faculdade de Psicologia e de ciências da Educação, Universidade de Lisboa, Lisboa. Retrieved from http://repositorio.ul.pt/bitstream/10451/2086/1/21849_ulfp034652_tm.pdf

The manufacturer's authorised representative in the EU is Springer Nature Customer Service Centre GmbH, Europaplatz 3, 69115 Heidelberg, Germany. If you have any concerns regarding our products, please contact ProductSafety@springernature.com

Printed and bound by CPI Group (UK) Ltd, Croydon, CR0 4YY
13/08/2026
02196029-0002